"WHERE'S YOUR WILL TO BE WEIRD?"
JIM MORRISON

"Pleasure to me is wonder—the unexplored, the unexpected, the thing that is hidden and the changeless thing that lurks behind superficial mutability."
— H.P. Lovecraft

"We read the weird tales in newspapers to crowd out the even weirder stuff inside us."
-- Alain de Botton

"There are more things in Heaven and Earth, Horatio, than are dreamt of in your philosophy."
— William Shakespeare

"The charm of horror only tempts the strong"
— Jean Lorrain

"But if what interests you are stories of the fantastic, I must warn you that this kind of story demands more art and judgment than is ordinarily imagined."
— Charles Nodier

"We lie to protect our children, and in lying we expose them to the greatest of harms"
— John Connolly

"There is no separate supernatural realm: all phenomena are part of one natural process of evolution."
— Julian Huxley

"The most merciful thing in the world, I think, is the inability of the human mind to correlate all its contents. We live on a placid island of ignorance in the midst of black seas of the infinity, and it was not meant that we should voyage far."
— H.P. Lovecraft

REAL

MASTER MAGICIAN

ALIVE

CABINET OF CURIOSITIES 2

ILLUSTRIOUS

AMERICA'S UNEXPLAINED IN 20 OBJECTS

TROY TAYLOR

THIS ONE IS FOR THE GIRLS... LAST TIME, I DEDICATED ONE OF THESE BOOKS TO
THE WOMEN WHO KEEP THINGS ON TRACK, BUT THIS TIME, IT'S FOR THE GIRLS
WHO MAKE DOING ALL OF THIS STUFF WORTHWHILE. THEY'RE THE DAUGHTERS OF
THE WOMEN WHO MAKE ME CONTINUE THE FIGHT...
– HELAYNA, MAGGIE, MADISON, JORDYN, CASEY, RACHAEL,
BETHANY, ELYSE AND LUX –
THE "GIRLS" THAT I'M LUCKY TO HAVE IN MY LIFE.

Original Cover Artwork Designed by
© Copyright 2014 by April Slaughter & Troy Taylor
Back Cover Author's Photo by Janet Morris

This Book is Published By:
Whitechapel Press
A Division of Apartment #42 Productions
Decatur, Illinois / 1-888-GHOSTLY
Visit us on the internet at http://www.whitechapelpress.com

First Edition - April 2014
ISBN: 1-892523-89-2

Printed in the United States of America

INTRODUCTION

And now for something completely different...

This is not my first attempt to unveil the history of the strange and unusual through a collection of objects - hence, the "II" in the title - but it is, by far, the strangest. In the first "cabinet of curiosities" book, I tackled the rather straightforward subject of ghosts and the supernatural. Since that's a subject that I have been researching and writing about for more than two decades now, I found that collection of tales to be an easy one to tell. This one? Well, not so much. I should note that this is not because of a lack of fascination when it comes to the subject matter (in fact, as a child, I was delving into the unexplained and the weird even before my interest was piqued by ghosts) but because the objects collected for this book, no matter how ordinary some of them they might seem at first, defy any sort of expertise about their nature.

Don't misunderstand, though, while there is no scientific proof that ghosts exist, the spirit world seems to be more easily understandable to us. There is lore about ghosts within just about every culture on the planet. We understand the idea of a belief in the afterlife, and can grasp the possibility that ghosts might exist, but that's not so easy to do when the subject turns to hairy giants lurking in the woods, vanishing towns, giant birds that attack small boys, a man-like, flying creature, fish and frogs falling from the sky, "mad gassers," and more. Such things should not exist and yet, within the weird confines of America, they apparently do.

Or at least so this collection of physical objects seems to prove.

This second book of curiosities fits more closely to the concept of what cabinets of curiosities historically were. They began during the Renaissance era as collections of marvels and unusual objects that symbolized concepts that were not yet clearly defined. Modern people would categorize the books and artifacts found in these cabinets (which were often large rooms instead of items of furniture) as examples of natural history, geology, archaeology, religious or historic relics, art and sometimes outright bits of humbug, like petrified mermaid carcasses and fish with fur. But no matter what the cabinets contained, they were collections of the unexplained. Everyone loves a mystery. Humans have always loved to question, to wonder and to be baffled by things they cannot understand. Cabinets of curiosities were all the rage among European rulers, aristocrats, scientists, wealthy merchants and anyone else who could afford them. They are considered to be an ancestor of the modern museum.

But that's not really where I drew my inspiration for this book. Believe it or not, it was at the Midwestern carnival sideshows of my youth. I was lucky enough to be around to experience the tail end of the waning days of the sideshows, before political correctness killed them off for good. During the heyday of the carnival sideshows, in the first half of the twentieth century, performers were usually people with physical deformities or abnormalities that made them unusual: "freaks," as they were called. Many of them chose to put themselves on display and most of the performers were enterprising, ingenious people who, for the most part, made a good living in the only way that they could during the era in which they lived. To the close community of sideshow performers, it was the rest of us, the "rubes" who came to gawk at them, who were the freaks.

I always gravitated to the sideshows when I was a kid. I marveled at the two-headed cows, the five-legged calves, the sheep with three eyes and of course, the more exotic stuff like the "smallest woman in the world" (who really wasn't), the "headless woman" (an illusion created with a mirror), the beautiful girl who turned into an ape "before your very eyes," and even the missing link, preserved in ice (who has his own chapter later in this book). Believe me, if at age eleven it had been possible for me to get a job with the carnival, and maybe take care of the two-headed cow, I would have done it.

It was those trips to the sideshows that inspired my fascination for the wonders contained in this book. Perhaps more than anything else, it was my first visit to a "pickled punk" show, as the carnies cheerfully called them. A "pickled punk" is a carny term for a human fetus preserved in a jar of formaldehyde, a longtime staple of the sideshows. Most of them displayed some sort of anatomical abnormality like conjoined twins, or enlarged heads, but the deformities wildly varied. It should be noted that there were a lot of fake pickled punks out there, too. The carnies called them "bouncers," because they were made from rubber or wax and had a tendency to bounce when they were dropped on the floor.

I can still vividly recall seeing my first "pickled punks." I remember buying my ticket and walking into the shadowy tent at the Illinois State Fair. I had pretty much exhausted my money on corn dogs, lemon shake-ups and sideshows by that point in the evening, but I'd deliberately held enough back to see the collection of "nature's freaks," which the barker stationed outside the tent promised were "Alive! Alive! Alive!" Well, as it turned out, most of them weren't. There were a couple of little people, and a handful of animals with various deformities, but the rest had clearly sprung forth from the taxidermist's shop. There were some pretty wild things that had been stuffed over the years, including a couple of the "jackalope" variety (rabbits with horns affixed to their heads) -- and then there was the thing in the dark corner in the back. I couldn't see much from around the heavy canvas curtain, but it looked like a big cabinet filled with glass jars. As I edged around the curtain, I got my first glimpse of those backlit, eerily glowing jars, each containing objects that were designed to give a kid nightmares for weeks. Babies with extra limbs, babies with two heads, an extra set of arms, bug eyes, cleft palates: the kind of stuff that you knew existed but never actually wanted to see.

But, of course, I couldn't look away.

By the time that I experienced my first pickled punk display, I was already well on my way to the life that fate had in store for me. I'm not sure how much it really affected the course of my life, except when it comes to this book, I guess. I've spent most of my life researching and writing about strange phenomena, weird crimes and unsolved mysteries. I've collected literally thousands of stories of hauntings, disappearances, odd events and bizarre happenings, and have collected a number of oddities that tell their own weird stories. My own "cabinet of curiosities" isn't filled with taxidermy specimens or pickled punks, but it's just as strange. My cabinet contains records and remnants of the unexplained: a curious collection of objects (both literal and figurative ones) that tell the story of the weird in our modern world.

So, let me sell you a ticket and I'll pull aside the tent flap and beckon you inside to examine the twenty objects that I have on display in my own little sideshow. Through the stories of these objects, you'll enter the lives of the men and women who came into contact with them, with the strange creatures often represented by them, and with the bizarre events that made these objects famous. Some items will be familiar: a plaster cast of a giant footprint; a carnival curiosity piece (or was it?); an elusive photograph; metal bolts from a fallen bridge; a handkerchief reeking with the fumes of a powerful, unknown gas. Others will be largely unknown and might not even constitute material that most historians would call important: nails from a cabin; stones from a cellar wall; a lock of white hair; a handful of discolored grass; a burned piece of furniture and a discarded shirt.

But each of them tells a story, and in this book, the twenty objects that I have chosen will offer a unique look at how our history has been shaped by the unexplained. In turn, I'll reveal how each of these objects marked a pivotal moment in our fascination with American mysteries. Every one of them represents a vivid event in the history of the unexplained, some of them tragic, some of them terrifying and all of them simply unexplainable.

You've bought your ticket, so step right in and take a look inside my cabinet of curiosities. Brush the dust off the artifacts on the shelves. Just be careful when you do. If you look too closely, there's a good chance that you'll never see the bizarre world of the unexplained in the same way again.

TROY TAYLOR
SPRING 2014

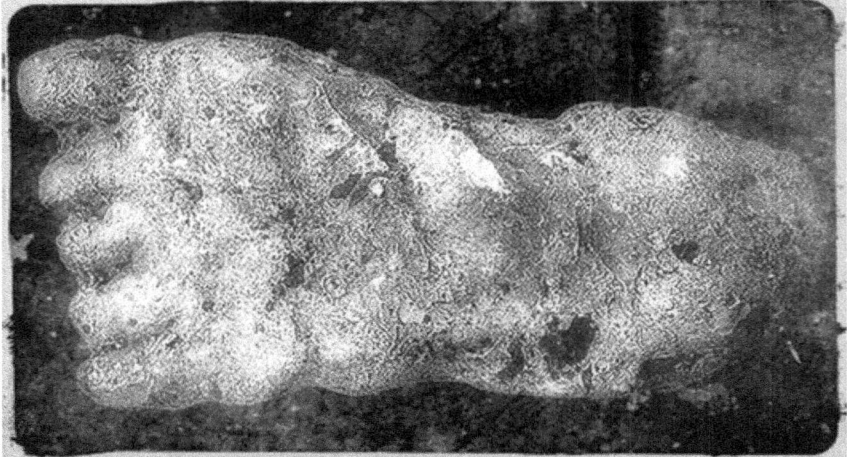

PLASTER CASTS

BIGFOOT IN AMERICA

It all started with a bunch of footprints at a construction site. Or at least the modern-day fascination with "Bigfoot" did. Stories of hairy giants in the woods and wandering "wild men" had been a part of American lore for nearly two centuries by the time the nickname "Bigfoot" was coined in the late 1950s. But it was then, with the advent of television and the modern media, that chasing down giants in the woods became a national craze.

It was the spring of 1957 and a road construction project was underway near Bluff Creek in northern California. The project was run by a contractor named Ray Wallace and his brother, Wilbur. They hired thirty men that summer to work on the project and by late in the season, Wilbur Wallace reported that something had been throwing around some metal oil drums at the work site. When winter arrived that year, cold weather brought the work to a halt, even though only ten miles of road had been completed.

In early spring 1958, some odd tracks were discovered near the Mad River close to Korbel, California. Some of the locals believed they were bear tracks. As it happened, this was close to another work site that was managed by the Wallace brothers.

Later on that spring, work started up again on the road near Bluff Creek. A number of new men were hired, including Jerry Crew, who drove more than two hours each weekend so he could be home with his family. Ten more miles of road were constructed, angling up across the face of a nearby mountain. On August 3, 1958, Wilbur Wallace stated that something threw a seven-hundred-pound spare tire to the bottom of a deep gully near the work site. This incident was reported later in the month, after the discovery of the footprints.

On August 27, Jerry Crew arrived for work early in the morning and found giant, manlike footprints pressed into the dirt all around his bulldozer. He was at first upset by the discovery, thinking that someone was playing a practical joke on him, but then he decided to report what he found to Wilbur Wallace. At this point, the footprints had not been made public. That occurred on September 21, when Mrs. Jess Bemis, the wife of one of the Bluff Creek work crew, wrote a letter to Andrew Genzoli, the editor of a local newspaper. Genzoli published her husband's "Big Foot" story and caught the attention of others in the area. One of these was Betty Allen, a newspaper reporter who suggested in a late September column that plaster casts should be made of the footprints. She had already talked to local Native Americans and interviewed residents about hairy giants in the area. She convinced Genzoli to run other stories and letters about Bigfoot. This would be the beginning of a story that would capture the imagination of America.

On October 1 and 2, Jerry Crew discovered more tracks, very similar to the first ones. In response to the new discovery, two workers quit and Wilbur Wallace allegedly introduced his brother Ray to the situation for the first time, bringing him out to show him the tracks. On the day after the last tracks were found, Jerry Crew made plaster casts of the footprints, with help from his friend Bob Titmus and reporter Betty Allen. He was irritated that people were making fun of him and wanted to offer the casts as evidence that he wasn't making the whole thing up. On October 5, Andrew Genzoli published his now-famous story about "Bigfoot." It was picked up worldwide by the wire services, and soon the term was being used in general conversation.

In 1959, famous zoologist Ivan T. Sanderson was touring the country for a planned book on ecology and used the time to also do some investigative work on unexplained phenomena. He had long been interested in the Yeti creatures of Asia and decided to stop off in Bluff Creek for a look at the site involved in Jerry Crew's accounts. He stayed at a local hotel for a little over a week, looking at files provided by Betty Allen and talking to witnesses from the area. When he left, he was supposed to make some candid assessments about the incidents to Tom Slick, a Texas millionaire who had funded some on-site investigation into the Bigfoot encounters, as well as a search for the Yeti in Nepal. When the report was made, though, what he called "various small items in the past" were left out. Sanderson was impressed by many of the people that he met, including Betty Allen and Jerry Crew, but he had some reservations about others -- especially Ray Wallace.

It's likely that he had good reasons for those reservations.

When Ray Wallace died in November 2002, newspapers across America ran stories that featured three words: "Bigfoot is dead!" When Wallace passed away, his son, Michael, told the *Seattle Times* that his father had been "Bigfoot" all along, and that the "reality is, Bigfoot just died." Needless to say, the media -- and those skeptical of the idea that a creature like Bigfoot could even exist -- went wild. Many hastily written stories followed that declared that Wallace, using a pair of crudely carved wooden feet, made phony tracks all over the

Pacific Northwest, and that his wife had donned a monkey suit and helped to hoax a controversial film that many respected researchers believe shows an authentic Bigfoot. The answer as to whether or not enormous, hairy, human-like creatures could be lurking in the woods and remote regions of the American continent had just been answered. There is no Bigfoot, the newspapers said; it had been a hoax all along. But had it really?

For many, Ray Wallace was the father of modern Bigfoot stories, but what happened at a construction site where he was a contractor was actually a minor event involving some mysterious footprints. The incident occurred at a time when Americans were ready for something exciting to grip their imaginations, and the media pounced on the discovery of the tracks. The word "Bigfoot" was coined and became a term that people have used ever since. No matter how you look at it, what happened in Bluff Creek in 1958 ushered in the modern era of Bigfoot and created an interest in the subject that is still alive today.

"Bigfoot" didn't die when Ray Wallace passed away in 2002. He'd already been with us for centuries and if many people - hunters, researchers and scientists - are to be believed, he is alive and well today.

In 2002, the media was trying hard to convince the general public that Ray Wallace was a highly respected figure in the world of Bigfoot research, but in truth, he had been regarded with suspicion by luminaries in the field like Ivan T. Sanderson, as far back as 1959. During his lifetime, Wallace claimed to have seen UFOs as many as two thousand times. He said he spotted Bigfoot hundreds of times and also claimed to have filmed footage of Bigfoot a year before Jerry Crew found the footprints at the construction site. At one point in 1959, he even claimed to have captured one! When Tom Slick offered him money for it, though, Wallace failed to produce the creature. He later claimed that he told amateur documentary maker Roger Patterson where to go to film Bigfoot in 1967, but few believed this. Wallace said that he had many films of Bigfoot but each turned out to be an obvious hoax. Later, a retired logger named Rant Mullens, who was known for perpetrating hoaxes, said that he often made large wooden footprints and gave them to Wallace, who then prepared plaster casts from them to put on display.

With his involvement in all sorts of questionable activities, Wallace had been regarded with suspicion by those with even a mild interest in Bigfoot for years. Sanderson was concerned about Wallace from the beginning, and became even more worried when he received letters about Bigfoot tracks being discovered in areas that turned out to be near other Wallace construction sites. He stated that everyone who did not believe the tracks were made by some sort of unknown, living entity believed that they had been made by Wallace. "He was a great 'funster,'" Sanderson wrote, and hinted that if there were enough problems on a work site, Wallace could get his work contracts changed and get no-cost extensions granted. Could this have been the motive for creating the phony tracks?

Unfortunately, the other things that Wallace got involved in from the 1950s until his death did not alleviate early suspicions about him. His continued involvement with fakes and frauds and his later claim that he hoaxed the tracks to bring attention to the plight of the real Bigfoot and to keep him from being killed by hunters, caused many to believe that the 1958 Bluff Creek tracks were a hoax. It also appears that Wallace planted phony prints at other worksites in the region over the years. This seems to mean that the so-called "birth of Bigfoot" was nothing more than a clever hoax: a hoax that managed to fool people all over the country and around the world.

So, if this is the case, does this mean that the existence of Bigfoot -- a giant, hairy creature that lives in the most remote regions of America -- is just a hoax? The skeptics would certainly like you to think so. But just as they, and the media, overlooked the fact that most Bigfoot researchers had already discredited Ray Wallace at the time of his death, they also overlooked the scores of reports, first-hand accounts and authentic evidence of the man-like creature that had been around for years.

Before we go any further, I should note that I'm not a Bigfoot researcher. While I have always been intrigued by the idea that such beings could exist, I have never encountered one, hunted for them, investigated case reports, picked up dung samples or took anything other than a mild interest in them. I have occasionally run across reports of Bigfoot creatures while researching other things, though, and being intrigued, have sometimes included accounts of Bigfoot in my writings.

However, I think it was my non-expert interest in Bigfoot that got me so upset in 2002 when Ray Wallace passed away. To be honest, I was alarmed by the revelation that Wallace had been involved in so many hoaxes over the years. Having no other knowledge about him or that he was already a suspicious figure to those in the field, I wondered about the damage this was going to do to Bigfoot research. Rather than jump to conclusions about the validity of Bigfoot study as a whole, however, I decided to do a little research into its history, which is probably something that the media should have been doing rather than printing half-baked theories about how Bigfoot had been a hoax from the beginning.

To "discover" Bigfoot, I turned to the past. How had history shaped the creature that we have come to know over the years, and in turn, how had Bigfoot shaped the unexplained in America? I began looking into the "history of Bigfoot" and what I found was fascinating. Bigfoot had not been "born" in 1958 but had been around for decades -- even centuries. I soon discovered some pretty amazing accounts of Bigfoot encounters from the past and it became obvious that the Bigfoot reports had not started in 1958, as the media claimed.

Before continuing, let me make it clear that I do not consider myself to be an expert on Bigfoot research. You won't find any technical writings here that delve into Bigfoot physiology or the best ways to capture one. What I have instead tried to do is to make the case that the existence of Bigfoot is possible -- even probable -- based on the fact that these creatures have been with us throughout the history of America. I have tried to collect the best, and most compelling, historical incidents of encounters with Bigfoot and have also included a few of the most interesting ones from modern times, as well.

Strange things are out there "in the wild" and the creatures that lurk in the dark woods and remote regions may even be stranger than anything you've ever imagined.

Where Bigfoot Walks

There was no question what the first entry in this book had to be. There is no greater mystery in the annals of the unexplained in America than Sasquatch, the creature most commonly known as "Bigfoot." Reports of giant, ape-like monsters have been documented all over the country, although primarily in the forested regions of the Pacific Northwest. There are tales of giant hairy figures in every state in America, although the "traditional" Bigfoot is believed to roam the vast regions of California, Oregon, Washington, Idaho and the western edge of Canada. The narrative that follows will include history and lore from a variety of locations.

Although most mainstream scientists maintain that no such creatures exist (and short of an actual specimen, their minds will not be changed), it is not inconceivable that undiscovered creatures could be roaming this wide region of mountains and forests. There are areas there that have been almost completely untouched by man and where few signs of the modern world can be found, even today. If we combine these remote areas with the hundreds of eyewitness accounts and pieces of evidence left behind, then we have no choice but to at least consider the idea that these creatures may actually be real. Of course, the reader is asked to judge for himself, but let's consider the history of Bigfoot in America.

According to many eyewitnesses, Sasquatch averages around seven feet in height, sometimes taller and sometimes a little shorter. They are usually seen wandering alone and hair covers most of their bodies. Their limbs are usually powerful, but they are described as being proportioned more like humans than like apes. However, their broad shoulders, short necks, flat faces and noses, sloped foreheads, ridged brows and cone-shaped heads make them appear animal-like. They reportedly eat both meat and plants, are largely nocturnal and are less active during cold weather. The creatures are most commonly reported as being covered in dark, auburn-colored hair, although reports of brown, black and even white and silver hair do occasionally pop up. The footprints left behind by the monsters range in size from about 12 to 22 inches long, with around 18 inches being the most common. Their tracks are normally reported to be somewhere around seven inches in width.

The stories of Sasquatch and other man-like creatures have been part of American history for generations. Native American legend and lore is filled with creatures that sound a lot like Bigfoot. One such creature was the "Wendigo." While this creature is considered by many to be the creation of horror writer Algernon Blackwood in his classic tale of the same name, this spirit was considered very real to many in the north woods and prairies. Many legends and stories have circulated over the years about a mysterious creature that was encountered by hunters and campers in the shadowy forests of the upper regions of Minnesota. In one variation of the story, the creature could only be seen if it faced the witness head-on, because it was so thin that it could not be seen from the side. It was said to have a voracious appetite for human flesh, and the many forest dwellers who disappeared over the years were said to be its victims.

The American Indians had their own tales of the Wendigo, dating back so far that most who were interviewed could not remember when the story was not part of their culture. The Inuit called the creature by various names, including Wendigo, Witigo, Witiko and Wee-Tee-Go, each of which roughly translates to mean "the evil spirit that devours mankind." Around 1860, a German explorer translated Wendigo to mean "cannibal" among the tribes along the Great Lakes.

Native American versions of the creature spoke of a gigantic spirit, over fifteen feet tall, that had once been human but had been transformed by the use of magic. Though all of the descriptions of the creature vary slightly, the Wendigo is generally said to have glowing eyes, long yellow fangs and a long tongue. Most are said to have sallow, yellowish skin, but others are said to be matted with hair. They are tall and lanky and are driven by a ravenous hunger. But how would a person turn into one of these strange creatures? According to the lore, a Wendigo is created whenever a person resorts to cannibalism in order to survive. When tribes and settlers were cut off from civilization by bitter snows and ice, they occasionally resorted to eating human flesh - and the Wendigo was created.

But how real were these creatures? Could the legend of the Wendigo have sprung up merely as a warning against cannibalism? Or could sightings of Bigfoot-type creatures have created the stories? While this is unknown, it is believed that white settlers to the region took the stories seriously. It became enough of a part of their culture that tales like those of Algernon Blackwood were penned. Purportedly real-life stories were told as well, and according to the settlers' version of the legend, the Wendigo would often appear, banshee-like, to signal an impending death in the community. A Wendigo allegedly made a number of appearances near a town called Rosesu in northern Minnesota from the late 1800s through the 1920s. Each time that it was reported, an unexpected death followed.

Even into the last century, Native Americans actively believed in, and searched for, the Wendigo. One of the most famous Wendigo hunters was a Cree Indian named Jack Fiddler. He claimed to have killed at least fourteen of the creatures in his lifetime, although the last killing resulted in his imprisonment at the age of 87. In October 1907, Fiddler and his son, Joseph, were tried for the murder of a Cree Indian woman. They both pleaded guilty to the crime but defended themselves by stating that the woman had been possessed by the spirit of a Wendigo and was on the verge of transforming into one. According to their defense, she had to be killed before she murdered other members of the tribe.

There are still many stories told of Wendigo that have been seen in northern Ontario, near the Cave of the Wendigo, and around the town of Kenora, where a creature has been spotted by traders, trackers and trappers for decades. There are many who still believe that the Wendigo roams the woods and the prairies of northern Minnesota and Canada. Whether it seeks human flesh, or acts as a portent of coming doom, is anyone's guess, but before you start to doubt that it exists, remember that the stories and legends of this fearsome creature have been around since before the white man walked on these shores. Like all legends, this one was likely started for a reason.

The Yakama Indians of the Pacific Northwest had a tradition of a "Qah-lin-me," which was a devourer of people and the Hupa Indians called the man-like beasts the "Omah," a demon of the wilderness. The Nisqually tribe of western Washington had the "Tsiatko," a gigantic, hairy beast, and the "Tenatco" was known by the Kaska. These creatures were known to dig a hole in the ground as a place to sleep and would sometimes kidnap women and children. Most of the woodland giants in the lore of the Native Americans seem to be more aggressive than the creatures we know as Bigfoot, but there is little mistaking them for something else. In fact, in 1934, author Diamond Jenness reported that the members of the Carrier First Nation of British Columbia, now generally referred to as the Dakelh, told of a monster that left enormous footprints in the snow, had a face like a man, was very tall and was covered in long hair. This hardly seems to be coincidence when compared to "modern" version of Bigfoot.

The legend of Bigfoot-type creatures is so mired in the history of American that even the Native American term "Sasquatch" is a bit of an extraction from mythological stories. The folkloric Sasquatch (the word is the Americanized version of a term used by the Coast Salish Indians of Canada) was introduced to the world in the writings of J.W. Burns, a schoolteacher at the Chehalis Indian Reservation near Harrison Hot Springs, British Columbia. Burns' Sasquatch was a legendary figure that he learned of through native informants and was really more man than monster. He was an intelligent "giant Indian" who was endowed with supernatural powers. Somehow, the name managed to stick for the huge beings that we would come to call Bigfoot.

"Wild Men of the Woods"

Legend has it that Bigfoot began to be encountered on this continent as early as the days when the first Vikings landed on our shores. Leif Erickson reportedly wrote of encountering hairy monsters with great black eyes, and in 1603, Samuel de Champlain was told of a giant, hairy beast that roamed the forests of eastern Canada. This creature was said to be much feared by the Micmac Indians of the region. In the 1790s, accounts told of large, hairy monsters in North and South Carolina and in that same decade, creatures were being reported in the Northwest by explorers and hunters who came to the region. While exploring the coast of British Columbia in 1792, naturalist Jose Mariano Mozino interviewed locals who spoke of the "Matlox," a large, hairy, human-like creature with huge feet, hooked claws and sharp teeth.

Throughout the nineteenth century, accounts of Bigfoot-type creatures continued to appear in newspapers and periodicals of the day. Obviously, the word "Bigfoot" had not been coined yet, and frankly, readers were not even familiar with any creature of this sort. The idea of even an "ape" was completely foreign to them, as the great apes of Africa were not officially "discovered" until later in the century, although there had been reports of them dating back to the fifth century B.C.E. by Greek explorer Hanno. For this reason, a search through old periodicals will not reveal historical Bigfoot accounts, but what did sometimes appear in newspapers of the 1800s were stories of "wild men" and beast-like creatures that were encountered, sometimes captured and occasionally killed. These reports likely thrilled readers of the day and may offer the modern researcher the first reports of Bigfoot in America.

Likely the oldest account of a man-like creature in North America appeared in the *London Times* in January 1785. The report stated that a wild man was caught in the forest, about two hundred miles from Lake of the Woods, Manitoba, by a party of Indians. The creature was said to have been seven feet tall and covered with hair. The wild man did not speak and seemed incapable of understanding his captors. It was found beside the body of a large bear, which it had just killed. This is unfortunately the extent of the information offered and no other news apparently followed.

The oldest known Bigfoot account in American newspapers appeared in September 1818 in Ellisburgh, New York. The incident apparently occurred on August 30. The story involved a local man of good reputation who had an encounter with an animal resembling a "wild man of the woods." The creature came out of the forest, looked at the man and then took flight in the opposite direction. He described it as bending forward when running, hairy, and having a narrow foot that spread wide at the toes. The article, which appeared in the *Exeter Watchman*, went on to say that hundreds of people searched for the wild man for several days, but no trace of it was found.

In the late 1830s, there were reports of a "wild child" around Fish Lake in Indiana. It was said to be four feet tall and covered in chestnut hair. The creature was often seen on the shore as well as swimming in the water. It made awful screeching noises, and no one was able to catch up with it because it ran so quickly. There were also reports in Pennsylvania of similar creatures, each much smaller than the typical Bigfoot creatures of the modern era. One of the creatures seen in Pennsylvania was covered in black hair and was said to have been the size of a six- or seven-year-old boy. Could these have been young Bigfoot, or perhaps, as authors Janet and Colin Bord have suggested, a different species of creature altogether?

The Bords also make reference to several wild men that were seen in Arkansas in the 1830s. The creatures were of gigantic stature and had been well known in St. Francis, Greene and Poinsett Counties since 1834. Two hunters had a close encounter with a wild man in Greene County in 1851, after seeing a herd of cattle that was apparently being chased by something. They discovered that the cows were being pursued by "an animal bearing the unmistakable likeness of humanity. He was of gigantic stature, the body being covered with hair and the head with long locks that fairly enveloped the neck and shoulders." Apparently, the wild man looked at the two hunters for a moment before running off into the forest. His tracks measured about 13 inches in length. Interestingly, the local explanation for this creature was that he was a "survivor of the earthquake disaster that desolated the region in 1811." The implication was that he was a human who had lost his sanity and home during the massive earthquake along the New Madrid Fault and had "gone native," living in the woods and growing his hair long.

Author and Bigfoot researcher John Green pointed out that some of the prospectors of the 1849 California Gold Rush were also encountering Bigfoot. According to a correspondent, his grandfather prospected for gold around Mount Shasta in the 1850s and told stories of seeing hairy giants in the vicinity.

In the late 1860s, residents in the Arcadia Valley of Crawford County, Kansas, were encountering their own wild man. What the newspapers were calling a "wild man or gorilla" or a "what is it?" was approaching the cabins of settlers, tearing down fences and generally wreaking havoc. The creature was described as being so near to a human in form that the "men are unwilling to shoot at it." However, it had a stooping gait, very long arms with immense hands and claws and an extremely hairy face. According to newspaper reports of the time, the settlers were divided as to whether or not the creature belonged to the human family or not. Some thought it to be an ape that had escaped from a menagerie that was located at a settlement east of the valley.

In the fall of 1869, a hunter from Grayson, California, wrote a letter to the *Antioch Ledger* and described his own experiences with a wild man in the forest. He returned to camp from hunting in the mountains around Orestimba Creek, and found that the ashes and burned sticks from his campfire had been scattered about. He searched around the area out of curiosity and a short distance away, he found "the track of a man's foot -- bare and of immense size." Thinking that he would try to catch a glimpse of the odd, barefooted visitor, he took up a position on a ridge overlooking his camp and waited there for nearly two hours. Suddenly, he was surprised by a shrill whistle and looked up to see a huge figure, standing erect by his campfire.

"It was the image of a man," the hunter wrote, "but it could not have been human." The creature stood about five feet high but was very broad at the shoulders. Its arms were of great length but its legs were short and his head seemed to be set upon his shoulders with no neck. It was covered with dark brown and cinnamon-colored hair that was quite long.

The wild man continued to make the odd whistling sound as he scattered the rest of the firewood and ashes. After a few minutes, he started to leave the clearing where the camp was located but went only a short distance before returning. This time, he brought with him another, similar figure, although this one was unmistakably female. The two creatures passed close to the hunter's hiding place and then disappeared into the forest.

Another wild man that was encountered in the late 1860s was seen in northern Nevada. The creature caused great excitement, and unlike most Bigfoot reports, this wild man carried a weapon. According to accounts, an armed party started off in pursuit of it shortly after it was spotted. The searchers concluded that it had once been a "white man, but was now covered with a coat of fine, long hair." It was seen carrying a club in one hand and a slain rabbit in the other. The moment that it caught sight of its pursuers, it let out a scream like "the roar of a lion," brandished the club, and attacked the men's horses. The men set their dogs after it, but the wild man managed to hide behind some fallen logs, uttering terrible cries throughout the night. It was gone by the following morning, leaving only "size 9" tracks behind.

In 1870, a report appeared in the Antioch, California, newspaper that spoke of a man seeing "a gorilla, a wild man, or whatever you choose to call it" in the forest. The creature's head "appeared to be set on the shoulders without a neck," which sounds remarkably similar to a modern Bigfoot report.

One wild man report from February 1876 was likely just that: a wild man. Except for the fact that the creature was covered with hair, it had no other characteristics of Bigfoot. While prospecting in San Diego County, a man named Turner Helm heard a whistling sound and came face to face with a wild man. He was sitting on a large boulder, and while Helm first assumed it to be an animal, he soon realized that it was a man. He was covered with coarse black hair, like that of a bear's fur, and had a beard that was long and thick. He was of medium size and had fine facial features, unlike those generally described for Bigfoot. Helm was startled but spoke to the man in both English and Spanish. He received no reply. The wild man looked at him for a few moments and then jumped down from the rock and vanished into the woods. Helm later stated that he and his prospecting partner had seen a man's tracks in the mountains many times, but had assumed they belonged to an Indian.

The rugged Green Mountains of Vermont have always had a reputation for strangeness. The area known as Glastonbury Mountain was once home to a small village of the same name. The town is long since gone and stories are told of how the residents were plagued with misfortune, disease, death and madness. It was near the vanished town that a coach full of travelers was attacked by the "Bennington Monster" in the 1800s and where, in 1892, Henry MacDowell went insane and murdered his friend, Jim Crowley. He was locked away in the Waterbury Asylum but he escaped and disappeared into the forests and rocks of Glastonbury Mountain and was never seen again.

These tales were recalled in October 1879 when two young men who were on a hunting trip south of Williamstown, Massachusetts, saw a wild man. They described the creature as being about five feet tall, and while he resembled a man in form and movement, he was covered with bright red hair, had a long beard and very wild eyes. When they first saw the creature, it sprang from a rocky cliff and began running toward the woods. Thinking that it was a bear or some other wild animal, one of the young men fired a shot and apparently hit it, because the creature let out a cry of pain and rage. It turned and then started toward the hunters in a furious state. The two men ran quickly in the opposite direction and lost their guns and ammunition on the way down the mountain. They never returned to retrieve them.

But one of the strangest of the early "wild man" reports is undoubtedly the "Jacko" story, which allegedly occurred in July 1884. According to the story, several men actually captured a young Bigfoot along the Fraser River outside of Yale, British Columbia. I remember reading this story when I was a kid in several books for young readers about the unexplained. I always considered it one of my favorites and always wondered what the eventual outcome of it was. In hindsight, the story was almost too good to be true, probably because it was. I was to be disappointed years later when I learned that respected Bigfoot author John Green revealed that it was likely a hoax.

The story appeared in Victoria's *Daily British Colonist* and told the story of several railroad workers, on the regular Lytton to Yale line, who found the creature lying alongside the tracks. Apparently, it had fallen from the steep bluffs and was injured, although when the train stopped, the creature jumped up, let out a sharp, barking sound and attempted to climb back up the bluff. The railroad men gave chase and managed to capture him.

They nicknamed the creature "Jacko" and described him as being "half man and half beast." He stood approximately four feet, seven inches tall and weighed about 130 pounds. He had long, dark hair and resembled a human, except for the fact that his body (except for his hands and feet) was covered with hair. His forearms were exceptionally long and he was very strong.

As no one was able to determine Jacko's identity or origin, he was eventually entrusted to the care of George Telbury, who planned to take the creature on tour or sell him to the circus. Some reports say that Jacko was on display in Yale for a time, but all trace of him later disappeared. At the time of the creature's alleged capture, newspapers reported that more than two hundred people came to the jail in Yale to see him. However, another newspaper, the *British Columbian*, stated that the only "wild man" present was the head of the jail, who had "completely exhausted his patience" with the curiosity-seekers. The *Colonist*, which originally ran the story, never disputed the criticisms of the other newspaper, and it was likely just another of the tall tales that were common in the Western papers of the late 1800s.

In the summer of 1885, hunters led by a man named Fitzgerald encountered a wild man in the Cascade Mountains. When spotted, the creature was eating raw deer flesh. Interestingly, the locals were so sure that this was a man, not a beast, that they even identified him as a missing person. The "wild man of the mountains" was said to be a man named John Mackentire, who had been lost in the forest while hunting about four years before. He and another man in his party had wandered off and were never seen again. The hunters claimed that the man they saw resembled Mackentire. He was naked but was "as hairy as an animal and was a complete wild man." He was bent down by the river and was eating part of a deer that had been recently killed. The hunters approached to within a few yards before he saw them and fled. According to the account, the wild man had been seen in the area as far back as two years before by other hunters, and it was believed that Mackentire had become deranged and was now living in a cave. A group of men organized a search party to go back and look for him but no other information was ever given about the result of the expedition.

In October 1891, a wild man encounter in Michigan had dire results for the dogs used to hunt down the creature. George Frost and W.W. Vivian ("both reputable citizens," the report added) were near the Tittabawassee River in Gladwin County when they ran into a naked man who was completely covered with hair. He stood over seven feet tall, with arms that hung down to his knees. Vivian released one of his bulldogs at the wild man, but with one mighty swing of his arm, the creature struck the dog and killed it.

Another hairy wild man appeared in late November 1893 in Rockaway Beach, New York. Both this report, and the one that follows, are important in that not every "wild man" report that appeared in newspapers of the period could have been a Bigfoot sighting. Some of the accounts, like these two, are just as strange, though, and are perhaps even more frightening.

A series of unprovoked attacks in Rockaway Beach were made by a "wild man of large stature, weird in appearance, with fierce bloodshot eyes, long, flowing matted hair and a shaggy beard." Armed with a "large cavalry saber," the wild man wreaked havoc in a saloon and later wrenched a shotgun out of a man's hand and fired it at him. According to witness descriptions, the man was about six feet tall and weighed about 200 pounds. Unlike most of the earlier reports about naked wild men, this one reportedly wore one shoe and a tattered oilskin jacket. The locals believed that he was a deranged sailor named James Rush, whose boat had been driven into shore during a recent storm and had gone missing.

This was obviously not a Bigfoot, but seemed to be strangely tied into another case that occurred just five weeks later. A similar wild man terrorized the Mine Hill-Dover area of New Jersey. In early January, three young women named Bertha Hestig, Lizzie Guscott and Katie Griffin encountered a wild man near the edge of town. He stormed out of the woods, completely naked and covered with cuts and bruises. With a shriek of terror at seeing the young ladies along the road, he ran back into the forest.

A few days later, two woodcutters were working near the Indian Falls clearing when their dogs began barking at a nearby rock. Thinking that a bear was nearby, the two men grabbed their axes and cautiously approached the area that seemed to be bothering the dogs. As they approached, a savage-looking figure jumped up from behind the rock. The stranger was said to be middle-aged, nearly six feet tall and weighing about 180 pounds. His face was covered with a long, unkempt beard. The wild man looked at the two woodcutters for a moment and then jumped onto the rock and began speaking loudly to himself in gibberish. Whenever the men got too close to him, he began to run back and forth yelling frantically, "all the time working his arms as though rowing a boat," they said. The woodcutters tried to seize the man but he picked up a club and swung it at them. The two men wisely fled and telephoned for help from a nearby store.

A search led by police officers commenced and lasted throughout most of the night, but no trace of the man was found. He appeared again on Saturday and tried unsuccessfully to break into the home of the Russell family. On Sunday, a man named William Mullen encountered the wild man when taking a walk. He appeared in front of him on the road and the two of them eyed one another uneasily for a few moments before the wild man shrieked loudly and ran into the woods.

The search continued for the man but only prints from his bare feet were discovered, along with a brush hut and an axe that may have belonged to the strange individual. The last sighting took place at the Dover Silk Mill when several ladies who were looking out the window saw the underbrush part and a naked man walk out. Their screams brought other employees but the wild man ran back into the woods. By the time the mill workers got outside, he was long gone. Various search parties continued to look for him, but he was never found. According to reports, inquiry was made at the Morris Plains Asylum but no inmates were missing. Who this man may have been is unknown but I suppose it's possible that he could have been the same wild man who was causing problems in New York just five weeks earlier.

In May 1894, a more classic Bigfoot-type of "wild man" report was recorded in rural Kentucky. For months, people around Deep Creek had been noticing that someone - or something -- was stealing chickens, eggs, young pigs, lambs and various food items from area farms. Finally, a man named Joseph Ewalt spotted a creature and reported that it had long white hair all over its body and wore only a piece of sheepskin for clothing. Ewalt said that a "light came from his eyes and mouth similar to fire," which may have been a bit of an embellishment on his part, or on the work of an imaginative newspaper reporter.

Some of the local men decided to try and capture the creature, but had no luck. One morning, Eph Boston and his sons saw it lurking around their barn. They described the creature the same way that Ewalt did, but added that it was about six and a half feet tall and had long claws. There was no mention of it having glowing eyes, though. A few moments after they spotted it, the wild man went running from the barn with three chickens clutched in its hands. Tom Boston shot at it but missed. He and his brothers and father, along with several neighbors, tracked the creature to a nearby cave, where a scattering of bones and feathers suggested that the wild man was living there. They walked a short distance into the cave but an "unearthly yell" sent them running. Efforts to try and capture the beast, including smoking it out of the cave, failed.

In 1897, a wild man sighting took place near Sailor, Indiana. A man took a shot at it and seemed to hit it, but no trace of the creature was found. The sighting occurred in late April when two farmers saw a hair-covered, man-sized beast walking near the edge of a field. When the wild man saw them approaching, it dropped from two legs to four and raced into the woods with great speed.

In April 1897, another wild man was seen in the woods near Stout, Ohio. Although covered with hair, the creature was said to be wearing a pair of tattered trousers. It attacked a young boy in the forest and then led a party of thirty men on a chase for several hours before disappearing. On May 26, the same creature may have appeared near Rome, Ohio. It was described as a "wild man" and "gorilla-like," and was spotted by two men who were cutting timber in the forest. They chased the figure into a rocky area along the Ohio River, where it vanished.

One of the final reports from the 1800s shows a traditional Bigfoot in a less threatening role than was noted in most of the previous encounters. In 1897, a Native American fisherman reportedly discovered an emaciated Bigfoot near Tulelake, California. The man took pity on the creature and gave it his catch. A few weeks after the encounter, the story goes that the fisherman awoke to find several fresh deerskins neatly arranged outside his cabin. In the following months, a nighttime visitor left firewood, pelts, berries and fruit for him to find each morning. The fisherman came to believe that it was the Bigfoot that he had helped who was leaving the gifts. Eventually, the offerings ceased and the man guessed that the creature had left the area. About a year later, though, the man was bitten by a rattlesnake and fell unconscious in the forest. He awoke a few hours later to find himself being carried by three large creatures, who took him to his cabin and wrapped his snake bite with moss, which drew out the poison. The monsters left him at his door and he never saw them again.

Teddy Roosevelt's Bigfoot

In his 1893 book, *Hunting the Grizzly*, Theodore Roosevelt relates a purportedly true story of a hunter who was abducted from his campsite and killed by an eerie creature that was covered with hair.

Roosevelt was born on October 27, 1858, and he spent his childhood as part of a privileged family in New York City. He was the seventh generation of Roosevelts to be born in Manhattan, and the second of four children in his household. Always a sickly child afflicted with asthma, the young Roosevelt was educated at home by private tutors prior to going to Harvard, where he excelled in boxing and academics.

After college, Roosevelt married Alice Hathaway Lee, a nineteen-year-old friend of his Harvard roommate. He then enrolled in Columbia Law School, but dropped out after one year to begin a career in public service, winning election to the New York State Assembly in 1882. A double tragedy struck Roosevelt in 1884, when his young wife died giving birth to their daughter, followed by the death of his mother - on the same day, in the same house. Devastated, Roosevelt left his daughter, named Alice after her mother, in the care of his sister and fled to the Dakota Badlands to forget.

After two years out West, where he "busted" cows as a cattle rancher and chased outlaws as a frontier sheriff, Roosevelt returned to New York rejuvenated and full of energy. He ran unsuccessfully for mayor of New York City, wrote three books about his adventures in the West, and campaigned for Republican presidential nominee Benjamin Harrison. When Harrison won the election, he appointed Roosevelt to the U.S. Civil Service Commission in 1889. His burgeoning career in politics would later lead him to the White House.

Roosevelt then married his childhood sweetheart, Edith Kermit Carow. He took little Alice and moved with Edith to a beautiful house at Oyster Bay, Long

Island, that he had built for his first wife. He called the house Sagamore Hill. The happy couple soon filled the home with four boys, another girl, and little Alice.

Even during his political career, the adventures that Roosevelt experienced in the American West left a permanent mark on him. His thirst for adventure would later lead him to act as the police commissioner of New York City, to fight bravely in Cuba with the "Rough Riders" and, later in life, to become renowned as a big game hunter.

In 1893, when he wrote his first books about his Western adventures, Roosevelt had already roamed most of the country in search of big game. He wrote: "In hunting, the finding and killing of the game is after all but part of the whole. The free, self-reliant, adventurous life, with its rugged and stalwart democracy; the wild surroundings, the grand beauty of the scenery, the chance to study the ways and habits of the woodland creature -- all these unite to give to the career of the wilderness hunter its peculiar charm." And "peculiar" would be the only word to describe a story that Roosevelt saw fit to include in one of the volumes of his Western accounts.

"Frontiersman are not, as a rule, apt to be very superstitious," Roosevelt wrote. "They lead lives too hard and practical and have too little imagination in things spiritual or supernatural.... but I once listened to a goblin story which rather impressed me. It was told by a grizzled, weather-beaten old mountain hunter named Bauman, who was born and had passed all his life on the frontier. He must have believed what he said, for he could hardly repress a shudder at certain points of the tale."

When the event occurred that Bauman related to Roosevelt, the mountain hunter was still a young man and was trapping with a partner among the mountains dividing the forks of the Salmon River from the head of the Wisdom River in Idaho. The two men worked the area for a time without much luck and then decided to try another location, where a branch of the Snake River ran through a particularly wild and lonely pass. The stream was said to be filled with beaver but was avoided by many of the Indian trappers in the region. The story went that a lone hunter had wandered into the pass the year before and had been killed by some wild beast. The man's half-eaten remains were discovered by a party of prospectors who had passed the man's camp only the night before.

Bauman and his friend decided to trap the stream anyway. They rode to the foot of the pass and left their horses tied in a meadow, because the rocky and heavily forested lands were nearly impassable for the animals. The trappers struck out on foot through the gloomy woods, finding the country dense and hard to travel through with their heavy packs and their need to bypass the stands of fallen timber and outcroppings of rock. After about four hours of walking, they found a small forest glade that offered easy access to the river.

An hour or two of daylight remained when they made camp, so they built a brush lean-to and unpacked their gear. Then they decided to take a short hike upstream and look for signs of game, returning to camp around dusk. They were surprised to find that in their absence, something, apparently a bear, had visited the camp and had rummaged through their things. The contents of their packs had been scattered about and the lean-to had been torn down. The beast had left a number of footprints behind but the men paid little attention to them as they had much to do to rebuild the camp before darkness fell. After starting a fire, they quickly rebuilt their shelter.

While Bauman began cooking supper, his companion studied the animal tracks more closely in the failing light. He was so intrigued by them that he lit a small stick in the fire and used it as a torch to follow the tracks to the edge of the clearing. When the light flickered out, he returned to the fire and ignited another stick, continuing his inspection of what appeared to be increasingly curious tracks. A few minutes later, he returned and stood next to where his friend was cooking dinner, peering uneasily out into the darkness. He suddenly spoke up. "Bauman, that bear has been walking on two legs," he said.

Bauman later recalled laughing at this, although his partner insisted that it was true. The two of them again examined the tracks and Bauman's partner showed him that they had been made by just two paws or feet. After discussing whether the prints could be those of a large person, and deciding that they could not be, the two men rolled up in their blankets and went to sleep beneath the shelter of the lean-to.

Around midnight, Bauman was suddenly awakened by a loud noise. He sat up quickly in his blankets and remembered later that he was struck by a strong, pungent odor. The horrible smell was soon forgotten, as the embers of the fire illuminated a large form looming at the entrance of the lean-to. Bauman grabbed his rifle and immediately fired off a shot. Almost as soon as he squeezed the trigger, the huge shape vanished and he heard the thing crashing through the undergrowth as it ran off into the night.

Not surprisingly, the two men slept very little after this. They sat up next to the rekindled fire, waiting and watching, but heard nothing more. In the morning, they checked the traps that had been put out the night before and began finding locations for new ones. By an unspoken agreement, they stayed within close proximity to one another all day and returned together to camp as night began to fall once again.

Again, they saw that the lean-to had been destroyed. The visitor from the previous day had apparently returned and had again scattered their gear and belongings. Whatever the beast was, it had left more of the large, two-legged tracks in the soft earth by the river but neither man had the nerve to follow them.

Instead, they gathered up as much wood as they could find and built a roaring fire that lasted throughout the night. One or the other of them stayed on guard during the darkest hours. At one point, both of them heard the creature approach once again, staying on the other side of the river. They heard it moving and crashing around in the forest and once it uttered a harsh, grating moan that chilled both men to the bone. This time, it did not venture near the fire.

In the morning, the trappers decided that they'd had enough. They were too almost too tired to tend to their work and believed that they could find just as good a location somewhere else. They discussed the strange events and decided that it would be best to pack up their gear and leave the valley by the afternoon. The men pulled their trap lines all morning, staying close together, and strangely, they found that all of the traps were empty and sprung. It looked as though they had snagged something but then the animals had been removed from the trap. Signs and tracks remained behind and the men hurried their work along even faster. Ever since leaving camp, they had experienced the uncomfortable sensation of being watched and followed. Occasionally, they would hear the snap or crack of a twig in the gloom of the forest, as well as the rustling of pine trees, and while they saw nothing, they became convinced that something was there.

By noon, they were within a couple of miles of the camp and there were still three beaver traps to collect from a little pond in a nearby ravine. Bauman offered to go and gather them while his friend went ahead to the camp and put their gear together. They planned to meet as soon as Bauman returned and then go down the mountain to the horses. His companion agreed and they parted ways.

On reaching the pond, Bauman found three beavers in the traps, one of which had pulled loose and had carried the trap into a beaver house. He spent the next several hours securing and preparing the animals and when he started back to camp, he experienced a sinking feeling as he saw how low the sun was beginning to dip in the sky. As he reached the clearing where the camp was located, Bauman called out to his friend but got no reply. The campfire had gone out and the packs lay nearby, all secured and ready to go. The woods were silent and Bauman called out again. Once more, he was met with silence.

The trapper looked around, at first seeing nothing, but then he glimpsed a splash of color at the edge of the camp. As he walked forward, he spotted the body of his friend. He was stretched out on the ground next to the trunk of a fallen spruce and blood was sprayed all over the ground and the surrounding trees and bushes. Bauman rushed over to the man and found that his body was still warm. His neck had been broken and his throat had been torn out with what looked to be huge, sharp teeth. The footprints of the beast that had been visiting the camp were marked deep in the surrounding soil and told the story of what had occurred.

Bauman's friend, having finished packing their gear, must have sat down on a log facing the fire, with his back to the woods, to await his partner. While he was waiting, the unknown assailant, which must have been lurking in the woods the entire time, came silently up behind the man and broke his neck, while burying its teeth in his throat. It had not eaten the body but had apparently tossed it around, rolling it over and over, before retreating back into the woods.

Bauman was utterly unnerved by his gruesome discovery. The creature, which they had assumed was a bear, was either something half-human or half-devil or some great beast from the stories of the Indian medicine men, who spoke of evil beings that haunted the forest depths. Roosevelt wrote that Bauman "abandoned everything but his rifle and struck off at speed down the pass, not halting until he reached the meadows where the hobbled ponies were still grazing. Mounting, he rode onward through the night, until far beyond the reach of pursuit."

Abducted by Bigfoot

In 1901, another account of a Sasquatch encounter appeared in the *Daily British Colonist*. In this story, a lumberman named Mike King stated that he was working alone on Vancouver Island, near Campbell River, because his Indian packers had refused to accompany him, due to their fear of the "monkey men" they said lived in the forest. Late in the afternoon, he observed a "man beast" washing roots in the river. When the creature became aware of King, it cried out and ran up a nearby hill. King described it as being "covered with reddish brown hair, and his arms were peculiarly long and were used freely in climbing and brush running; while the trail showed a distinct human foot, but with phenomenally long and spreading toes."

Three years later, on December 14, 1904, the *Colonist* again featured a Sasquatch story, this time from "four credible witnesses" who saw a man-like creature on Vancouver Island. In 1907, the newspaper told of the abandonment of an Indian village due to the inhabitants being frightened away by a "monkey-like wild man who appears on the beach at night, who howls in an unearthly fashion."

One of the most bizarre Bigfoot encounters in history occurred in 1924, although it would not be reported until many years later, in 1957. It involved a man who claimed to have been abducted and held captive by a party of the creatures while on a prospecting trip in British Columbia. Although such tales seem to stretch the limits of believability, those who interviewed the man years later, including esteemed investigators John Green and Ivan T. Sanderson, did not for a moment doubt his sincerity or his sanity. Primatologist John Napier remarked that the man gave a "convincing account... which does not ring false in any particular."

The same cannot be said for all alleged Bigfoot "abductions," though. In 1871, a young girl named Seraphine Long was said to have been kidnapped by a male Bigfoot and taken to a cave where she was held prisoner for a year. She eventually got sick and so her captor allowed her to leave. However, when she returned home, it was discovered that she was carrying the creature's baby. She gave birth to the child but it only lived a few days. Of course, that was the story. The reader asked to judge the validity of it for himself.

A story with a much more authentic feel to it took place in 1924. That summer, a man named Albert Ostman was prospecting for gold near the Toba Inlet in British Columbia. He claimed that he was abducted by Bigfoot, and his detailed accounts of the creature's habits and activities remain unique to this day, leading many of the most respected authorities in the field to wonder if perhaps he was telling the truth about this adventure.

Toba Inlet was a secluded wilderness in 1924 when Albert Ostman decided to visit the area during a much-needed vacation. The construction worker and lumberjack liked to prospect for gold as a hobby, and in addition to doing some hunting and fishing, he planned to search for a legendary lost gold mine that was rumored to be in the area. Ostman hired an Indian guide to take him to the head of the inlet and on the way, the Indian told him about a white man who used to come out of the area laden with gold. When Ostman asked the guide what happened to the man, the guide replied that he had disappeared and had probably been killed by Sasquatch. Ostman scoffed at the story, not believing a word of this tall tale.

When they reached the inlet, the guide helped Ostman to set up his base camp and then he departed. Ostman had paid him to return in three weeks. For the first week or so, he hunted and fished a little and spent quite a bit of time hiking in the woods and searching for any traces of the lost mine. He was quite casual about the search, though, enjoying the outdoors and the freedom away from his work. Then one day, he returned to camp to find that his gear had been disturbed. Nothing was missing, but it had all been moved around. Ostman assumed that a porcupine or some small animal had been looking for food. He tried to stay awake for two nights to try and catch the annoying animal but each time, he fell asleep. On both mornings when he awoke, he discovered that food was missing from his pack.

Now irritated, and determined to trap the culprit, he loaded his rifle and shoved it down in his sleeping bag, along with his clothes and some of his personal belongings. He planned to stay awake the entire night and drive off the pesky animal. Despite his good intentions, however, Ostman fell asleep. Later on that night, still half asleep, Ostman awoke to find that he had been picked up, still inside his sleeping bag, and was being carried through the woods. He first assumed that he had been tied up and thrown over the back of a horse, but then realized that he was pinned into his sleeping bag by two large arms. Unable to reach his rifle, or his knife, he was trapped in the bedroll. There was no sound but the huffing of breath from the figure who carried him, the sound of powerful feet trudging through the forest and the occasional rattle of a fry pan and canned food in Ostman's pack, which the giant had also picked up from the camp.

Ostman traveled for several hours and estimated that he journeyed about thirty miles inland. Eventually, he was dumped onto the ground and he slowly crawled out of the sleeping bag in the darkness. His whole body ached from being jostled, and as he was trying to massage some feeling back into his legs, the sun came up and the prospector got his first good look at his abductors. Squatting nearby were four hairy giants, the same type of creatures that had been described to Ostman by the Indian guide.

They sat there looking at Ostman with curiosity, but did not seem threatening in the least. The two older creatures were male and female and the two younger ones were also of both sexes. The oldest male stood nearly eight feet tall and weighed an estimated 750 pounds. The oldest female was slightly smaller and had large, hanging breasts. The younger creatures were of smaller proportions than what Ostman assumed were the parents and the younger female had no breasts. All four of them had coarse, dark hair that covered their bodies.

Ostman later recounted that the older female seemed to object to his presence during the first day of his captivity. She chattered and grunted angrily at the male like a nagging housewife displeased by the presence of an unwanted guest. Eventually, her mate seemed to win the day and was allowed to keep Ostman around. The two females avoided him as much as possible, spending their time hunting for roots, nuts and berries. The two male creatures were curious about everything the prospector did and found the contents of Ostman's pack and sleeping bag to be quite fascinating. He had carried along with him his food, his rifle, a few pots and pans and his knife. They often looked at these items but never touched them, although the oldest creature was very interested in Ostman's snuff box and its contents. This keen interest would eventually prove to be integral in Ostman's escape.

Two days into his captivity, Ostman tried to run away. The Sasquatch lived in a small ten-acre basin that was cut between two cliff walls. A narrow break in the rock provided the only entrance. When Ostman tried to slip out of the valley, the oldest male quickly caught him and pulled him back into the basin. He considered using his rifle and trying to shoot his way out, but knew that if he did not kill the creature with the first couple of shots, the beast would surely tear him apart.

After six days, Ostman had another idea. He was becoming increasingly nervous of the creatures because he was starting to get the impression that he had been captured in order to provide a mate for the younger female. Not wanting to spend the rest of his life in captivity, he began working on a plan to break free. He knew that the elder Bigfoot was very interested in his chewing tobacco. Each day, he gave the creature a small amount of it to chew on. He wondered if there might be a way to use the Bigfoot's interest in his snuff to his advantage.

On the morning of the seventh day, Ostman made a fire for the first time since he had arrived. He decided to make some coffee, which interested the two males. As he was eating his breakfast and drinking coffee, he decided to try out his idea. He reached over and offered the older creature some of his snuff. He held on tightly to the box so that the creature could only take a small amount, which irritated him. He jerked the box from Ostman's hand and proceeded to devour the entire contents. He liked the taste so much that he literally licked clean the inside of the container.

It only took a few moments for the creature to become violently ill. Retching and coughing, he ran towards the stream and collapsed on all fours. At the same time, Ostman grabbed his rifle and his pack and began to run. He shot towards the narrow entrance but his escape attempt was noticed by the older female, who set off after him. He made it to the gap in the rock just seconds before she caught up with him and turning quickly, he fired a shot over her head. The creature stopped in her tracks and let out a squeal. She did not pursue him any farther.

Using his compass, Ostman managed to make his way back to civilization. After three days, he met up with a party of lumberjacks and told them that he had gotten lost while prospecting. He was sure that no one would ever believe his account of what really happened and he remained silent for more than thirty years, finally telling his story in 1957.

Although Ostman has long since passed away, Bigfoot researcher John Green knew him for more than twelve years and questioned him extensively about his captivity. He had no reason to consider him a liar and neither did the police officers, primate experts and zoologists who also looked into his account. None of them ever believed that he was lying. The truth of his story remains for the reader to decide.

Encounter at Ape Canyon

In July 1924, a weird incident involving a group of Bigfoot occurred in the Mount St. Helens region of southwestern Washington. The incident involved an all-night assault by unknown creatures on a cabin where a group of miners were staying. The men had been prospecting a claim on the Muddy, a branch of the Lewis River, about eight miles from Spirit Lake. One of the most interesting parts of the story is that there are detailed news articles that exist from the time of the incident, and there has been much since then to substantiate the events of that summer. An article in the *Portland Oregonian* for July 12 noted that the encounters with the creatures were not the first. The article begins by calling these "the fabled 'mountain devils' or mountain gorillas of Mount St. Helens" and mentions that "Smith and his companions had seen tracks of the animals several times in the last six years, and Indians have told of the 'mountain devils' for sixty years."

In the news article, the "devils" are described as "huge animals, which were about seven feet tall, weighed about four hundred pounds, and walked erect." Tracks "thirteen to fourteen inches long" were found where the animals were seen.

In 1967, Fred Beck, who was one of the miners, and his son, R.A. Beck, privately published a small booklet about the incident called *I Fought the Apemen of Mt. St. Helens*. For many years, prior to the advent of the internet, it was extremely hard to find. Since then, the story has become a classic of Bigfoot literature and is essential to the narrative of Bigfoot in historical terms.

But this case may be even stranger than most people believe. And when it comes to Bigfoot stories, that's really saying something.

Starting in 1918, Fred Beck and his partners - Marion Smith, his son Roy Smith, Gabe Lefever and John Peterson - began prospecting for gold in the Mt. St. Helens and Lewis River area of southwestern Washington. Before they built a cabin, they lived in a tent below a small mountain called Pumy Butte. There was a small creek nearby and a sandbar that was about an acre in size where they went to wash their dishes and get drinking water.

Early one morning in 1922, one of the men came back to the camp and urged the others to follow him back to the creek. When they got to the sandbar, he showed them two huge, human-like tracks that were sunk about four inches deep into the sand. Strangely, there were no other tracks nearby. Because the nearest place where someone could have jumped and landed in the center of the sandbar was 160 feet away, the men reasoned that the creature either had a huge stride, or "something dropped from the sky and went back up." As time passed, the miners came upon similar tracks, which they could not identify. The largest of them was nineteen inches long.

After they had built their cabin, Beck and the other four miners who were working the claim would hear a strange "thudding, hollow thumping noise" in broad daylight. They could not find the cause, though they suspected one of their number might be playing tricks on them. That proved not to be the case, since even when the group was gathered together, the sound continued all around them. They thought it sounded as if "there's a hollow drum in the earth somewhere and something is hitting it."

These were not the last strange sounds they would hear. Early in July 1924, a shrill whistling, apparently coming from atop a ridge, was heard in the evening. An answering whistle came from another ridge. These sounds, along with a booming "thumping," as if something huge was pounding its chest, continued every evening for a week.

Thoroughly unnerved by what they were hearing, the men began carrying their rifles with them when they went to the spring that was located about one hundred yards from the cabin. Beck and a man only identified as "Hank" in order to protect his anonymity (it was later revealed that it was Marion Smith) were drawing water from the spring when Hank yelled and raised his gun. Beck looked across a little canyon and saw a seven-foot-tall apelike creature standing next to a pine tree. The creature, about one hundred yards away from the two men, ducked quickly behind the tree. When it poked its head out to get a look at them, Hank fired three quick shots, hitting the tree but apparently missing the creature, which momentarily disappeared from sight. It then reappeared about two hundred yards down the canyon, and this time Beck managed to get off three shots before it was gone.

Unnerved by the encounter, Hank and Beck ran back to the cabin and spoke to the other two men there. The third member of the party was absent. They agreed to abandon the cabin, but not until daybreak. It was too risky to try and make it back to their car after dark. They went ahead and packed up most of their gear, ate some supper and then settled down to try and get some sleep.

Around midnight, they awakened to a tremendous thud against the cabin wall. Whatever it was, it hit the wall with such force that some of the chinking between the logs fell out and landed on Hank's chest. The impact was followed by what sounded like a group of people tramping about and running around outside. The men grabbed their guns, fearing the worst. Since the crude cabin had no windows, Hank tried peering out through the gap that had been opened between the logs when the chinking had been dislodged. He said that he spotted three of the "apes" outside. From the sounds the men could hear, there were likely many more of them.

The creatures pelted the cabin with rocks. The men inside were terrified - in fact, two of the miners cowered in fear in the corner - but Beck said that they should only fire at the creatures if they physically attacked the cabin. This would show that the miners were only defending themselves.

A short time later, Beck's worst fears came true. The "apes" began to attack the cabin. Some of them jumped up and down on the roof, trying to get it to collapse. Hack and Beck fired upwards through the roof, hoping to scare them away. In the meantime, other creatures were trying to break down the door, slamming against it as they tried to smash it open. The miners inside braced the door with a long board that was taken from a bunk bed. It seemed to hold, but Beck and Hank riddled the door with bullets in an attempt to frighten the invaders away.

The attacks continued all night, pausing only for short periods of eerie silence. At one point, a creature reached through the gap between the logs and grabbed an axe by the handle. Beck lunged forward and turned the axe upright so that the creature couldn't get it out. As he was doing so, a bullet fired by Hank barely missed the creature's hand. It quickly withdrew its arm and retreated.

Finally, just before daybreak, the attack ended. The beleaguered miners waited for the sun to rise and then cautiously stepped outside, guns in hand. A few minutes later, Beck saw one of the creatures about eighty yards away, standing near the edge of the canyon. Taking careful aim, he fired three times and then watched as it fell over the cliff and plunged down into the gorge four hundred feet below.

The men hastily departed, heading for Spirit Lake, Washington, and leaving $200 worth of supplies and equipment behind. They never returned to retrieve any of it.

At Spirit Lake, Hank told a forest ranger about their experience. Once back home in Kelso, the story leaked to the newspapers and caused a sensation. Reporters found giant tracks at the scene, but no other evidence of the creatures. The canyon where the incident allegedly occurred became known as Ape Canyon and it still bears that name today.

As mentioned, the tale has become a classic of Bigfoot literature and while it's certainly strange, it's gotten even stranger over the years. In the 1967 booklet that Beck wrote with his son, he gave the experience a completely different spin, noting that even prior to the encounter, he had numerous psychic experiences, including many with supernatural "people." He was convinced that the "apemen" were "not entirely of this world... I was, for one, always conscious that we were dealing with supernatural beings." Beck stated that he believed that creatures known as Sasquatch were from "another dimension" and were a link between human and animal consciousness. They are composed of a substance that ranges between the physical and the psychical, sometimes more of one than the other, he said, and because of their peculiar nature, none will ever be captured, nor will their bodies ever be found.

According to the booklet, Beck saw the entire experience as spiritual, with the thumping as poltergeist activity and the Bigfoot as spirits. It's hard to say whether or not Beck's 1967 booklet was merely the fantasy of an old man, or was due to the contemporary 1960s influences of his son, who wrote a large section of it. But he had certainly changed his views on the 1924 events during the four decades after they happened. It should be noted that Fred Beck never mentioned the paranormal when Bigfoot researchers interviewed him about his experiences in the early 1960s. The paranormal elements popped up when Beck and his son decided to tell the story in 1967. The news stories of the 1920s seem to be closer to the actual details of the event.

Those stories told of ape-like creatures that were far shorter than our standard idea of Bigfoot, with smaller strides and footprints. The articles, which were a series of stories from the Kelso area between 1918 and 1924, also mentioned four stubby toes, as opposed to the five toes normally included in modern Bigfoot reports. According the newspaper articles, the Native Americans in the region called the reported creatures *Seeahtiks, Siatcoes* and *Selahtiks*. In July 1924, the sheriff sent out search parties, but only footprints were ever found.

Regardless of how you look at it, the story of Ape Canyon is a strange tale and presents another classic example of the historical Bigfoot.

Sasquatch sightings and encounters continued and were occasionally mentioned in newspaper accounts, most of them issuing from Canada. Bigfoot did not enter the American mainstream until 1958, when the now-infamous tracks were discovered at Bluff Creek. This was a time when America's fascination with Bigfoot was only beginning. Through the remainder of the 1950s, the 1960s and the 1970s, interest in these elusive creatures reached its high point. After a cooling down period of about two decades, when only Bigfoot hunters and diehard enthusiasts were seeking information about Sasquatch, public interest began to rise in the late 1990s and continues today.

But that interest has not been without controversy.

The Patterson Film
By the decade of the 1960s, Bigfoot was firmly entrenched in the American imagination. Though scientists refused to admit that what witnesses were seeing was actually what they claimed to see, a number of investigators had begun seeking out sightings and venturing into the forest, hoping to catch a glimpse of one of the monsters. Books began to appear and articles began to generate even more interest with readers of magazines like *True* and *Saga*.

Among the amateur investigators who went looking for Bigfoot was Roger Patterson, a onetime rodeo rider, amateur documentary film maker and Bigfoot hunter. In 1967, Patterson was barely scraping by as an inventor and promoter when his interest was piqued by a 1959 *True* magazine article about Bigfoot. From them on, he devoted as much of his spare time as possible to roaming the woods of the Pacific Northwest in search of the elusive creature. Patterson always carried a motion picture camera with him on his expeditions, hoping that he might be able to catch one of the monsters on film.

Around 1:15 in the afternoon on October 20, 1967, Patterson and a friend, Bob Gimlin, were riding on horseback north along a dry stretch of Bluff Creek in the Six Rivers National Forest of northern California. At one point, a large pile of logs in the middle of the stream bed blocked their path, and they had to maneuver their horses around to the east. As they rode along the logs, they veered left and resumed their original course, only to see something that still has investigators and researchers puzzled today.

A female Bigfoot stood up from the creek where she had been squatting and walked away from the approaching men and horses, moving briskly and swinging her arms as she moved toward the forest. At the same time this occurred, all three horses (including the pack horse) began to panic. Patterson's horse reared up and fell over sideways, but managed to stagger back to its feet again. As it did, Patterson quickly reached for the 16mm camera in his saddlebag and began to follow the creature, filming as he went. Unfortunately, only 28 feet of film remained in the camera but Patterson managed to use it to record the Bigfoot's escape from three different positions.

After his return to civilization, Patterson enlisted the help of researcher John Green to get some sort of scientific confirmation of the evidence that he had captured, without any luck. The amateur investigator was ignored and berated by the established scientific community, so in 1968, he took his case to the public. After padding his film footage with a documentary-style look at other evidence gathered in the search for Bigfoot, he went on a tour of the American West, renting small theaters and auditoriums for one-night shows and lectures. Since that time, the footage has gone on to become one of the most famous -- and most controversial -- pieces of Bigfoot evidence.

Patterson's life was cut short in 1972 when he died, nearly broke, from Hodgkin's Disease, but he swore to the end that the sighting and the film were authentic. Bob Gimlin also maintained that the events really took place and that his friend's film was the genuine article. Gimlin did not start out as a believer in the creature. He was interested but unconvinced and only came along on Patterson's expeditions out of friendship, rather than a belief that they would actually find anything. "He'd talk about it around the campfire," he said in an interview. "I didn't care, but after a time you'd find yourself looking for the doggone thing too."

The first investigator on the scene of the sighting was a man named Bob Titmus, who found tracks that matched the creature's stride depicted in the film. He made ten casts of them and discovered that the footprints led up a small hill, where the creature had paused to look back on the men below. Patterson and Gimlin had elected to recover their horses rather than pursue the Bigfoot and risk being stranded in the wilderness.

The legacy of Patterson's film lives on, despite the fact that it has never settled the question as to whether or not Bigfoot exists in the forests of America. Researchers have argued about the speed of the film, the gait of the creature, the length of its stride and more. Most biologists and zoologists who have studied it remain noncommittal. Film experts and individuals experienced with hoaxes have been unable to find evidence that it is not authentic. For this reason, the film has never been successfully debunked.

Of course, that's not for lack of trying. Recent claims against the validity of the film have stated that the Bigfoot was actually a man in a monkey suit. Some maintain that Patterson and Gimlin were knowing participants in the hoax, and that they rented the suit with the idea of profiting from the resulting film. This is in spite of the fact that the men made very little money from it and Patterson died nearly broke. Regardless, this theory has it that Patterson and Gimlin (who were both barely making ends meet as rodeo riders in 1967) rented an expensive costume, transported it to an area that was nearly inaccessible by car and cleverly shot the grainy, jerky and poorly executed film.

Defenders of the film believe this is ridiculous and state that a frame-by-frame analysis of the footage shows a creature that does not walk like a man. Anthropologist Grover Krantz demonstrated that humans lock their knees when they walk, but the filmed Bigfoot does not do this. It would have been very difficult for a hoaxer to pull off and still walk as smoothly as this creature does. In addition, after viewing the film with Bigfoot investigator Peter Byrne in 1973, the chief technician at Disney Studios stated that "the only place in the world a simulation of that quality could be created would be here, at Disney Studios, and this footage was not made here." If the Bigfoot was a fake, it was one that was very, very well done.

And while the Disney tech may have been overstating the importance of his studio, there were very few places that such a film (or a suit like that) could have been made in the late 1960s. Even the detractors grudgingly agree that Patterson and Gimlin did not have the resources to pull off a hoax of that magnitude, and certainly could not have paid to have such a convincing-looking suit created. Only two companies could have created a costume of that type, at that time, and both claimed that they did not do so. To make matters more mysterious, the person in the suit (if there was one) has remained silent for more than thirty-five years, ignoring the opportunity for financial gain by confessing.

Interestingly, a more popular theory as to who made the suit has emerged within the last few years. According to some conspiracy theorists, the Patterson Bigfoot was actually a man wearing a suit created by master makeup artist John Chambers, who created the makeup for the classic film *Planet of the Apes*, along with numerous other makeup credits. The debunkers have fixed on Chambers for a couple of reasons, including his award-winning makeup effects for the movie and also for the fact that the movie finished filming on August 10, 1967, just a couple of months before Patterson's encounter. The idea is that Patterson could have easily rented one of the surplus monkey suits for his own purposes.

Even though this seems somewhat plausible, the theory has its problems. For one thing, the Bigfoot in Patterson's film looks nothing like the apes that were created for the movie. The apes in *Planet of the Apes* were not suits but were mostly facial makeup. The Bigfoot in Patterson's film does not resemble these apes at all. The idea that Chambers may have created the Bigfoot suit was apparently the result of director John Landis joking about it to some friends at a party. As anyone who knows anything about Hollywood knows, you can't take every rumor you hear seriously in that town. To complicate things further,

Chambers repeatedly denied the claims until his death. He told interviewers that he was "good, but not that good" in response to the story. It has been the general consensus that Chambers enjoyed having people think that he *might* have made the suit because it bolstered his skills as an artist. The truth is that it's very unlikely that he made it. In spite of this, the story lives on.

To this day, the debate continues to rage. Many Bigfoot experts believe that it is valid footage of an unknown creature, but just as many people laugh when the subject is brought up. While I see that it might be possible for Chambers to have created the suit and helped to perpetrate a hoax, I really have to ask if it's plausible. I have no hard evidence to back up my opinion that the film is genuine. I have followed the debate for quite some time and have found nothing to convince me that this is a person wearing a costume. Based on the time period, I don't think that enough information had been made available to the general public for someone to have imitated a creature in the way that the Bigfoot moves in the Patterson film. Just because Chambers *could* (and this is debatable) have made the suit does not mean that he did.

The Bossburg Tracks

After the remarkable film footage obtained by Roger Patterson began making the rounds, the feeling in Bigfoot circles seemed to be that they were close to catching the animal. Over the years, there have been literally thousands of fraudulent footprints, photos and film that have been "discovered" since Bigfoot entered the mainstream. While much of the alleged evidence appears dubious at best, other Bigfoot so-called "evidence" has managed to defy easy explanation. When such evidence appeared, it gave researchers the feeling that anything could happen next.

In the wake of the Patterson film, the next major event to occur was in Bossburg, in the extreme northwest corner of Washington State. On November 24, 1969, near Bossburg's town dump, a butcher named Joseph Rhodes found a bizarre set of tracks. They appeared to belong to a creature that walked on two feet, one of which was deformed. The word spread quickly among Bigfoot researchers, including Rene Dahinden, a Canadian who spent decades conducting field investigations and interviews throughout the Northwest. He was a major advocate for the authenticity of the Patterson film and the character of the French Canadian Bigfoot hunter in the film *Harry and the Hendersons* was based on him.

When Dahinden arrived in Bossburg, he found and covered one of the better pair of tracks. One clearly shows that the right foot that had made the track was deformed. It looked as if it had two bumps out to the side and only four toes showing. Using what he had available (a cardboard box), Dahinden casually preserved what many consider to be one of the best pieces of Bigfoot evidence ever found.

From seven hundred miles away, in western British Columbia, Bob Titmus, a taxidermist and Bigfoot researcher who taught Jerry Crew how to make plaster casts of the tracks at Bluff Creek in 1958, made his way to Bossburg. His behavior seemed eccentric to Dahinden, who wrote that Titmus, "went out and bought an eight-pound slab of beef and hung it in a tree. I believe that he was sitting out there at night in a panel truck, watching the meat, thinking that if this thing was a cripple and was living off the garbage dump, when it came along, he would just grab it by the arse and throw it in the truck and run off home with it."

Another Bigfoot hunter named Norm Davis had a similar plan. He put out a big bowl of fruit in the hope of luring Bigfoot. Titmus left within three days. Dahinden and Davis became friendly and began sharing a trailer, which they moved onto land that belonged to Ivan Marx, who had been part of the Tom Slick expedition to look for the Yeti a few years before. The three of them combined resources to continue the search around Bossburg.

On December 13, 1969, after a significant snowfall, Dahinden, Marx and a local man named Jim Hopkins went scouting for signs of Bigfoot around Roosevelt Lake. It was there that they stumbled upon a series of 1,089 tracks: the remains of the best footprints ever discovered in America. They measured 17-1/2 inches long and about seven inches wide and seemed to indicate that the creature that left them had a right clubfoot, the result, some surmised, of a childhood injury. This minor detail seemed to rule out any chance of a fraud for it's unlikely that any hoaxer would have gone to the trouble to include this deformity in such a huge number of tracks.

The unusually long trail followed waterways, going around a lake and along a river. It crossed railroad tracks, and stepped over a five-wire fence that was forty-three inches high. Then, the creature rested, apparently in a depression in the floor of the pine forest, before going up a hill, then back down, leaving a patch of yellow snow where it had relieved itself. From there, the Bigfoot appeared to backtrack, going through some underbrush, and to an overhang by the river's edge. The trail of tracks finally vanished where the creature descended the river's bank to the rocky edge where the trail could not be followed.

Dahinden photographed the tracks carefully and examined each print along the route. The three men did not have many resources, so they kept some of the prints from the snow in Marx's freezer. They were later inadvertently destroyed. Regardless, plenty of proof existed to show that the prints were real. Their sheer number and occurrence in a remote and seldom-traveled area argued against a hoax. Why would someone go to the trouble of creating phony Bigfoot tracks in a place where no one would likely ever see them?

Not surprisingly, when word of the tracks leaked out, tourists with cameras descended on the area, ruining and trampling the fragile evidence. But the Bossburg events continued anyway. A U.S. Border Patrol officer found new tracks on the far side of the river on December 18. The distinctive prints of the crippled right foot could be seen, though a recent rain had mostly washed them out. More Bigfoot hunters arrived, including Roy Fardell and Roger St. Hillaire, a young zoologist from San Francisco; Roger Patterson and his associate, Dennis Jensen. Patterson came and went, but Jensen stayed behind to "protect" Patterson's role in the hunt. Ohio millionaire Tom Page pledged money to the hunt and soon off-road vehicles and snowmobiles arrived and the hunters were backed up by air searchers.

Dahinden, Patterson, Marx, Jensen, Fardell, St. Hillaire and others held together as a loosely-knit group of hunters through most of early January 1970. Then on January 27, a startling announcement was received at the hunters' camp.

On that day, Joe Metlow began claiming that he had found a cream-colored Sasquatch, discovered where it lived, and had captured it in its cave. He wanted the researchers to start bidding for the cave's location. Patterson was being marginally funded by Tom Page and he was on the telephone to Page right away. Page flew out to meet him and the big split between the Patterson camp and the Dahinden camp began.

Page was initially willing to spend $35,000 for a Bigfoot, dead or alive. Then Dahinden got into the bidding and researcher John Green came to Bossburg. Green essentially served as a mediator between the two camps. The bidding had reached $55,000 for the Bigfoot. Page's helicopter was standing by at Colville airport to take the creature away. Things were reaching circus-like proportions.

The problem was that Metlow's story kept changing. Dahinden, during a moment of truce with the Patterson camp, paid a visit with Dennis Jensen to Metlow's home. Conversation was general and friendly until Metlow casually mentioned that he had a Sasquatch foot in his freezer. Dahinden became excited and offered $500 for a look at the specimen. Metlow demanded $5,000. Before anything could be confirmed, a crony of Metlow had a contract sketched out that would include John Green to write a book about the discovery, Bob Titmus to skin and dissect the owner of the foot - presumably stashed in a cave somewhere above the snow line - and Dr. Grover Krantz to present the creature to science. Dahinden was soon shut out of the mix, and so was Patterson.

After a series of fruitless searches, following instructions provided by Metlow, the Bigfoot hunters figured out that there was nothing to his wild claims and things grew heated and raw in Bossburg. A lot of time, money and energy had been wasted. The hunters left town discouraged, but a little more aware of the shenanigans that would often run rampant in the Bigfoot hunting field.

But that wasn't the end of the Bossburg story.

Rene Dahinden kept in touch with Ivan Marx throughout 1970 and Marx always had some new, exciting find to tell him about: a new footprint, some handprints and even a new Bigfoot film in 1971. Tom Page returned to the area, offering Marx $25,000 for the film, but it turned out to be a hoax. Researcher and author John Green called Marx "the biggest, well, yarn-spinner in California."

Marx had lived in California for many years but had moved to Bossburg in 1969. The famed Bossburg "crippled" footprints started soon after and continued until 1971, with Dahinden, Krantz, Green, Patterson and others finding their way to the area. Millionaire Bigfoot enthusiast Tom Page made an appearance and researcher Peter Byrne reportedly put Marx on a $750 monthly retainer as a

Sasquatch hunter after the 1971 film surfaced. But Byrne soon discovered that the film was a fake.

Were the Bossburg prints authentic, or were they, as some researchers came to believe, the product of Ivan Marx? In 1978, John Green simply stated: "I tend to write off the whole Bossburg episode to entertainment." But not everyone agreed. Many believe the prints were genuine, their reputation damaged by the questionable activities (and people) that surrounded the incident. The casts that still exist of the crippled tracks led authorities like Grover Krantz, the late anthropologist who was one of the first academics to consider the possibility that Bigfoot exists, to believe in their reality. Anthropologist John Napier also felt the tracks were genuine. He wrote, "Either some of the footprints are real, or all are fakes. If they are all fakes, then an explanation invoking legend and folk memory is adequate to explain the mystery. But if any of them is real, then as scientists we have a lot to explain. Among other things we will have to rewrite the story of human evolution. We shall have to accept that *Homo sapiens* is not the one and only living product of the hominid line, and we shall have to admit that there are still major mysteries to be solved in the world we thought we knew so well."

The Grover Krantz-certified footprints have become famous in the Bigfoot community and have been largely accepted as authentic, at least to everyone who considers the possibility of the existence of Bigfoot. But the question still remains: was Ivan Marx merely lucky once and then attempted to stay in the limelight through hoaxes later on? Or was the Bossburg incident, from start to finish, just an entertaining episode that we can only view today as a cautionary tale? The reader will have to be the judge.

Bigfoot on the Back Roads of Illinois

Growing up in Illinois, and always being in search of the strange and unusual, I discovered the works of author Loren Coleman, another central Illinois native who went on to write a number of books and articles on the state's mysterious monsters. Loren's passion for high strangeness was infectious, and I was soon tracking down the sources of his stories - as well as stumbling into a few of my own.

For more than a century, reports have filtered out of rural and southern Illinois about strange, man-like beasts that resemble a cross between man and ape. Most witnesses talk of their odd appearance and the horrible odor that seems to accompany them. The stories of these Bigfoot creatures have been passed along from generation to generation and have long been chronicled by both professional and amateur researchers. There are so many reports of Bigfoot in Illinois that it is only rivaled by the Pacific Northwest for its number of creature sightings. Some of the classics of Bigfoot literature stem from Illinois, which makes it worth mentioning in this chapter.

The earliest sighting that I could find from this region comes from Centreville in September 1883 and concerned a "wild man" that was seen in the nearby woods. He was described as a "naked roaming madman," who had been "roaming around the country" for several days and had been causing "intense excitement and consternation" among the rural folks who lived in and around this small community. The man was described as having a long, dark beard and his body was covered with matted hair. He had a tall "athletic form" and a fierce look in his eyes that "make him exceedingly unpleasant to meet in a lonely spot." The creature was first seen by the wife of Dr. John Saltenberger, who was returning home shortly after nightfall when she saw him creeping out of the orchard on her property. As he made a quick rush toward her horse and buggy, Mrs. Saltenberger lashed frantically at him with her whip and then snapped the reins. The horse picked up the pace but the creature stayed close behind and then, suddenly, it leapt onto the back of the carriage. He only remained there for a few moments before jumping down and running into the woods. Needless to say, Mrs. Saltenberger was terrified by the encounter. The following day, her husband placed a telephone call to Belleville and asked the sheriff to come and capture the creature. He was joined in his hunt by several young men from the area but despite a thorough search of the woods around Centreville, the monster never turned up.

After that, the next report dates to around 1912. A woman named Beulah Schroat reported that she and her brothers had often encountered hairy creatures in the woods near their home outside of Effingham when they were children. According to her description, the beasts stood on their hind legs and were about as tall as a normal people, with large eyes and copious amounts of hair. The creatures seemed very shy and harmless and always ran away whenever they were approached. The children usually saw them near a small creek on the farm, where they waded and splashed about. Mrs. Schroat said that her brothers would often run to the house after an encounter to report the sighting, but their parents dismissed the stories as practical jokes until they found an article about similar monsters in a Chicago newspaper.

The next documented account was a brief report about a man-like beast covered in brown hair and with an apelike face that was spotted near Alton in 1925. There are unfortunately no other details to accompany this account.

Another report comes not long after the Alton sighting. In this brief snippet, we find that a "huge gorilla" was seen in the woods near Elizabeth in July 1929. Then, in 1941, the Reverend Lepton Harpole was hunting squirrels near Mt. Vernon when he encountered a large creature that "looked something like a baboon." He struck it with the butt of his rifle and fired a warning shot that sent it scurrying back into the underbrush. More sightings of the same creature occurred the next year, and searches were conducted along the Gun Creek Bottoms in hopes of tracking the creature down. More than 1,500 men attempted to flush out the beast, which was said to have a "wildcat's scream," combing the bottoms with shotguns and rifles at the ready. The animal was blamed for the death of a dog in the vicinity. No trace of it was ever found.

From the 1940s and into the 1960s, huge prints were discovered along the marshy areas of Indian Creek in southwestern Illinois. The creature leaving the tracks was dubbed the "Gooseville Bear," taking its name from an area of farmland and small businesses that were located about three miles east of Bethalto at the intersection of Route 140 and Indian Creek. Some identified the tracks as belonging to a bear but others insisted that they were man-like. Whatever the beast was, it was never seen, and after leaving its mark on the area for almost two decades, it disappeared.

In 1962, a grayish-colored creature was spotted by Steven Collins and Robert Earle standing in a riverbed east of Decatur, just off of East Williams Street Road. The monster was looming upright in the water, looking straight at them. At first, they thought it was a bear, until they noticed its strange, human-like features. The creature vanished into the woods and the astonished witnesses told the local newspaper that it was "like no other animal we had ever seen before."

In September 1965, four young people were parked in a car near an undeveloped area outside of Decatur called Montezuma Hills. The area would later become a housing addition but at that time, it was a secluded lovers' lane. The young couples were sitting in the car when a black, man-like shape approached the vehicle. The creature seemed massive and it frightened the teenagers badly. They drove off in a panic, but after dropping off their dates at home, the two young men returned to the area for another look. They once again saw the monster, and it walked up to their car as though it were curious. The boys were too scared to get out, but even with the windows rolled up, they gagged at the monster's horrible stench. They quickly summoned the police, and with several officers as support, they made a thorough, but fruitless, search of the woods. The police officers said they had no idea what the young people had witnessed, but they were obviously very frightened by whatever it had been.

Another man-like creature was encountered near Chittyville in August 1968. Two young people, Tim Bullock and Barbara Smith, were driving north of town on August 11 when they spotted a ten-foot-tall monster that was covered with black hair and had a round face. It threw dirt at their car and they quickly left to summon the police. When the authorities returned, they found a large depression in the grass that was apparently a nest. Local residents claimed that their dogs had been "carrying on" for the two weeks before the encounter.

Another frightening encounter occurred about one month later, in September 1968, a few miles outside of Carpentersville in Cook County. Two young men were driving along some back roads, searching for a party they had been invited to, and got lost somewhere east of what is now Barrington Hills. As they drove along the wooded roads, they stopped and then started to turn around and drive back towards Carpentersville when they saw something at the edge of the road. A creature, which the witnesses stated was "about as tall as our Ford van," started out across the roadway, about fifteen to twenty feet in front of their vehicle. The creature had a long stride, stood upright and was covered with dark brown (almost black) hair that was matted and longer in some spots. It swung its arms as it walked, in a manner that suggested they were too long for its torso. As it crossed the road, it turned and looked at the two men. Its face was covered with hair, except around the eyes, nose and mouth. Its face was flat, they said, more like an ape's than a man's.

As the driver was backing up and turning the vehicle around, the passenger looked to his right as they pulled away. What he saw gave him quite a fright: the creature had changed direction, as if to chase their van! They were terrified as "it looked so powerful that it could have torn the doors off the van with no trouble whatsoever." They immediately left the area and did not return for another look at whatever they had encountered there in the woods.

A violent encounter with some sort of hairy monster occurred about one month later, in October 1968, just outside Lewiston in Fulton County. At about 9:30 p.m. one Friday evening, three high school boys in a truck were following a friend in his car near the Dutch Henry crossing. All at once, the boys in the truck were forced to stop, as they saw their friend's car was now parked crossways in the road in front of them. In the headlights, they could see their friend lying on the road, seemingly unconscious. The boys got out of the truck and were walking toward the other boy when something came out of the darkness and knocked them to the ground. Each time they tried to get up, they were knocked back down again. The boys later reported that, whatever it was, it did not hit them with its fists but backhanded them with terrific force. At one point, the boys managed to wrestle the creature to the ground, but it knocked them aside with ease.

During the fighting, the first boy, whom the others had discovered lying on the ground, ran for the truck and locked the doors. He said he got a fairly good look at the creature, and that it was not too tall but was very strongly built and seemed to be very hairy. Too terrified to get out of the truck, he remained there until something frightened the monster away. It vanished into the woods. The boys were not badly harmed but they were shaken up and the incident was reported to the local police. No trace of the creature was ever found.

One of the strangest Illinois incidents took place in July 1970, near Farmer City. Early that spring, three sheep had been killed near town. Local officials dismissed it as the work of wild dogs, which had been known to roam the area. Outside the small town, near Salt Creek, was a ten-acre section of woods and fields that was a popular parking spot for teenagers.

Three teenagers decided to camp out there one night. Very late in the evening, they reported hearing something approaching their campsite in the tall grass. They turned a light in that direction and saw a huge, black shape crouching near their tent. The shape had a pair of gleaming, yellow eyes, which was a color that would be repeated in every account to follow. The terrified screams of the teenagers scared the creature and all of them ran off in different directions.

Stories about the "Farmer City Monster" quickly spread. Dozens of people reported seeing the creature over the next several days, with all of the sightings taking place near the wooded area outside of town. Robert Hayslip, a Farmer City police officer who investigated the scene, reported his own encounter. In the early morning hours of July 15, he saw the broad back of the creature moving along the trees. The creature turned in his direction and Hayslip noted its yellow eyes. The local police chief, who until that point had been skeptical about the sightings, decided to close off the area. The creature was soon to move on.

On July 24, a couple driving near Weldon Springs State Park, outside of Clinton, saw what looked like a huge bear in the river. Later, a policeman and a conservation officer found tracks along the water's edge that definitely did not belong to a bear. They were reportedly very large and human-like.

A few days later, farther north, a woman caught the reflection of eyes with her car headlights as she was traveling outside Bloomington. She thought the eyes might belong to a dog that had been injured by a passing car, so she stopped and approached the ditch where she had seen the eyes shining. Suddenly, a large creature jumped out of the ditch and ran away on two legs. She was unsure about what she had seen, but whatever it was, it seemed ape-like. Later that same week, another witness reported seeing an identical creature near Heyworth.

On August 11, three young men reported seeing a large, dark-haired creature near Waynesville, and five days later, construction workers saw the creature near the same location. It ran across the highway in front of their truck and disappeared into the forest. That was the last report of the so-called "Farmer City Monster." One can't help but wonder if it continued its strange journey northwest across central Illinois. If it did, it was never reported again.

In May 1972, there were new reports coming in from the Pekin and Peoria areas. In late May, a young man named Randy Emmert, along with some of his friends, reported a large, hairy creature near Cole Hollow Road. This monster was eight to ten feet tall and whitish in color. The witnesses stated that it made a loud, screeching sound and they suspected that it was living in a hole beneath an abandoned house. It left very unusual tracks, having only three toes on each foot. Soon, others were reporting the same monster and it became known as "Cohomo," short for the "Cole Hollow Road Monster".

On May 25, local police logged more than two hundred calls about the monster, including one where the creature destroyed a fence. The police departments were naturally skeptical, but the calls kept coming in. By July 1972, there had been so many sightings that nearly one hundred volunteers were organized to search for Cohomo. Tazewell County sheriff's officers eventually sent the volunteers home after one of them, Carl R. Harris, accidentally shot himself in the leg with a .22 caliber pistol.

The sightings continued and they couldn't be written off to local panic, either. One witness, from Eureka knew nothing about the creature, yet happened to be in Fondulac Park, in East Peoria, for a birthday party when he spotted it. He reported the creature and, strangely, a set of strange lights that seemed to descend vertically and land behind some trees. Were the two sightings connected? No one knows, but whatever the creature was, it was gone.

In the summer of 1973, the town of Murphysboro in southwestern Illinois became the scene of a series of monster sightings. The enigmatic creature, now recalled as the "Murphysboro Mud Monster," or the "Big Muddy Monster," appeared without warning and then suddenly disappeared two weeks later, seemingly without a trace. In its wake, the monster left a number of confused and frightened witnesses, baffled law enforcement officials and an enduring legend.

The monster that wreaked havoc in Murphysboro was first seen around midnight on Monday, June 25, 1973. On that humid and steamy night, a young couple, Randy Needham and Judy Johnson, were parked near a boat ramp into the Big Muddy River near Murphysboro. The night was quiet until a strange, roaring cry shattered the stillness. It came from the nearby woods and Randy and Judy looked up to see a huge shape lumbering toward them from out of the shadows. Whatever it was, it walked on two legs and continued to make the horrible sound. They later described the noise as "something not human."

According to their account, the monster was about seven feet tall and was covered with matted, whitish hair. The "fur" was streaked with mud from the river. As it lurched toward them, the tone of the creature's cry began to change, alarming them even further. When the creature approached to within twenty feet of them, they quickly fled the scene, and went directly to the Murphysboro police station.

"They were absolutely terrified," former Police Chief Ron Manwaring recalled in 2003, the thirtieth anniversary of the sightings. The retired officer agreed to be interviewed about the case and remembered all that he could about what happened. "I'm convinced that they saw something that night... I can't tell you what it was that they saw, whether it was a bear or something else. But something was definitely there."

A short time later, Officers Meryl Lindsay and Jimmie Nash responded to the area and surveyed the scene. Although skeptical, they were surprised to find that a number of footprints had been left in the mud. The footprints were "approximately 10-12 inches long and approximately three inches wide." At 2:00 a.m., Nash, Lindsay, a Jackson County sheriff's deputy named Bob Scott, and Randy Needham returned to the scene. This time, they discovered more tracks and Lindsay left to go get a camera. The others followed the new footprints, tracing their path along the river.

Suddenly, from the woods about one hundred yards away, they heard the creature's terrifying scream. They didn't wait to see if they could spot the monster. They made a quick retreat for the patrol car instead. Needham later recalled that the sheriff's deputy was so scared that he dropped his gun into the mud. After waiting in the darkness for a little while, they got back out of the patrol car and spent the rest of the night trying to track down a splashing sound they heard in the distance. Things quieted down after daylight, but the next night, the creature was back.

The first to see the monster this time was a four-year-old boy named Christian Baril, who told his parents that he saw a "big white ghost in the yard." They didn't believe him, but when Randy Creath and Cheryl Ray saw an identical monster in a neighboring yard just ten minutes later, Christian's parents, and the police, quickly reconsidered the little boy's statement.

Randy and Cheryl spotted the monster at about 10:30 p.m. while sitting on the back porch of the Ray house. They heard the sound of something moving in the woods near the river and then spotted the muddy, white creature staring at them with glowing, pink eyes. Cheryl would insist that the eyes were actually glowing and were not reflecting light from some other source. They estimated that it weighed at least 350 pounds, stood seven feet tall, had a roundish head and long, ape-like arms. Cheryl turned on the porch light and Randy went for a closer look. The creature seemed unconcerned and finally ambled off into the woods. Investigators would later find a trail of broken tree branches and crushed undergrowth, along with a number of large footprints. They also noticed a strong odor left in the monster's wake, which lingered for a short time.

The officers who arrived on the scene, Jimmie Nash and Chief Ron Manwaring, quickly summoned Jerry Nellis, a local dog handler who often assisted the police department in searching buildings and tracking suspects. He brought a German shepherd to go in pursuit of the monster. The dog followed a trail through the weeds and then managed to track the creature through the woods and down a hill to a small pond. Eventually, the trees and undergrowth became too thick for the dog to continue and he was put back on the leash after almost pulling Nellis off a steep embankment. The officers began searching the area with flashlights, and the dog began sniffing near the trees, hoping to pick up the scent again. He then set off toward an abandoned barn, but refused to go inside. Instead, the animal began shaking with fear and started barking.

Nellis called the two officers over and they opened the barn and went inside. After a few moments, they realized that it was empty. The three men were puzzled. The dog had been trained to search buildings and Nellis could not explain why it had refused to enter the barn. A short time later, the search was called off for the night.

The Mud Monster was reported two more times that summer. On the night of July 4, traveling carnival workers stated that they spotted the creature disturbing some Shetland ponies that were being used for the holiday celebration at Riverside Park. This report actually came in on July 7, because the carnival owner was concerned that the sighting might scare away potential customers. However, he did tell the police that several of his workers noticed the ponies attempting to break loose from the trees where they had been tied up for the night. According to the police report, the workers described the monster as being seven to eight feet tall with light brown hair all over its body. It stood erect on two legs and weighed at least 300 to 400 pounds. The creature stood very close to the ponies and while it seemed curious, it did not advance on them or threaten them in any way.

Then, on July 7, Mrs. Nedra Green heard a screaming sound coming from a shed on her rural farm. She did not go out to investigate but the description of the cries matched the description given by Randy Needham, Judy Johnson and the police officers who also heard it. This was the last incident connected to the monster to occur that summer.

As the story leaked out, it turned up in the newspapers, got posted to the wire services and soon made headlines across the country. Even the *New York Times* sent a reporter to investigate. The story of the Big Muddy Monster made it around the world and soon letters came pouring into the Murphysboro Police Department from as far away as South Africa. Researchers, curiosity-seekers and even scientists were pleading with the local authorities to release more information.

They received letters from hunters and trappers who offered to track down the monster and kill or capture it. Two men from Oregon offered to do the job and wrote that they "would be willing to take on this adventure at only the cost of expenses and materials for doing so." Some wrote suggesting that the police try using bait to snare the creature. A Florida man suggested, "Why don't you put bread and cheese and eggs out for your creature? You would have a splendid attraction if you could have it in a little hut, to show people."

Assistant professor Leigh Van Valen, from the University of Chicago's Biology Department, also wrote to Chief Manwaring. "I have heard of your creature," his letter stated, "which could be of considerable scientific interest. There have been many reports of such animals but no real specimens have been available for scientific study." Professor Van Valen went on to explain how the creature, if circumstances required shooting it, should be properly embalmed or "preserved in good condition." The professor agreed to cover the necessary expenses to procure the monster for scientific study.

In the end, all of the ideas and suggestions didn't matter, for the monster never returned to Murphysboro. There was only one other sighting that could possibly have been the creature. It occurred in the fall of that same year, a number of miles southwest of town, near the Mississippi River. A local truck driver told police that he saw a monster that resembled the Murphysboro creature along the edge of the road. It vanished before he could get a good look at it, but it left behind a number of large tracks in the mud. The authorities made casts of the impressions but they were unable to determine if they matched the previous footprints or were the work of a prankster. After that one last gasp, the Big Muddy Monster simply faded away.

So what was the Murphysboro Mud Monster? Local authorities admitted that they didn't know then and to this day, no one has offered a logical explanation for the sightings. One of the police officers involved in the case said, "A lot of things in life are unexplained and this is another one. We don't know what the creature is, but we do believe what these people saw was real."

Some of the locals were skeptical. Jerry Nellis, the dog handler, said many years that that, "in my opinion ... we were tracking a bear."

But Randy Needham, one of the first to see the monster, disagreed. He stated with certainty, "It would be kind of naïve for us to think that we know everything that's out there." Needham added that after his encounters in 1973, he never went into the woods at night again. And even in the daytime, he never went alone. "I always look for way out in case I need to leave fast," he said.

American Apes

Many Bigfoot researchers, like author and cryptozoologist Loren Coleman, have come to believe that perhaps the Sasquatch of the Pacific Northwest and the creatures sighted in some other parts of the country may be different monsters entirely. The creatures of many of the southern and central states (like the so-called "Skunk Apes" of Florida) seem to be different than the traditional Bigfoot. They have been seen and tracked throughout the South and lower Midwest, usually in the swampy woods, bottomlands and along the rivers. The classic Bigfoot stands upright, walking on two legs, and averages between six and eight feet tall. It leaves a giant print that looks like an oversized human footprint, complete with five toes. However, what Coleman called the "North American Apes," are more ape-like, shorter (as has been noted in some of the previous accounts), and are sometimes seen walking on all fours. It often leaves a footprint that is more like a hand - that is, with the big toe sticking out to the side, like a thumb.

In many reports, the word gorilla was used to describe these river-bottom dwelling creatures. In Boone County, Indiana, in 1949, two fishermen were chased away from Sugar Creek by a brown "gorilla." In 1962, a Kentucky farmer named Owen Powell spotted a "gorilla" that was six feet tall, walking on its back legs and having front legs or arms that hung down to its knees. In 1968, a Kinloch, Missouri, boy was allegedly snatched and then released in the backyard of his home by what he called a "gorilla." The creature was frightened off by a barking dog and the screams of the boy's aunt. In 1968, newspapers near Hamburg, Arkansas, printed stories about a prowling "gorilla." Over a three-year period from 1967 to 1970, a Calumet, Oklahoma, man believed that he was seeing an ape on a regular basis. He left out bananas and oranges for the animal, which he hoped to capture. The effort ended without success. These reports - along with many others - are often buried in among the traditional Bigfoot accounts because that term is more widely used today.

In many such cases, sightings and reports have become part of the folklore of the area in which they occurred. In Allen County, Kentucky, the name Monkey Cave Hollow was given to an area northeast of Scottsville. Early settlers to the area stated that it was inhabited by a tribe of beings that they identified as some kind of monkey. The creatures foraged in the woods and took refuge in small caves. An account from an "old-timer" recalled seeing the carcass of the last "monkey." A hunter had brought the body to his father's house when the man was only seven or eight years old. He could not remember exactly what it looked like after nearly eighty years, but said that the creature had hands and feet "like a person," was about the same size as the boy, had no tail, but was covered in brown hair.

In some cases, the old events become cloudy with the passage of time. An incident from 1900 in Hannibal, Missouri, said that local residents noticed a mysterious animal moving about on a large wooded island on the Mississippi River near the town. The sheriff was notified and he said that he thought it was a hyena, except that it was eating grass. When the sheriff and a few other men captured it, it turned out to be "the man from Borneo," who had allegedly escaped from a circus, which was happy to get him back. In those days, the "man from Borneo" was a common nickname for an orangutan - which would have been incapable of swimming the Mississippi or any other river.

Despite the fact that the known species of great apes do not swim, the North American apes never seem to have a problem doing so. They are very often found up and down the Mississippi waterways, as well as in the forests that border the river systems. A high percentage of sightings take place in the river and creek bottoms of rural America. The popular film *The Legend of Boggy Creek* (a docudrama in that it was mostly factual in the details, but melodramatic in the re-creations), is about Fouke, Arkansas', ape-like "monster." It noted several times that "he always travels the creeks."

A sighting of a swimming ape in 1969 reinforces the point. On November 7, a man named Charles Buchanan was camping on the shore of Lake Worth in Texas when he awoke around 2:00 a.m. to see a hairy creature that looked "like a cross between a human being and a gorilla or an ape" towering above him. Buchanan had been sleeping in the bed of his pickup truck when the beast suddenly jerked him out and pulled him to the ground, still trapped in his sleeping bag. Gagging from the creature's foul stench, Charles did the only thing that he could think of and grabbed a bag of leftover chicken and shoved it in the creature's face. It took the sack in its mouth, made some grunting sounds and then ran off through the trees toward the lake. It first splashed into the water, then began swimming with powerful strokes toward Greer Island.

Out in the Woods

The authentic tracks and credible sightings of these mysterious apes seem to suggest that there may be another creature lurking out there in woods and forests of America, along with Bigfoot, the most elusive of the hairy bipeds. Are such creatures real, the product of wild imaginations run amuck, or could they be an almost-vanished race of unknown animal that is encountered on rare occasions in remote and isolated areas?

Believe it or not, evidence suggests that there really is something out there. In addition to the numerous eyewitness accounts, there are the hundreds of plaster casts and photographs of giant, unexplained footprints. Other evidence that has been discovered consists of feces and hair samples that are either associated with sightings or may have been indications of a Bigfoot's recent passing. Many of these samples seem to resist identification.

But what about the body of a Bigfoot? Debunkers and skeptics say that Bigfoot cannot exist for if it did, then someone would have found the corpse of one by now. Jeffrey Meldrum, an associate professor of anthropology at Idaho State University, disagrees. "Think about it," he said in an interview. "It's rare, reproduces infrequently, and if it's like other apes, it may live for fifty years. It's at the top of the food chain, so death most likely comes from natural causes. When an animal is ill or feeble, it'll hide somewhere safe, which makes it more difficult to find any remains. Scavengers strip the carcass and scatter the bones.

Rodents chew up what's left for the calcium. Soil in the Northwest is acidic, which is conducive to plant fossilization but not to bones. They disintegrate."

Beyond the physical evidence, there have also been recordings that have been made by Bigfoot hunters of what is alleged to be the "voice" of the creature itself. Many of the tapes have been analyzed, including one notable recording that was obtained on October 21, 1972 in California's High Sierra Mountains. That night, investigators recorded a series of moans, whines, growls and grunts that were coming from the darkness. Two electronic specialists, one from the University of Wyoming and one from Rockwell International, came to the conclusion that the sounds came from "more than one speaker, one or more of which is of larger physical size than an average human male. The formant frequencies found were clearly lower than for human data, and their distribution does not indicate that they were a product of human vocalization and tape speed alteration."

But, no matter how convincing the pieces of evidence might be, the real proof of the creature's existence would be not just capturing its footprints - but the creature himself. If someone could find one and bring it back, it would be the ultimate evidence that Bigfoot really exists.

Today, there are still many researchers out there hunting for Bigfoot, hoping to bring back remains, tracks or anything else that will prove these creatures exist. As mentioned already, the reader is asked to judge the existence of these creatures for himself, for short of solid evidence, we can only surmise that the mysterious giants are out there in the forests of the Northwest. Until one is found, though, they have to remain one of the greatest of the mysteries in the annals of the unexplained in America.

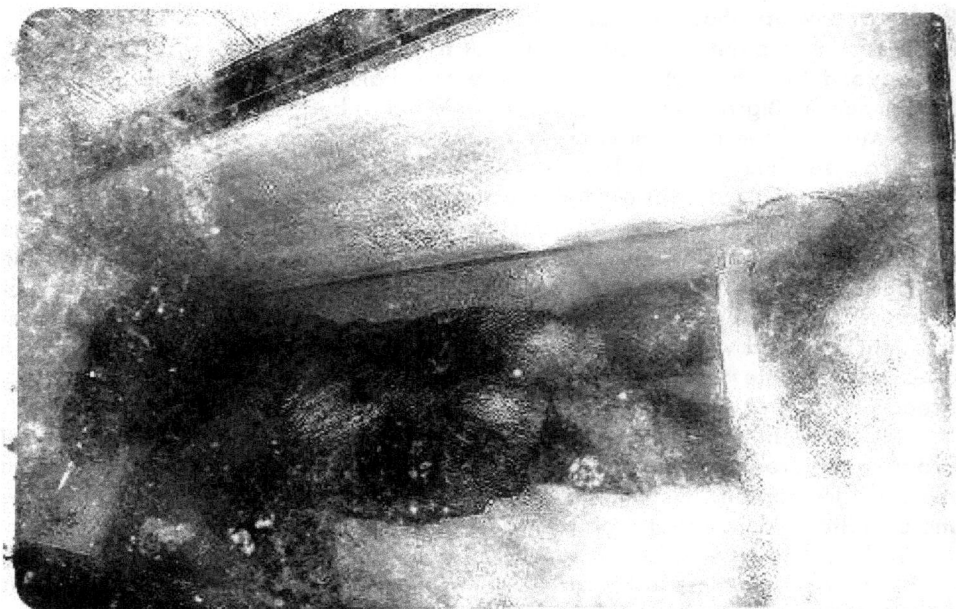

MINNESOTA ICEMAN
WAS THE CARNIVAL ATTRACTION TRUTH OR FICTION?

As I wrote in the introduction to this book, much of my fascination for the weird was fueled during the waning days of the carnival sideshow circuit. In the late 1970s, when I was about 12, I attended the Illinois State Fair and wandered down into an area that was known at the time as "Happy Hollow." This was the best part of the fair for a young boy, for it was where the carnival rides, games of chance and sideshows were located. The late 1970s were a fading time for the carnival sideshow. Political correctness had forced most of the old-time "freak shows" out of business. Occasionally, you still saw someone claiming to be the "world's smallest woman" or a collection of two-headed calves and five-legged pigs or jars of "pickled punks."

More common in those days - and they hung on until the middle 1980s - were the crazy grind shows where a woman supposedly turned into a gorilla or a girl was "Alive! Alive! Alive!" - even though she had no head. Even at twelve years old, I knew such shows were simply illusions, fun romps to part the "rubes" from their money, but I was happy to hand over my hard-earned allowance anyway. In addition to the tent shows, there were also the trailers that claimed to hold giant alligators, rare animals and in one case, the frozen body of the "missing link."

I'll never forget my look through the murky glass at the body of what could only be Bigfoot, shot to death and then frozen in the ice. It certainly seemed real, but was it? I'll likely never know, although chances are what I saw at the state fair that year was merely a dummy - a dummy made up to look like the real thing!

The creature that achieved fame as the "Minnesota Iceman" was one of the first exhibits that ever claimed to be the body of some sort of Bigfoot-like creature, but it was not the last. In recent years, a thriving market has appeared for phony Bigfoot carcasses. With the field sadly filled with hucksters, self-promoters and publicity seekers, it seemed almost inevitable that someone would appear on the scene and (once again) claim to have a dead Bigfoot on ice. In 2008, two Georgia men, Matt Whitton and Rick Dyer, did just that. Unfortunately, only days after the men announced their frozen find at a press conference, their "evidence" was exposed as a rubber ape costume.

Ironically, the hoax was exposed by the very company that the two men teamed up with to announce their supposed find. Searching for Bigfoot, Inc., which was managed by "Sasquatch Detective" Steve Kulls stated that he realized the Bigfoot "corpse" was a fake when the frozen body began to thaw–after the press conference had already taken place. Kulls said that he and a colleague had plucked a few hairs from the defrosting body and burned them for analysis, but became suspicious when they "melted into a ball uncharacteristic of hair." More ominous signs emerged as the ice encasing the body began to melt away. After about another hour of thawing, one of the team members noticed how unnatural one of the "corpse's" feet looked, reached in and confirmed that it was made out of rubber. According to Kulls, that was the first time that the team had been able to investigate the body. He stated that he immediately informed Tom Biscardi, the founder of Searching for Bigfoot, Inc., about the discovery. When confronted, Whitton and Dyer reportedly admitted to the hoax.

The problem was that many of the elements of Kulls' account sharply contradicted earlier statements by Biscardi, who had stood alongside Whitton and Dyer at the earlier press conference in Palo Alto, California. At the conference, Biscardi said he had flown to Georgia and had actually seen, touched, and prodded the body and was satisfied it "was not a mask sewn on a bear hide." He also added that Whitton and Dyer had already given him the Bigfoot body and that it was being kept at an undisclosed location. This was certainly not what Steve Kulls had told the press when it was discovered that the body was a fake.

For many Bigfoot researchers, though, Biscardi's role in the hoax was not a surprise.

Biscardi, a Las Vegas promoter and internet radio host, described himself as a "real Bigfoot hunter" who developed a taste for the search while watching television in 1967 and seeing the first 8mm footage that Roger Patterson took of the Bluff Creek incident. His first search for Bigfoot was reported in the magazine *Saga* in 1973 and in 1981, he produced a documentary film called *In the Shadow of Bigfoot.*

It was in 2005 when Biscardi first got into trouble. On July 14, he appeared on the Coast to Coast AM radio program and claimed that he was "98-percent sure" his group would be able to capture a Bigfoot near Happy Camp, California. On August 19, he returned to say he knew of the location of a captured Bigfoot and that he planned to air footage of the creature through a pay-per-view webcam service. However, on the day the footage was to be distributed, Biscardi claimed he was "hoodwinked" by a woman in Stagecoach, Nevada, and that the Bigfoot did not exist. Coast to Coast AM host George Noory demanded that Biscardi refund the money to people who had paid for the web-cam subscription, and he did - but only to those who subscribed after August 19.

Then, in 2008, came the Whitton and Dyer hoax. In August, the two men announced that they had discovered the carcass of a 7-foot-7-inch, 500-pound creature while hiking through the northern mountains of their state. They said they had placed the body in a freezer in an undisclosed location. Biscardi teamed up with them to promote the claim that they had a Bigfoot corpse, and promised the media DNA evidence. The three held a press conference in Palo Alto, California, where they showed photographs of the alleged creature. Biscardi (despite what Steve Kull would later say) reassured the press of the corpse's authenticity. He stated, "Last weekend, I touched it. I measured its feet. I felt its intestines." Soon after, Whitton and Dyer admitted that it was a rubber costume. Biscardi claimed that he was deceived.

Then, in late 2012, a wilderness tracker appeared in the press and announced that he had shot and killed a Bigfoot. He had it stored in a freezer and planned to hold a press conference to show off the body. Once it was confirmed as authentic, he was going to take the body on tour across the United States and show it off. If all of that sounds familiar, it should. The tracker was Rick Dyer, one of the two men who perpetrated the same dead Bigfoot hoax in 2008. This time, Dyer insisted, he had the real deal.

At the time of this writing, the "authentic evidence" has yet to be revealed, but needless to say, this author has little doubt about how things are going to turn out.

Which brings us back full circle to the "Minnesota Iceman" - one of the most compelling, weirdest and most mysterious tales in the annals of the unexplained in America. What was it? What happened to it? And most of all, could the thing in the ice have really been either Bigfoot or the "missing link?" Researchers are always looking for solid proof that Bigfoot exists in the form of either a live specimen or a dead one. Did someone actually have that evidence at one time? As mentioned, it's likely we'll never know, but the story itself is nearly as compelling as what the answers might be.

The tale really has to begin with the discovery of the "Iceman" by Milwaukee zoology student Terry Cullen in December 1968 at Chicago's International Livestock Exhibition and Fair. The Iceman had already appeared on the scene prior to this, but it was at this exhibition that it really entered the public spotlight.

However, everything that occurred before Cullen found the creature on display at the fair is definitely open to question and conjecture.

There are three different versions of the story as to how the Iceman ended up in the freezer of a Minnesota man named Frank Hansen. The convoluted history of the Iceman has only added to the mystery of the creature's authenticity over the years. According to one ridiculous version, the Iceman was a Bigfoot-type creature that attacked a woman named Helen Westring while she was alone on a hunting trip in the woods near Bemidji, Minnesota, in 1966. According to her story, the beast grabbed her, ripped off her clothes, and raped her. Ms. Westring avenged her honor by taking up her rifle and shooting the creature through the right eye. She took the body back to town and it eventually came into the hands of Frank Hansen.

Another version of the story states that the creature was not from Minnesota at all but was reportedly found frozen in a block of ice in the Sea of Okhostok, near eastern Siberia. The body was discovered by either Russian seal hunters or Japanese fishermen, who smuggled it to Hong Kong. After that, it was purchased by an American millionaire who lived on the West Coast. The unnamed millionaire in turn rented the curiosity to Air Force veteran Frank Hansen of Winona, Minnesota, who exhibited the frozen specimen. Hansen reportedly came up with this story to appease the FBI when he was questioned about transporting what he was claiming was a frozen carcass back and forth over the Canadian-American border.

The third (and "official" version) was recounted by Frank Hansen himself in the pages of *Saga* magazine in 1970. According to Hansen, the story of the Iceman began in 1960 when he was an Air Force captain and pilot assigned to the 343rd Fighter Group in Duluth, Minnesota. During the 1960 deer hunting season, Hansen was staying at a small resort on the shores of the Whiteface Reservoir, about sixty miles north of Duluth. Three other Air Force personnel, Lieutenant Roy Aafedt, Lieutenant Dave Allison and Major Lou Szrot, were also part of the hunting party.

The men left the cabin at about 6:00 a.m. on the second morning of the trip and Hansen started off for a narrow neck of swamp that he hoped would be a good location for game. He sat motionless on a hillside for almost two hours when a slight movement at the edge of the swamp caught his eye. He looked up to see a large doe staring at him. At that same moment, a shot was fired on the opposite side of the swamp and the deer ran in Hansen's direction. He opened fire and hit the animal just as it was reaching the edge of the trees and it fell to the ground. Hansen bolted his rifle to take another shot, but before he could, the deer sprang up and ran out of sight in the heavy brush.

Walking toward the thicket, he found large spots of blood on the grass and trampled brush that indicated which direction the deer had vanished into the woods. The animal had left a clear trail into the swamp and Hansen decided to follow it. He said later that he pushed along, always thinking that the wounded animal would be just around the next bend in the trail until he realized that he had been walking for almost an hour. He decided to check his bearings and then retrace his trail out of the swamp. He knew that he would never be able to pack the animal out of the forest, even if he did find it.

Stepping over a small cedar log, he heard a strange gurgling sound ahead. Thinking that it might be the deer, he pushed aside the brush and peered into a small clearing. There, in the center of the area, were three large creatures that he first thought were bears. Two of them were on their knees, tearing at the insides of the deer that Hansen had shot. The gurgling sound had been noises the creatures made as they drank the deer's blood.

The third beast was crouched at the edge of the clearing, about ten feet away from the hunter. When it saw Hansen watching, it began to let out a weird screeching sound. It screamed with its arms raised above its head and charged at Hansen. Without thinking, he raised his rifle and fired the chambered shell. The explosion carried the bullet into the creature's eye and the beast was sent spinning to the frozen ground. Apparently, the two remaining creatures ran one way and Hansen ran the other. Blind with fear, he crashed back through the swamp until he fell to the ground. Now lost, as well as terrified, he passed out.

When Hansen came to, he fired three shots into the air (the signal for a hunter in distress) and then fired off three more. Eventually, after traveling some distance, he heard a voice calling out and he emerged from the woods and into a hunting camp. He explained that he had become lost but he never mentioned the strange creatures that he had encountered. One of the hunters said that he knew where Hansen and his friends had parked their truck that morning and offered to drive him there. When he arrived, his friends were waiting and while he good-naturedly took their ribbing about becoming lost, he never told them about what he had seen and what he had done in the swamp.

Time passed and the truth gnawed at him. What had the creature been? Was it an escaped gorilla? Was it a man dressed up for a prank? Except for the fact that it was covered with hair, the beast had seemed to be a human being. Had Hansen committed murder or had the whole thing been the product of his fevered imagination? For the next two months after returning home, he was plagued with migraine headaches and had trouble concentrating on flying and flight instruction. He knew that he had to return to the swamp, but he hesitated to do so unless he would be able to find his way out again. Then, on November 29, the area was covered with five inches of fresh snow and Hansen returned to the region near Whiteface on December 2.

He brought along a swamp buggy with his pickup and he drove the vehicle into the forest, re-tracing his route from the hunting season. He eventually found the creature's body, proving to himself that the encounter had been real after all. He brushed away the snow and found that the corpse had been frozen, covered with blood, and that one eye was missing as a result of his rifle shot. As he inspected the creature, he realized that it was not a human but what he called a "freak of nature." Even so, he didn't want to leave it in the swamp. He feared that hunters might stumble across the corpse and contact the authorities. If they did, an investigation might lead back to Hansen. With that in mind, he left the swamp buggy in the woods and returned to Duluth. He told his wife that the vehicle had gotten stuck and he needed to return with a pick, shovel, ax and chainsaw to get it out. When he returned to Whiteface, Hansen chopped the body from the frozen earth and loaded it onto the rear platform of the swamp buggy. He tied it down with cargo straps and then hauled the creature back to his truck, cutting a trail as he went. Using nylon straps, he moved it into the truck's bed and covered it up with tarps to conceal it from curious eyes on his drive home.

It was nearly dark when he returned home to Duluth. Needless to say, his wife was almost hysterical when he told her about what had happened to him and showed her the gigantic corpse. The Hansens had recently purchased a new freezer and because they couldn't bury the beast in the frozen ground, they decided to remove the meat in the freezer and replace it with the body, at least until spring. After their children had gone to bed, Hansen and his wife, Irene, hauled the body out of the truck and into the basement. The creature was beginning to stink but they managed to hold their breath as they bent the arms and legs of the corpse and forced it into the freezer. They covered it with a blanket and left it there for over a month.

Hansen still planned to bury the corpse somewhere in the spring but after checking on its condition, he saw that it was beginning to dehydrate and decay. He and Irene decided that the body would be better preserved if they filled the freezer with water and encased the cadaver in ice. They began pouring about twenty gallons of water into the freezer each day until it was a solid block of ice. This seemed to be the perfect plan, until the spring thaw arrived and Hansen began to wrestle with the idea of trying to thaw out the body and transport it somewhere and bury it. His plans continued to be delayed until his retirement approached and the family purchased a farm near Rollingstone, Minnesota.

Hansen realized that he could not risk hiring a moving company to transport the freezer, so he rented a truck and moved it himself. Friends helped to move the locked, "meat packed" freezer into the truck and then into the basement of the new house. During the seven-hour ordeal, the top layer of ice began to melt, and while Hansen was able to quickly re-freeze the body, he became so paranoid about the beast unthawing that he purchased a generator for his new home so that the power would never go out. He was now sure that the monster would never be discovered.

In November 1965, Hansen retired from the Air Force and joined his family on the farm. Now, with time on his hands, he began to do some reading and ran across some books and articles on the "abominable snowman." The more he read, the more certain he was that the creature in his freezer was one of these elusive beasts. He made a few discreet inquiries about the statute of limitations on murder in Minnesota and learned that there was none. Even though he was sure the creature was not human, he decided to keep the corpse hidden in the freezer for a while longer.

A little over a year later, Hansen met an unnamed "veteran showman" who, recognizing his boredom with civilian life, suggested that Hansen exhibit a rare old John Deere tractor that he had acquired and had loaned to the Smithsonian

Institution. It had been returned to him from Washington and he had been showing it on a limited basis. The showman suggested that Hansen take the tractor on the state fair circuit. He wouldn't make much money at it, but it would keep him busy. Hansen was pleased with the idea but had other things in mind. He asked his friend if the body of a hairy creature that resembled a prehistoric man would make a good attraction. The showman assured him that it would, but when he asked Hansen where he would get something like that, Hansen told him that he could have a model made.

Hansen decided to consult with his attorney concerning the legalities of displaying the creature he had killed in the woods. The lawyer didn't believe a word of the story until Hansen drove him out to the farm and showed him what was in the freezer. Not surprisingly, the attorney was stunned. He advised Hansen that he could possibly get into legal trouble by displaying the body. There could be a murder charge if the creature was determined to be human, he said, and there were also laws about transporting dead bodies.

Hansen continued to press him about displaying the body as an exhibit. The attorney thought things over for a moment. "You have the original body," he finally said. "The authorities will be after it because this thing is the scientific find of the century. However, it might be possible to create a model as you suggested. Maintain a record of the model's construction but show the real creature instead. If the officials pressure you, it's a small matter to produce photos of the model taken during different phases of fabrication." Hansen agreed and then came up with an even better idea. He would exhibit the model only for the first year so that the carnival people would accept it as a bogus sideshow exhibit.

In January 1967, Hansen made sketches of the creature and then went to Hollywood to confer with some makeup artists who created special effects for the movies. He spoke with George "Bud" Westmore, the head of makeup effects for Universal Studios. Westmore is credited with doing the makeup for hundreds of movies, including *Creature from the Black Lagoon*. He told Hansen that a believable model could cost as much as $20,000 to produce. He said that he didn't have time to make the model himself but if needed, he would provide technical support. Hansen then consulted with the Los Angeles County Museum and it was suggested that he contact Howard Ball, an independent artist who had created life-sized animal exhibits for the La Brea Tar Pits. Hansen hired Ball to make the model, and was also told that a small wax studio in Los Angeles could implant the hair according to Hansen's specifications. He then hired Pete and Betty Corral, who implanted each strand of hair on the model individually with needles.

Hansen now had a model that he had spent thousands of dollars on, but there was no guarantee that he could make any money on it. He decided to put the final touches on the creature himself rather than spend more money. He and a friend from Pasadena added bloody eyes, a broken arm and blood-soaked hair to make it look as close to the original in Hansen's freezer as possible.

Hansen then rented a freezer where he could encase the model in ice to get it ready for its debut on the West Coast.

The exhibit debuted on May 3, 1967 as what the carnival folks called a "What is it?" show. Hansen explained that the creature had been found frozen in the Bering Straits by Japanese fishermen. He stuck to this story for the next two years. The tour continued until November 1967, when Hansen closed at the Louisiana State Fair and returned home to Minnesota. By March 1968, he had convinced himself that it was now safe to replace the model with the real specimen for the upcoming fair season. He had been told by carnival personnel that the model was a sensational attraction but that it had too many flaws to fool anyone with an expert knowledge of anatomy. Hansen felt relieved. He was sure that word had gotten out that the exhibit was a fake and that it would now be safe to put the real cadaver on display.

Hansen got to work unthawing the real body so that he could cut the tendons in the arms and legs and make it look like the model. He froze it again and then prepared to hit the fair circuit. This time, the attention that the exhibit got was different than when Hansen had been showing the model. While most of the onlookers had been impressed with the old exhibit, the real corpse was drawing a different crowd. Now, doctors, college students and scientists were coming to examine and photograph the "missing link." At the Oklahoma State Fair, one prominent surgeon visited the exhibit on nine separate occasions, each time bringing a different colleague with him. At the Kansas State Fair, the county pathologist was so intrigued that he sent many of his associates to see the display.

By now, Hansen was asserting that the creature as the "real thing," although he continued his cover story that the monster was actually owned by a California millionaire, and that it had been recovered in the icy waters of the ocean. While the creature was drawing attention, Hansen was still able to keep its existence quiet and to maintain that it was merely a carnival exhibit. However, that was about to change.

In December 1968, a college student named Terry Cullen became more than a little intrigued by the exhibit that he saw in Chicago. Like everyone else, he paid his 25 cents to see the "man left over from the Ice Age." He filed past the frozen block of ice that Hansen had secured in a refrigerated glass coffin. He was not convinced that this was some carnival sideshow fake and began to try unsuccessfully to interest some mainstream academics in what he had found. Finally, Cullen alerted famed naturalist Ivan T. Sanderson. Sanderson was intrigued. He had written a book on the mysterious creature called the abominable snowman and was the founder of the Society for the Investigation of the Unexplained. As it turned out, his house guest at the time turned out to be Dr. Bernard Heuvelmans, a respected cryptozoologist and the author of *On the Track of Unknown Animals*. After hearing from Cullen, the two men immediately traveled to Chicago to see first-hand what Hansen was putting on display.

After viewing the frozen creature, they contacted Hansen and asked for permission to study it closer. Hansen agreed but would later admit that "this was a grave mistake on my part." Both men were very impressed with the creature, Hansen said, but neither of them made mention of publishing a scientific report about the Iceman. That was the last thing Hansen wanted.

Sanderson and Heuvelmans spent three days examining the creature in Hansen's trailer. The corpse was that of an adult male with large hands and feet. Its skin was covered with dark brown hair that, for the most part, was three to four inches long. The creature had been shot through one eye and it had a gaping wound and a fracture to the left arm. In places where the ice had melted, the two investigators could smell putrefaction, leading them to believe that the body was authentic. They could hardly believe what they saw. Heuvelmans would later publish a report on the creature in the February 1969 bulletin of the *Royal Institute of Natural Sciences of Belgium*. He called the creature the "*Homo pongoides*" and stated that "the long search for the rumored live 'ape-man' or 'missing link' has at last been successful."

Sanderson wrote his own article for the May 1969 issue of *Argosy*. He stated that "one look was actually enough to convince us that this was -- from our point of view, at least -- the 'genuine article.' This was no phony 'Chinese' trick or 'art' work. If nothing else confirmed this, the appalling stench of rotting flesh exuding from a point in the insulation of the coffin certainly did."

Hansen's problems began with the publication of Heuvelmans' article and escalated when Sanderson's piece hit the newsstands. To make matters worse, Sanderson mentioned the Iceman during an appearance on the *Tonight Show*. Soon, newspapers, television shows, radio stations and magazines from all over the world began trying to verify the creature's authenticity. Calls poured in daily and both the FBI and the Smithsonian Institution requested permission to examine the body, along with dozens of scientists who asked for blood and hair samples. Hansen refused them all. Heuvelmans had stated in this article that it appeared the creature had been shot. Because of this, newspapers began to speculate on the possibility that law enforcement officials should investigate just how Hansen had obtained the creature if it was actually real. An article in the *Detroit News* declared, "If the body is that of a human being, there is the question of who shot him and whether any crime was committed."

On that note, the body of the genuine Iceman vanished. The model was again put on display in its place and Hansen kept quiet as investigators tracked down the Hollywood makeup artists who had created the fake. He now began spreading the story that the body had been returned to the possession of the mysterious California millionaire who owned it. No further examinations would be made. According to Hansen, this was done on the advice of his attorney, who told him that he should substitute the model for the real thing and "take a long vacation." The actual corpse was hidden somewhere "away from the Midwest" and the model was re-frozen and put on display in its place.

Debunkers quickly asserted that the exhibit had been a fake from the very beginning, although Sanderson and Heuvelmans would never waver in their belief that the Iceman was very real. Photographs that were taken of the model in 1969 show at least fifteen technical differences between the original that was studied by Sanderson and Heuvelmans and the replacement body. Terry Cullen wholeheartedly agreed that what he had seen in Chicago had once been a living creature. In addition to the smell noted by the later investigators, Cullen had become intrigued by the body because he could see plant matter in the creature's teeth, along with traces of lice on its flesh. These were details would not have been evident in a carnival "gaff."

So, was the Iceman real -- or was it an elaborate and expensive hoax? Obviously, we are never going to know for sure unless the real specimen eventually turns up somewhere. But if the whole thing was a hoax and the body never existed, then why would Hansen create such an elaborate and damning story to explain it? Was he simply trying to cash in on the model that he had created? This seems unlikely, since Hansen was never able to make much money on it. The admissions fees barely reimbursed him for the cost of having his model made. The only way that Hansen could have gotten rich from the creature was by selling the genuine body, which he never did. He seemed to be more worried about criminal charges that might threaten his Air Force retirement pension than he was about getting rich off the corpse.

The biggest question that remains in my mind is what happened to the original body? According to Hansen in 1970, he had been pressed for the conditions or circumstances under which he would consider giving up the specimen for scientific evaluation. He stated that he had to be assured he would be given complete amnesty for any possible violation of federal or state laws for either the murder of the creature (if it was deemed to be human) or for transporting and exhibiting the corpse. Whatever became of his requests and whether or not they were granted is unknown. As far as I know, the real body --- if there was indeed a real body -- was never seen again.

As for the fake body, the intricate model fashioned for Hansen by Hollywood, it continued to turn up at state fairs and traveling exhibits and was last seen in a Minnesota storage warehouse in 2002. Was the fake body the one that I saw at the Illinois State Fair in the late 1970s? I'm sure it was. Was there ever a real body? Probably not... but then again, who knows? If a real monster ever existed, Frank Hansen took the secret of what became of it to his grave in 2003.

And as for me, the monster - real or not - helped put me on the path that I'm still walking today, always on the lookout for weirdness and enigmas.

A BROKEN SHIP'S COMPASS
THE MYSTERY OF THE MARY CELESTE

History is filled with many mysteries of ships and the sea. But of all of the ships in history, none has a more haunting reputation that the infamous *Mary Celeste*, a vessel from which the entire crew inexplicably vanished and was never seen again. Discovered floundering in the waters of the North Atlantic in December 1872, the ship soon became an enigma, a much-talked-about puzzle that still intrigues historians and sailors well over a century later. Most consider it the greatest nautical mystery of all time, one that will never be solved.

On the chilly afternoon of December 4, 1872, the British brigantine *Dei Gratia* cut through the waters of the North Atlantic. She was on a course from New York to Gibraltar and the weather promised smooth sailing with sunny skies and a good wind. Suddenly, a two-masted square-rigger appeared over the horizon. The ship's course was unsteady and as the wind veered, the vessel shifted aimlessly. The strange ship was under short canvas in the brisk wind, yawing heavily while lurching along at only two knots. Two of her sails were missing and the lower foretopsail hung slackly at the corners.

The captain of the *Dei Gratia*, David Reed Morehouse, could see no one at the helm. He ran up a signal, but there was no reply. Captain Morehouse, along with First Mate Oliver Deveau, raised their telescopes for a look. He recognized the ship as the *Mary Celeste*, but could see no one on board. Morehouse was stunned. He knew the captain of this ship, Benjamin Spooner Briggs, and in fact, had a passing friendship with him. The two men had dined together less than a month before, when their ships had been loading cargo at neighboring piers in New York. The *Mary Celeste* had set sail for Genoa, Italy, on November 5, eight days before the *Dei Gratia* had left port.

Deveau pointed out that there seemed to be no distress signal. As the two ships approached within hailing range, Captain Morehouse broke out his speaking trumpet. "Celeste ahoy!" he called out. "Can you hear me?"

There was no reply from the other ship, only the creaking and flapping of plank and canvas. Morehouse called again but nothing stirred on the ship. The captain could see that the *Mary Celeste* was on a starboard tack, but the jib sail was set to port. To the experienced seaman, he knew this meant only one thing: the ship was out of control, and the crew was either incapacitated or dead. He ordered his first mate to take two men with him and board the ship. "Find out what's amiss," he instructed Deveau.

A boat was lowered and the first mate and two crewmen cast off toward the silent ship. The dinghy was tied up to the *Mary Celeste* and the three men climbed aboard. What they found has remained a mystery ever since. The deck was empty. No crew member came forward to meet them. They shouted, but no one answered. The wheel stood unattended, spinning idly as the waves slapped at the rudder. The only sound was the groan of wood and rope. The silence was uncanny.

They searched the ship from stem to stern, but there was no one on board. The vessel was absolutely deserted, but if the crew had abandoned her, they had left everything behind.

The hull, masts and remaining sails of the *Mary Celeste* were all sound. The cargo, which consisted of 1,701 barrels of industrial alcohol, was all intact - except for one barrel, which had been opened. There was a six-month supply of food and water. Sea chests and clothing lay dry and undisturbed. In the galley, a meal was being prepared and still hung over a dead fire. The bed was unmade in the captain's quarters and the table had been set for breakfast and then abandoned. There was porridge on one of the plates and the remains of eggs on another. Next to one plate was an open bottle of cough medicine with its cork and a spoon lying beside it. In the deck cabins, the skylight stood wide open and rain and sea water had soaked the bedding and clothing, forming large pools on the floor.

The ship itself was seaworthy and most things were in their proper place. It looked as though the entire crew had suddenly winked out of existence. Whatever had occurred, the searchers realized, had taken place a short time before. None of the food had rotted and none of the metal surfaces had rusted in the sea air. Everything on the ship, including money and valuables, was intact. The only things that seemed to be missing were the ship's chronometer and the lifeboat. Deveau knew that the *Mary Celeste* had carried a boat lashed to the main hatch and now that spot was empty. A piece of railing parallel to it had been removed, apparently in order to launch the craft.

The crew, it seemed, had managed to leave the ship in a single lifeboat and they must have done so in a feverish hurry. Not only had they left behind their personal belongings, including their pipes and tobacco, which most sailors did not abandon unless in fear of death, but the ship had a disturbed look about it that suggested possible violence. Rope and canvas was scattered about on the deck. The ship's compass had been smashed into pieces. In one cabin, they found a cutlass that was smeared with what could have been blood. They found similar stains on the starboard deck rail, near a cut that looked as though it had been made with an ax. On each side of the bow were strips of wood that had been cut from the deck. The strips were six feet long, but why they had been cut was anyone's guess. The windows in the captain's cabin had been boarded up with canvas and heavy planks.

Had the crew abandoned ship in fear of an attack or some other calamity? If so, how had they escaped? It was unlikely that everyone on board could have fit into the single lifeboat. There had been a crew of seven on the ship, along with 37-year-old Captain Briggs, his 30-year-old wife and first cousin, the former Sarah Elizabeth Cobb, and their two-year-old daughter, Sophia Matilda. The Briggs' other child, seven-year-old Arthur, had been left at home with his grandmother, so he could attend school.

Deveau checked the ship's log and found the last entry was dated for November 24, ten days before. At that point, the Mary Celeste was passing north of St. Mary's Island in the Azores, which was more than seven hundred miles away. If she had been abandoned after the entry, then the ship had sailed itself, unmanned and unsteered, for more than a week and a half. Such a feat seemed impossible. Deveau believed that someone had to have been on the ship for at least several days after the final log entry. But who had it been? And where had everyone gone? Were they stricken with disease, madness, or had something far more sinister happened?

Deveau returned to the Dei Gratia and made his report to Captain Morehouse. Although saddened by the disappearance of his acquaintance and his family, Morehouse saw an opportunity and money to be made. He ordered Deveau to return to the Mary Celeste with two crewmen and then follow the Dei Gratia to Gibraltar. He would claim the ship as salvage, which would bring him a sizable reward.

Both of the ships arrived in the Gibraltar harbor one week later. Instead of salvage money, though, Morehouse was met with an official order from the British Admiralty's office to seize the Mary Celeste for an immediate investigation.

The Mary Celeste had always been known as an unlucky ship. Originally called the Amazon, her first captain died just forty-eight hours after his appointment. On her maiden voyage, she collided with a fishing boat off the coast of Maine and damaged her hull. During the repairs, a fire broke out below decks. Her third captain managed to run into another ship off the Straits of Dover. Her fourth captain ran the ship aground on Cape Breton Island and she was wrecked, nearly beyond repair. After all that, the Amazon was salvaged and repaired. She was given a new name and an experienced captain in Benjamin Briggs and was put back into service.

At that point, the ship not only had a reputation for being accident-prone, and therefore unlucky, it was probably considered to be even more unlucky due to the name change. Among sailors, who tend to be a superstitious lot, changing a ship's name is thought to bring bad luck.

The investigation in Gibraltar uncovered little more than theories as to what had become of the *Mary Celeste's* crew. They considered mutiny or perhaps some plot by the American crew to steal the ship's cargo or to sink the ship and collect the insurance. Finally, mutiny was thought to be the solution. The Admiralty believed that the crew had murdered the captain and his family and then had escaped in the single lifeboat. There was no explanation as to why valuables, including jewelry and an expensive Italian sword, were left behind on the ship.

The American merchant navy was angry over the finding of mutiny. Captain Briggs was not only a fair and decent man, he was well-liked by all of the men who served with him. He also ran a "dry" ship. The only alcohol that was aboard the *Mary Celeste* was the cargo and it was crude alcohol and impossible to drink. To do so would cause severe stomach cramps and possibly even blindness.

Finally, in March 1873, the British Admiralty admitted that they had no solution to the mystery. It was the first time in history that the court had failed to come to a definite conclusion over maritime law. The owners of the *Dei Gratia* were awarded one-fifth of the value of the *Mary Celeste* as a salvage fee and the ship was returned to her owner. He wasted no time in selling the cursed ship.

Over the next decade, no new evidence was unearthed about the abandonment of the ship. No one from the crew was ever seen again and finally interest in the story began to fade.

However, in 1882, the strange story of the *Mary Celeste* took an unusual turn. A seemingly unrelated event occurred in England, in the small town of Southsea. This event was the moment that a newly licensed doctor named Arthur Conan Doyle put up a nameplate on the wall outside of his office door, where he hoped to specialize in opthalmology. Doyle would then spend days and weeks waiting for patients and prosperity, only to find neither one. Instead, he would discover a love of writing and would chase away the boredom of his lackluster medical practice by penning stories. Doyle would go on to become a prolific writer of mystery and horror novels, the creator the legendary detective Sherlock Holmes and an outspoken proponent of the Spiritualist movement. In those days, however, he was simply a penniless doctor with a taste for strange tales.

In the fall of 1882, he would pen one of these strange stories and it would go on to not only create a sensation, but would also earn a unique place in history. In fact, Doyle's harmless story would jumble the facts of the *Mary Celeste* mystery so badly that many believe that the blame for the case never being solved rests squarely on Conan Doyle's shoulders.

The story, titled "J. Habakuk Jephson's Statement" appeared in the *Cornhill Magazine* of January 1884. The tale was not only one of Doyle's best early tales, but he used a fictional setting to create a theory about what happened to the crew of the real-life *Mary Celeste*. To do this, he created an entirely different scenario. In the first sentence alone, he changed the location of where the ship was found, the circumstances behind her discovery and even the name of the ship itself from "Mary Celeste" to "Marie Celeste."

The public and the popular press immediately seized upon the story. It was published anonymously and accepted as truth with the fictional Jephson claiming to be on board the "Marie Celeste" when she is taken over by a black radical leader with a hatred for whites. No one seemed to notice the obvious changes that Doyle had written into the story. It was taken very seriously and debated by people as the true story of the real Mary Celeste.

The adventures of Jephson created a storm of controversy for the British Admiralty. The chief investigator in Gibraltar, Frederick Solly-Flood, in his role as Queen's Counsel, was so outraged by the story that he sent a flurry of public telegrams denouncing Jephson's "true account" as an outrageous lie. He followed these rather embarrassing telegrams with an official report to the Admiralty, pinpointing each of the mistakes in the account. Needless to say, when the real details of the fictional story were learned, the press was delighted, as was Conan Doyle. The story would go on to launch his literary career.

In addition, the story turned out to be the catalyst for a new wave of interest in the mystery of the Mary Celeste. In the years that followed, a number of other hoax accounts of the last days of the ship (none as successful as the first) emerged. Nothing was ever heard from any known member of the ship's crew again, but there was a steady surfacing of Mary Celeste survivors whose names, somehow, had been left off the ship's register. They popped up all over the world, with stories that ranged from the impossible to the ridiculous.

Charles Fort, an avid collector of newspaper accounts of odd occurrences and the author of several books on anomalous phenomena, suggested that the missing passengers and crew could have been whisked off the ship by what he called a "selective force," which left the ship itself untouched. In 1926, Adam Bushey claimed that the Mary Celeste had been "dematerialized" en route but when it returned to solid form, the crew did not return with it. Other weird stories emerged of strange accidents, giant squids, krakens, time warps and abductions by aliens.

Countless serious theories were also expressed as to the fate of the ship's crew. James Briggs, the brother of the ship's captain, was convinced that the solution to the mystery lay in the ship's last log entry. It stated that the wind had dropped after a night of heavy ocean squalls. If this is correct, it could have meant that the ship lost speed and drifted toward the rocks of Santa Maria Island. The ship's hull may have been breached, explaining the pools of water that Dei Gratia First Mate Deveau found below decks. The crew may have believed the Mary Celeste was sinking and abandoned ship.

Another explanation claimed that the ship was struck by a waterspout. This would explain the water below decks and the damage done to the sails. Or the crew may have panicked in the storm and abandoned ship.

There is one feasible explanation for what happened that takes into account everything that was discovered by the Dei Gratia crew. There was no structural damage to the ship, and yet it had apparently been abandoned in great haste. For this reason, it seems that the evacuation was not carried out because of something that had already happened - but because of something they were afraid was going to happen. The only potential for danger on board the *Mary Celeste* was her cargo.

Captain Briggs had never carried crude alcohol before and was likely unfamiliar with its chemical reactions. He had come from the cold weather of New York to the much warmer region of the Azores, and the barrels, shaken by stormy weather, may have started to leak fumes into the hold. It's possible that Briggs feared that the vapors could either poison the crew, or that the barrels might explode. One of the barrels, it will be remembered, was opened, probably during an inspection. If the inspection had taken place by candle light, the open flame could have caused the fumes to burst into flame - which may have convinced the captain that the entire ship was in danger of exploding.

Terrified for the safety of his men, not to mention his wife and daughter, he may have ordered everyone into the lifeboat. In all likelihood, Briggs intended to stick close to the ship so that they could get back on if no further explosion occurred, but it would not have taken much wind to send the *Mary Celeste* sailing away from the lifeboat, abandoning the crew at sea. The crew almost certainly would have tried to catch up with the ship, but rough seas may have prevented them from doing so, and the crew and passengers of the *Mary Celeste* were lost forever.

This theory was first offered by James Winchester, the ship's owner, and it has since been considered by several authors. Somehow, though, it's never been generally accepted, perhaps because pirates, sea monsters and time warps are much more exciting than an ordinary, yet fatal, accident.

So, what became of the *Mary Celeste* after the court of inquiry was finished with her? Her owner sold the ship as soon as he arrived back in New York, some say at a great loss. But perhaps the most unlucky person in the deal was the man who bought her. The *Mary Celeste* was rumored to be jinxed from the beginning and the events that followed the vanishing of her crew continued her run of terrible luck.

The new owner loaded the ship with a cargo of lumber and sent her to Montevideo. During a storm that occurred while en route, the deck cargo, and a good amount of the ship's rigging, was lost. The voyage turned out to be a total loss. On the return trip, carrying a load of horses and mules, most of the animals died in the hold and a few days later, the new owner followed suit.

From that point on, the *Mary Celeste* changed hands so quickly and so frequently that it became almost impossible to keep track of who owned her and when. She continued to sail up and down the American coastline, slowly falling apart.

Then, in 1884, she was purchased by an old seaman from Massachusetts named Gilman C. Parker. For most of his sixty-one years, Parker had dabbled in almost every kind of illegal activity on the sea, except for outright piracy. He and some of his friends concocted a scheme to make some money off the notoriously unprofitable *Mary Celeste*. They loaded her with a cargo of junk, worth less than a few hundred dollars, but insured the cargo as being worth nearly $27,000. After that, Captain Parker took the ship on her death voyage to the Caribbean.

In Haiti's Gulf of Gonave is a coral reef called Rochelois Bank, which had proven fatal to scores of ships over the years. Parker set a course for the reef and the brigantine was grounded on the razor-like coral. With the waves crashing around her, the ship began to settle. There was no immediate danger and the crew had plenty of time to row the cargo ashore. When everything worthwhile had been salvaged, Parker ordered kerosene poured onto the decks and then he lit a torch. The *Mary Celeste* burst into flames. By evening, she was nothing but a charred skeleton.

Back in Boston, Parker and his associates filed their insurance claim. The company was suspicious and dispatched detectives to question the crew. The sailors, who were not getting a share of the money, freely talked about what they had seen. Soon after, Parker and his partners were in federal court, facing a charge of barratry - an act of gross misconduct committed by a master or crew of a vessel which damages the vessel or its cargo. In those days, this was a hanging offense.

The jury was unable to reach a verdict, however, and Parker and the other conspirators were set free. They never collected their claim and the notoriety of the case killed their reputations. Eight months later, Parker died in disrepute and poverty. One of his friends was confined to an insane asylum and another committed suicide.

Even after she was destroyed, the *Mary Celeste*, the most famous cursed ship in history was still bringing bad luck to anyone connected to her.

STONES FROM A CELLAR WALL
THE STORY OF DUDLEYTOWN

For many years, those of us with a penchant for the unexplained have been fascinated by the tales of a lost settlement called Dudleytown - a vanished Connecticut settlement that was apparently plagued by ghosts and demons, and whose residents vanished without a trace. In the northwest region of the state, in the shadows of mountains, remnants of the lost community still exist as cellar holes, stone foundations and crumbling walls. The roads that once brought residents to this place are now little more than narrow trails where only a few adventurous hikers dare to wander. Although it is forbidden, the most hardened curiosity-seekers still dare to venture down Dark Entry Road and into these shadowy woods at night.

They come here in search of the unexplained and an answer to the mysterious events that created Dudleytown's reputation as an evil place. Those terrible events were said to be caused by a curse that was brought by the Dudley family to the New World. Unfortunately for the yarn-spinners, the so-called "curse" was nothing more than the product of active imaginations - but that doesn't seem to matter.

One thing is certain: something very strange occurred in Dudleytown, whether the land was cursed or not.

Dudleytown, or at least the area where it was located, was first owned by a man named Thomas Griffis, one of the first white men to settle in the region, in the early 1740s. There are no records to say that he ever lived where Dudleytown later stood, but he did own half of the land in 1741. A few years later, with the arrival of Gideon Dudley in 1747, the village would gain a name. Gideon was followed to the region by his two brothers, and the Dudleys have become known over the years as the men who brought a curse to Dudleytown - a curse that has allegedly plagued the region ever since.

According to what have turned out to be both recent and fanciful accounts, the "curse" had its beginnings in England in 1510. At that time, Edmund Dudley was beheaded for being involved in a plot to overthrow King Henry VIII. Supposedly, a curse was placed on his family, which stated that all of the Dudley descendants would be surrounded by horror and death. Proponents of the curse claim that the Dudleys then began to experience a rather disquieting run of bad luck.

Edmund's son, John Dudley, also attempted to control the British throne by arranging for his son, Guilford, to marry Lady Jane Grey, next in line for the crown. After Edward VI died, Lady Jane became the queen for a mere nine days before the plan failed, ending with the execution of Lady Jane and the two Dudleys. To make matters worse, Guilford's brother returned from France, where he had been serving as a military officer, and brought home a plague that he spread to his officers and troops. The sickness wiped out massive numbers of British soldiers and eventually spread throughout the country, killing thousands.

John Dudley's third son, Robert, Earl of Leicester, a favorite of Elizabeth I, wisely decided to leave England and travel to the New World. It would be his somewhat luckier descendant, William, who would settle in Guilford, Connecticut. Three of William's descendants, Abiel, Barzallai and Gideon, would later buy a plot of land in Cornwall Township.

While there are undoubtedly some grim events that surrounded the Dudley family in England and France, questions have been raised about whether or not a "curse" really followed them to America. The problems with the story came about because in order for the curse to have been passed along, William Dudley would have had to have been the son of Robert, Earl of Leicester - but he wasn't. Robert Dudley had only two sons and one of them died while still a child. The other went to Italy and while he had children, all of them remained in that country. This means that there was no link between William, his sons who founded Dudleytown, and any so-called "curse."

But while we may have established the fact that Dudleytown was never "cursed," this does not mean that it was not "tainted" in some other way. There are many places across the country where odd things happen and where the land does not seem quite right. Records indicate that the land around Dudleytown was once Mohawk Indian tribal grounds but tell us little else before the coming of the first white settlers. This region has gained a chilling reputation over the years. Could the weird stories and strange disappearances here be connected to the past in some way, or are they nothing more than just coincidence and imagination?

In the early 1740s, Thomas Griffis bought a parcel of land that would later be considered the first lot in Dudleytown. The land today looks much as it did when Griffis first came here. It is covered in thick forest and the ground is strewn with rocks. The nearby mountains (Bald mountain, Woodbury mountain, and the Coldfoots triplets) heavily shadow the area, so it receives little sunlight. The woods were later dubbed with the ominous name of "Dark Entry Forest."

In 1747, Gideon Dudley bought some land from Griffis to start a small farm. By 1753, Gideon's two brothers, Barzallai and Abiel Dudley, from Guilford, Connecticut, also purchased land nearby. A few years later, a Martin Dudley from Massachusetts moved to the area, but he was from a different line of the family. He later married Gideon's daughter.

One thing that should be mentioned was that Dudleytown was never an actual town. It was a loose community in an isolated part of Cornwall. The village rested in the middle of three large hills, which accounts for the recollections of it being nearly dark at noon time. Cornwall Township was never a good area for farming, as is apparent by the large rocks that were used to build the foundations and stone walls that still stand today. In spite of this, settlers began to trickle into the area. The Tanner family, the Joneses, the Pattersons, the Dibbles and the Porters all took up residence there. The community grew larger after iron ore was discovered nearby and farming became a secondary concern. However, there were never any stores, inns, schools or churches in Dudleytown. Provisions had to be purchased in nearby towns and when someone died, a trip to Cornwall was necessary because, in addition to there being no church in town, there was no cemetery either. The population of Dudleytown was never large, and according to an 1854 map, the peak number of families who lived there only reached twenty-six.

In spite of all of these things, the area did thrive for a time. Dudleytown was noted for its timber: gigantic white pines, hemlocks, chesnuts and oaks, which were burned and used as fuel for the nearby Litchfield County Iron Furnaces in Cornwall and other towns. The furnaces later moved closer to the railroads and the more industrial towns, and lumber from Dudleytown was no longer needed. Iron ore was used from the area for a time, and there were three water-powered mills in Dudleytown. Most of the mills eventually closed because it was necessary to make a long trip down the mountain in order to deliver their goods.

Despite the outward signs of prosperity, there were strange deaths and bizarre occurrences at Dudleytown from the start. Some historians have attempted to downplay the unusual events in recent years. They will debunk the legends of the town by first stating how few people ever lived there and then will try and downplay the disappearances, cases of insanity and weird deaths, as if such things happen all the time. And perhaps they do - but why so many unusual happenings in such an isolated area with so few people living in it? The number of deaths that occurred in the community would not seem so high in a larger town but in this small settlement, one can't help but wonder what exactly was going on. There are also, I believe, an inordinate number of people who went insane in this area, as well as people who simply vanished without a trace. It's no wonder - bogus or not - that a story started about a Dudleytown "curse."

Three of the Dudleys moved out of the region and lived long and full lives, dying of natural causes and forever diminishing any possibilities of a curse. Only

Abiel Dudley remained in town and after a series of reverses, lost his entire fortune - and his mind. Abiel died in 1799 at the age of ninety and when he was no longer able to pay his debts, the town took his property, sold it, and then made him a ward of the town. Toward the end, Abiel was senile and insane and would not be the last to suffer from this affliction.

In 1792, seven years before Abiel Dudley passed away, his good friend and neighbor, Gershon Hollister, was killed falling from the roof while building a barn at the home of William Tanner, Abiel's closest neighbor. Tanner was also said to have gone insane, although likely from old age and senility rather than from supernatural influences. He lived to the age of 104, and according to records, he was "slightly demented" at the time of his death. There have been stories that have circulated claiming that Tanner told other villages of "strange creatures" that came out of the woods at night. If this is true, there is no way for us to know if these "creatures" were real or were products of Tanner's feeble mind.

The Nathaniel Carter family moved to Dudleytown in 1759 and lived in a house that was once owned by Abiel Dudley before he was made a ward of the town. A mysterious plague swept through Dudleytown and Cornwall and took the lives of the Adoniram Carter family, relatives of Nathaniel. Saddened by the loss, they moved to Binghampton, New York, from Dudleytown in 1763. Those who believe in the "curse" say that the taint of Dudleytown followed them, but their tragic fate was actually far too common during the early days of the frontier. The Carters later moved to the "Delaware wilderness," in the heart of Indian territory. Indians attacked and slaughtered Nathaniel, his wife and an infant child. The Carters' other three children were abducted and taken to Canada, where two daughters were ransomed. The son, David Carter, remained with his captors, married an Indian girl and later returned to the United States for his education. He went on to edit a newspaper and became a justice on the Supreme Court.

Another bizarre tragedy affected one of the most famous residents of the region, General Herman Swift, who had served in the Revolutionary War under George Washington. In 1804, his third wife, Sarah Faye, was struck by lightning and killed instantly while standing on the front porch of their home near Dudleytown during an April thunderstorm. Swift went insane and died soon after. Many have dismissed this incident as not being connected to the other unusual events, saying that Swift did not actually live in Dudleytown but on Bald Mountain Road (where his house remains today) and that he only went insane when he became old and senile. But in an area this sparsely populated, the records indicated three people to have gone insane in the space of less than a half century. Could this be mere coincidence? And does a person being struck by lightning while standing on their front porch qualify as being "unusual?" I would say that it does and our story is not yet complete.

Another famous personage allegedly connected to Dudleytown was Horace Greeley, the editor and founder of the *New York Tribune* - or so the stories of the "curse" go. In this case, the story deserves to be debunked. Greeley married a young woman named Mary Young Cheney, who the stories of the "curse" say was born in Dudleytown. In truth, she was born and raised in nearby Litchfield and never lived in Dudleytown. She left the area as early as 1833 and went to live in a vegetarian boarding house in New York City that was owned by Dr. Graham of "Graham Cracker" fame. While there, she met and married Horace Greeley. In 1872, Greeley ran for president against Ulysses S. Grant, crusading against the corruption of his administration, but died one week before the election. One month before, Mary Greeley, a longtime tuberculosis sufferer, succumbed to the disease. Her death occurred in New York City with her husband and their daughters, Ida and Gabrielle -- the only survivors of the couple's seven children -- in attendance. She was buried in Brooklyn's Green-Wood Cemetery. The legends claim that she committed suicide by hanging, but this was not the case.

After the Civil War, Dudleytown began to die, as many of the villagers simply packed up and moved away. The demise of the town is hardly surprising, whether you believe in the so-called "curse" or not. Its geographical location was foolhardy at best. Surrounded by hills and at elevations of more than 1,500 feet, there was little chance that the settlers could sustain themselves by farming the thin, rocky soil. The winters were harsh and even the hardy apple trees were stunted from months of cold. To make matters worse, the area was plagued by too much water, much of it run-off from snow melting on the mountains. It pooled into tepid swamps and seeped into the earth, creating a damp morass.

But even if you overlook the idea of an actual curse, and admit that the location of the town must have had a hand in its undoing, the sheer number of unusual deaths (leaving out that of Mary Greeley) and insanity in such an isolated area more than suggests that something out of the ordinary was occurring. And no matter how hard the debunkers try to disregard the next mysterious event to occur in Dudleytown, their efforts fall short.

This event occurred in 1901, at a time when the population of Dudleytown had dwindled away to almost nothing. One of the last residents of the town was a man named John Patrick Brophy. Tragedy visited swiftly and in several blows. First, his wife died of tuberculosis, which was not uncommon in those days. There was nothing strange about her ailment, as she had been suffering from it for years. This did not lessen Brophy's grief, however, but he was soon further stricken when his two children vanished into the forest a short time after the funeral. And while their disappearance could have been voluntary (they had been accused of stealing sleigh blankets, a minor offense), there is nothing to indicate that it was. They vanished and were never found. Shortly after, Brophy's house burned to the ground in an unexplained fire and not long after, Brophy himself vanished into the forest. He was never seen again.

By the early 1900s, Dudleytown was completely deserted. The remaining homes began to fall into disrepair, and soon, the forest began to reclaim the village. But there was still one other death that proponents of the "curse" have connected to Dudleytown and while the curse may be unlikely, it does mark an additional case of insanity for an isolated region that was already riddled with them.

Around 1900, Dr. William Clarke came to Cornwall and fell in love with the forest and the quiet country life. Clarke had been born in 1877 and grew up on a farm in Tenafly, New Jersey. He later became a professor of surgery and taught at Columbia College of Physicians and Surgeons, as well as earning a reputation as the leading cancer specialist in New York. He purchased 1,000 acres of land in the wilds of Connecticut, which included Dudleytown, and began construction of a vacation home. Over the next few years, he and his wife, Harriet Bank Clarke, visited the house on weekends and during the summer until it was completed. After that, it became mostly a holiday house for short stays in the summer and for Thanksgiving. Together, they maintained an idyllic second life near Dudleytown until 1918.

One summer weekend, Dr. Clarke was called away to New York on an emergency. His wife stayed behind. According to the story, he returned thirty-six hours later to find that she had gone insane, just as a number of previous residents of the village had done. The story also claims that she told of strange creatures that came out of the forest and attacked her. She committed suicide soon afterward. But how much truth is there to this tale? Perhaps more than some would like you to believe. It has been recorded that for several years before her suicide, Mrs. Clarke suffered from a "chronic illness." There is nothing to indicate what this ailment might have been or whether it was a physical or mental one. I think that it is safe to say, though, that mentally stable individuals do not ordinarily take their own lives. As far as whether or not she saw "strange creatures in the woods" - well, we will never really know for sure, but even if we disregard this, we still have one more suicide of a resident of the nearly nonexistent village of Dudleytown.

While undoubtedly shattered by his wife's suicide, Dr. Clarke continued to maintain his house in Dudleytown and continued to make visits there. He remarried and returned to stay at his summer house until a larger home was completed nearby in 1930. In 1924, he and his second wife, Carita, as well as other doctors, friends and interested landowners formed the "Dark Entry Forest Association." It was designed to act as forest preserve so that the land around Dudleytown would remain "forever wild." They held their first meeting in 1926 with forty-one members. Dr. Clarke died in Cornwall Bridge in February 1943 and Carita passed away five years later. A number of their children and family members still reside in the area.

Today, Dudleytown is mostly deserted, except for the curiosity-seekers and tourists, who come looking for thrills. The Dark Forest Entry Association still owns most of the land on which the village once stood. There are a group of homes on Bald Mountain Road that are very secluded from the main roads that belong to the closest residents. These locals maintain that nothing supernatural takes place in this region and perhaps they are right. It seems unlikely that the "curse" on Dudleytown ever really existed, but on the other hand, it is strange that such a small area experienced so many disappearances, unusual deaths, suicides and cases of insanity. The stories of a "curse" had to have gotten started for some reason, and perhaps this was why.

As far as we know, the ghostly tales began to surface in the 1940s. It was at this time that visitors to the ruined village began to speak of seeing wispy apparitions in the woods. Even today, those who have visited the place boast of having taken paranormal photographs, and having experienced overwhelming feelings of terror. They have reported seeing mysterious lights, hearing unexplained sounds and even of being touched, pushed and scratched by unseen hands. Some researchers refer to the area as a "negative power spot," or a place where entities enter this world from the other side. They say this may explain the strange events in Dudleytown's history, like the eerie reports, the strange creatures and perhaps even the outbreaks of insanity and madness. The place is often thought of as "tainted" in some way, as if the ground has somehow spoiled, or perhaps was sour all along.

Most historians dismiss such reports and theories and maintain that since the so-called "Curse of Dudleytown" never existed, then nothing strange has ever occurred there either. However, an open-minded look at some of the things that have happened do seem to show that this is a strange place, one that has been an enigma from the earliest days of its history. Whether or not there is any truth to the accounts of people who have come here since the days when the village was abandoned and say they have experienced paranormal phenomena is up to the reader to decide.

I should warn you, though, that trying to visit Dudleytown today can be hazardous - and not because of any curse. It should be noted that the members of the Dark Forest Entry Association have forbidden trespassing on their property. In 1999, they announced that they would no longer allow hikers on the land. In spite of this, many still go - now daring not only the spirits, but the authorities, too. Unfortunately, the ruins of Dudleytown have been vandalized in recent years and the constant stream of trespassers has had a negative effect on the ecology of the area. My advice - in spite of how tempting it might be to go there - would be refrain from visiting this area until methods can be devised to better preserve this wilderness region and until this unsettled corner of New England has been opened to the public again.

STEPHEN DECATUR'S CANNONBALL
THE LEGEND OF THE JERSEY DEVIL

The historic states along America's Atlantic Seaboard have given birth to hundreds of weird tales and unusual stories over the years. One of the strangest is undoubtedly that of the Jersey Devil, a being that is believed by some to be a mythical creature and by others, a real-life monster of flesh and blood. Its origins date back to when New Jersey was still a British colony and has its roots in a wild and overgrown region called the Pine Barrens.

This rugged place is one of vast forests, sandy soil and patches of swamp, where streams that are stained orange from iron ore and cedar slither through the shadows. It is a place that is often forgotten by man. The ruins of small settlements vanish into trees and undergrowth, leaving behind little but names that are now nothing more than crossroads in the wilderness. Among the places are Hog Walllow, Ongs Hat, Sooy Place and Mary Ann Furnace, as well as many others. They date back to the colonial days, when settlers actually attempted to farm the Barrens. The sandy soil, dense with pine and cedar, never took to crops other than the cranberries that flourish in the bogs, and so the colonists moved on, taking harsh memories of the place with them.

The Pine Barrens stretch across more than 1,700 square miles of southeastern New Jersey. The region lies within one of the most densely populated states in the country, and yet the desolation here is ominous. It is not difficult to travel for many miles without ever encountering a single sign of civilization. It is a place where one can easily vanish into the wild and never be seen again -- as many have.

What makes the Pine Barrens different than other wild regions of America is its unique history. At a time when the country was overwhelmingly made up of farms, the Pine Barrens supported literally dozens of industrial towns and villages. Furnaces and forges throughout the region turned out munitions for the American cause during the Revolution, during the conflicts with the Barbary pirates and the War of 1812. In the middle nineteenth century, though, a better grade of iron ore was found in the west and production in the Pine Barrens went into a decline. There were efforts to keep the paper and glass works going, but eventually they proved to be unprofitable and one by one, the factories closed down. What was already a rugged area in which making a living became difficult with the collapse of the local industries, and many moved away. Those who remained slipped deeper into poverty. They left the crumbling towns and moved into the forests and the swamps to eke out a living. These "Pineys," as they were called, remained here for generations, often living in horrific destitution. They hunted and fished, working at seasonal jobs to survive, while keeping completely to themselves until the modern roads of the twentieth century finally breached the isolation of the Pine Barrens.

It was at this time, as civilization began to encroach on this anomalous region, that stories began to filter out about a strange creature that lurked in the swamps and forests of the Barrens. As time has passed, countless stories of this monster have circulated throughout southern New Jersey, changing little as they pass from one person to the next. The stories all tell of a mysterious beast that has long terrorized communities in south Jersey and eastern Pennsylvania, always returning to its lair in the Pine Barrens.

This legendary creature is known as the Jersey Devil.

The origin of the Jersey Devil is as shrouded in mystery as the very existence of the creature itself. According to one version of the legend, Mrs. Jane Leeds came from a poor family who eked out a precarious existence in the Pine Barrens. In 1735, Mrs. Leeds discovered that she was pregnant with her thirteenth child. Overwhelmed with trying to keep her large brood fed and clothed, she told her friends and relatives that "the Devil can take the next one," and he did, or so the story went. When the baby was born, he was monster. He immediately took on a grotesque appearance and grew to more than twenty feet long, with a reptilian body, a horse's head, bat wings and a long, forked tail. There is no record of Mother Leeds' reaction to her infant's startling metamorphosis. He thrashed about the Leeds home for a bit and then vanished up the chimney to terrorize the surrounding regions, proving that it's a good idea to be careful what you ask for, especially where the Devil is concerned.

Other versions of the story tell similar tales but often with varying birthplaces and sometimes with families other than the Leeds. Regardless of its beginnings, though, the creature, or the "Jersey Devil" as he was dubbed, began haunting the Pine Barrens. As the story of the monster spread, grown men declined to venture out at night. It was said that the beast carried off large dogs, geese, cats, small livestock and even occasional children. The children were never seen again, but the animals' remains were often found. The Devil was also said to dry up the milk of cows by breathing on them and to kill off the fish in the streams, threatening the livelihood of the entire region.

In 1740, the frightened residents begged a local minister to exorcize the creature and the stories stated that the exorcism would banish the monster for one hundred years, however the Devil returned to the Pine Barrens on at least two occasions before the century was over. Legend has it that naval hero Commodore Stephen Decatur visited the Hanover Iron Works in the Barrens in 1800 to test the foundry's cannonballs. While on the firing range, he allegedly saw a strange creature flying through the sky overhead. Ordering his men to take aim and fire on the creature, Decatur watched as the monster crossed the sky. His men would later swear that the beast was struck by Decatur's cannonball, but the Devil continued on its path.

The second sighting took place a few years later. This time, the Devil was seen by another respected witness, Joseph Bonaparte, the former king of Spain and the brother of Napoleon. Bonaparte leased a country house near Bordertown from 1816 to 1839. He reported seeing the Jersey Devil while hunting game one day in the Pine Barrens.

In 1840, as the minister warned, the Devil returned and brought terror to the region once again. It snatched sheep from their pens and preyed on children who lingered outside after sunset. Livestock vanished and were found slaughtered and residents caught glimpses of a winged monster that were accompanied by chilling screams and inexplicable, cloven hoof prints that were left behind. People all across south Jersey locked their doors and hung a lantern on the doorstep, hoping to keep the creature away.

In 1859, an article appeared in the *Atlantic Monthly* that testified to the fact that fear of the Jersey Devil in the region had not diminished over the last two decades. The author of the article, W.F. Mayer, visited the Hanover Iron Works and found about fifty people living in squalor near the old mill. He found that few of them would venture out into the woods after dark.

That same year, the Jersey Devil was seen in Haddonfield and then vanished until the winter of 1873, when it was seen in Bridgeton. Throughout the 1880s, frequent reports continued to surface and in 1894, the Devil was often sighted lurking about Smithville, Long Beach Island, Brigantine Beach, Leeds Point and Haddonfield again. In 1899, after frightening people in Vincentown and Burrsville, the creature winged its way north and was seen along the New Jersey and New York border. A local newspaper printed the account of a man named George Saarosy, who claimed that his sheep were disturbed over several nights by horrifying screams that came from near the Lawrence Street Bridge over the Pascack River in Spring Valley, New York. Saarosy, who spotted the source of the screams, said that it resembled a "flying serpent." Those who had heard of the Jersey Devil recognized the description, and even though it was far outside of its usual territory, believed that the beast had come calling.

As the turn of the new century dawned, stories of the Jersey Devil continued to be told and the belief remained strong in South Jersey that the Pine Barrens definitely confined some sort of eerie inhabitant that occasionally got free and spread chaos through the region. For many, though, the Devil was little more than a legend -- until that legend came to life in 1909. In that year, the Jersey Devil returned again and literally hundreds of people spotted the monster or saw his footprints. It became so bad that schools closed across portions of the state and people refused to go outside after dark, or often even in the daytime. "Jersey Devil" hysteria gripped the region - and it may have been for good reason.

The first sighting occurred in the early morning hours of January 17. A man named Thack Cozzens of Woodbury was leaving the Woodbury Hotel when he heard a strange hissing noise and saw a blur of something white crossing the street. As the object vanished into the darkness, he saw it turn and caught a flash of two, glowing white eyes.

On that same morning in Bristol, Pennsylvania, within hours or even minutes of the Woodbury sighting, a man named John McOwen was awakened by the sound of his baby daughter crying. He went to calm her and heard odd noises coming from the Delaware Division Canal, which ran behind the house. He described the noises as scratching and whistling sounds and when he looked outside, he got the shock of his life. There, on the edge of the canal, was a large creature with wings that was hopping along the tow-path.

Nearby, a police officer named James Sackville also spotted the monster while walking his beat that night. He was passing along a dark alley when the winged creature hopped into the street and let out a horrific scream. Sackville, who later became the chief of Bristol's Police Department, got a closer look at the monster than either Cozzens or McOwen did and said that it had wings like a bird but the features of a peculiar animal. He ran toward the creature and it hopped backward in retreat. He then fired his revolver at the beast, but it spread its wings and vanished into the air.

Not long after the Devil escaped from Sackville's gunshot, it was spotted by E.W. Minster, the postmaster of Bristol. He stated that he awoke around 2:00 a.m. and heard an "eerie, almost supernatural" sound coming from the direction of the Delaware River. He looked out the window and saw what looked to be a "large crane" that was flying diagonally and emitting a curious glow. The creature had a long neck that was thrust forward in flight, thin wings, long back legs and shorter legs in the front. The creature let out a combination of a squawk and a whistle before disappearing into the darkness.

Other Bristol residents found their yards covered with abnormal-looking hoof prints the following morning. Few could provide a reasonable explanation as to where they had come from.

After leaving Bristol, the Jersey Devil next turned up in Burlington, New Jersey, a city that became the center of its activities in the days to come. Late on the night of January 17, Joseph W. Lowden and his family, who lived on High Street in the middle of town, heard noises like something heavy trampling the snow in their backyard. The sounds circled the house and then scraped against the back door, as if someone was trying to open it. When they examined the yard the following morning, they found strange tracks everywhere. Something had scuffled in the snow around their trash cans and the garbage had been half eaten. The tracks defied all explanation --- and the Lowdens were not the only ones to find them.

Hardly a yard in Burlington seemed to be untouched by the weird hoof prints. They climbed trees, skipped from one roof top to another, trampled across fields, into streets, over fences and then vanished, as if whatever had made them simply flew away. To add to the mystery, the size of the tracks varied. Some were as large as horse's hooves, but others were quite small. One thing was sure, though, they were frightening and a general panic gripped the town that day. Doors and windows were bolted and people refused to leave home, especially after dark. Those who did venture out went in search of the creature. Attempts to capture and kill it were made, or at least vowed, but all were unsucessful.

Reports of more tracks poured in from surrounding communities and in Jacksonville, a hunt for the Jersey Devil was organized. Strangely, dogs brought in for the search refused to follow the trail left by the monster and so their handlers followed the prints for nearly four miles before the tracks disappeared. Farmers set out steel traps but - luckily for them - they never caught anything in them.

The sightings continued and a flurry of them took place on January 19. At around 2:00 a.m., Nelson Evans, a Gloucester City paper hanger, and his wife were awakened at their home on Mercer Street. Strange noises were coming from outside and the couple nervously peered out their window to see a large animal on the roof of their shed. They watched for a full ten minutes as the Jersey Devil stomped back and forth. They described the beast as: "about three and a half feet high, with a face like a collie and a head like a horse. It had a long neck, wings about two feet long and its back legs were like those of a crane and it had horse's hooves. It walked on its back legs and held up two short front legs with paws on them." Mrs. Nelson also added that as the creature flapped its wings, it made a muffled sound "like a wood saw makes when it strikes a rotten place." A drawing based on the Nelson's description appeared in the *Philadelphia Evening Bulletin* and became the most famous rendition of the creature.

Yet another hunt was started for the Devil that day near Gloucester. Muskrat hunters Hank White and Tom Hamilton tracked the creature for close to twenty miles through the forest. They were amazed to see the tracks jump over eight-foot fences and then duck under spaces no more than eight inches high. By the time the hunt was called off, White stated that he would not venture outside his home without a gun until the Devil had left the region.

Sightings of the monster's hoof prints continued all over southern New Jersey. The daughter of William Pine, from Camden, was bringing her father his dinner pail when she stumbled across a series of strange tracks in the snow. She became so frightened that she fell into a dead faint. Her father and others examined the tracks and stated that they resembled those of a donkey with only two legs. One of the tracks, they said, was larger than the other, which made it seem "obviously deformed."

Early Wednesday morning, January 20, an unidentified Burlington policeman spotted the creature and said that it "had no teeth and its eyes were blazing coals." That same morning, Reverend John Pursell spotted the beast in Pemberton. He said that he had "never saw anything like it before."

Predictably, more hunts were organized that day. Haddonfield, New Jersey, was the scene of two search parties, led by a Dr. Glover and a Mr. Holloway. They found many tracks in the fields and woods around town but all of the trails ended suddenly, when the creature apparently took flight. Another search party hunted the creature near Collinswood and while they found many tracks, they only got a fleeting glimpse of the Devil as it winged its way north toward Moorestown.

The Devil's only stop in Moorestown was in Mount Carmel Cemetery, where it was spotted by John Smith of Maple Shade. Smith claimed to have chased the creature until it vanished around a nearby gravel pit. Moments later, the Devil crossed the path of George Snyder, who had been fishing in the same gravel pit. Both his and Smith's description of the monster matched, stating that it was three feet tall, covered in black hair, had a face like a dog's, split hooves, wings and a tail.

The Devil was seen again late that night, this time in Springside, just south of Burlington City, by a trolley car operator named Edward Davis. He was shocked when he saw a strange shape leap across the tracks in front of the trolley and then disappear into the shadows. Davis said that he shape resembled a "winged kangaroo with a long neck."

That same night, residents in Riverside, New Jersey, discovered a series of odd tracks leading throughout the town, especially near chicken coops, buildings and even outhouses. Joseph Mans found the tracks had paced a circle around the body of his dead puppy. Mans at first attributed the dog's death to some people against whom he had recently testified in court, and told police officers that the prowler had worn what seemed to be small horse shoes on the bottom of his boots. The dog killer had "left tracks everywhere, including the rooftop." The judge before whom Mans had testified, Justice Ziegler, became interested in the investigation and came over to the house. Curious, he made a half-dozen plaster casts of the footprints, and when word of this got out, crowds came to his office to see the casts. It was soon realized that the dog's death had not been the work of Mans' enemies at all.

In the early morning hours of Thursday, January 21, the Jersey Devil put in a frightening appearance in Camden. Members of the Black Hawk Social Club were at a meeting around 1:00 a.m. and a Mr. Rouh was distracted by what he called an "uncanny sound" outside the back window. He turned to see a gruesome face staring in at him and he let out a scream. The other club members fled in terror but Rouh grabbed a club and waved it at the creature. He stated that it flew off, emitting "bloodcurdling sounds."

An hour later, a Public Service Railway Trolley was pulling out of Clementon and heading for Camden. It had just passed Haddon Heights when a passenger yelled out and pointed to the window. Everyone on board crowded up to the glass to see a winged creature swoop past them. The trolley traveled another two hundred yards before it stopped and when it did, the Devil circled above the car, hissing loudly. A few moments later, it flew away and headed north. Within days, trolley cars began carrying armed guards on board to protect the passengers.

A short time later, the creature turned up again, this time on the road between Trenton and Ewing. William Cromley was returning home from his job as the doorkeeper at the Trent Theater in Trenton when his horse panicked and stopped in the road. He climbed out of the buggy to see what was wrong and saw "a sight that froze the blood in his veins and caused his hair to stand upright." Confronting him on the road was a winged beast that was larger than a big dog with glowing, sparkling eyes. The beast growled at him and then spread its wings and flew off.

Not long after this sighting, Trenton City Councilman E.P. Weeden was awakened by the sound of someone trying to forcibly enter his home. Banging and crashing sounds were heard coming from the back door and he sprang out of bed to see what was going on. Weeden flung open a second-floor window and looked out, only to see a black shape suddenly vanish into the darkness. The movement was accompanied by the sound of beating wings and the next morning, he found cloven tracks in the snow of his yard and on his roof.

Later that afternoon, Mrs. J.H, White was taking clothes off her line when she noticed a strange creature huddled in the corner of her yard. She promptly screamed and fainted. Her husband rushed out the back door to find his wife on the ground and the Devil close by, "spurting flames." He chased the monster with a clothesline prop and it leapt over the fence and vanished. White ran out into the alley in pursuit but soon quit the chase and returned to his wife, who was still unconscious. He called the family doctor, who spent more than an hour reviving Mrs. White from her terrifying experience.

A short time later, the Devil was seen in West Collingswood. Charles Klos and George Boggs were walking down Grant Avenue when they saw what they first thought was an ostrich perched on the roof of the fire chief's home. Concerned, the two men called in a fire alarm and when a department truck arrived, they turned their hoses on the creature. At first it fled some distance down the street and then the beast ignored the water and charged directly at the now-frightened men. As they ran for cover, the Devil spread its wings and soared over them, disappearing into the dusk.

Leaving the vanquished West Collinswood firemen behind, the Devil traveled up Mount Ephraim Avenue and attacked a dog belonging to Mrs. Mary Sorbinski in South Camden. When she heard the dog's cries in the darkness, she dashed outside and drove the Devil away with a broom. The creature fled, but not before tearing a chunk of flesh from the dog. Mrs. Sorbinski carried her wounded pet inside and immediately called the police. By the time that patrolmen arrived, a crowd of more than one hundred people had gathered at the house. The crowd was witness to the piercing screams that suddenly erupted from nearby. The police officers emptied their revolvers at the shadow that loomed against the night sky, but the Devil escaped once again.

In the days that followed, eyewitness accounts of the Jersey Devil filled the newspapers, as well as photos and reports of cloven footprints that had been found in yards, woods and parking lots. The Philadelphia Zoo offered a $10,000 reward for the beast's capture, but there were no takers. Many people refused to leave their homes, even in broad daylight, and many schools closed down, due to a lack of students. Theaters canceled performances and mills in Gloucester and Hainesport were shut down when workers refused to report for their shifts.

Then, as suddenly as it had come, the Devil vanished into the Pine Barrens again.

The stunning events of 1909 had come to an end. Up until that time, it was always assumed that the Jersey Devil was nothing more than a legend, an old wives' tale from the rugged, remote Barrens. But now, the entire region had been the scene of this mythical beast's rampage, leaving hundreds of believable eyewitnesses in its wake.

The creature did not return again until 1927. A cab driver was changing a tire one night while headed for Salem. He had just finished when his cab began shaking violently. He looked up to see a gigantic, winged figure pounding on the roof. The driver, leaving his jack and flat tire behind, jumped into the car and quickly drove away. He reported the encounter to the Salem police.

In August 1930, berry pickers at Leeds Point and Mays Landing reported seeing the Devil, crashing through the fields and devouring blueberries. It was reported again two weeks later to the north and then it disappeared again.

In November 1951, a group of children were allegedly cornered by the Devil at the Duport Clubhouse in Gibbstown. The creature bounded away without hurting anyone. Reports claimed that it was spotted by dozens of witnesses before finally vanishing again.

Sightings continued here and there for years, and then peaked once more in 1960 when bloodcurdling cries terrorized a group of people near Mays Landing. State officials tried to calm the nervous residents but no explanation could be found for the weird sounds. Policemen nailed signs and posters everywhere stating that the Jersey Devil was a hoax, but curiosity-seekers flooded into the area anyway. Harry Hunt, who owned the Hunt Brothers Circus, offered $100,000 for the beast's capture, hoping to add it to his sideshow attractions. Needless to say, the monster was never snared.

One of the most recent sightings of the creature occurred in 1993 when a forest ranger named John Irwin was driving along the Mullica River in southern New Jersey. He was startled to find the road ahead of him blocked by the Jersey Devil. He described it as being about six-feet tall with horns and matted black fur. Could this have been the reported Jersey Devil, or some other creature altogether? Irwin stated that he and the creature stared at one another for several minutes before the monster turned and ran into the forest.

Today, there are only a few, isolated sightings of the Jersey Devil. It seems as though the paved roads, electric lights and modern conveniences that have come to the region over the course of three centuries have driven the monster so far into hiding that it has vanished altogether. The lack of proof of the monster's existence in recent times leads many to believe the Devil was nothing more than a creation of New Jersey folklore and a product of mass hysteria. But was it really?

If it was merely a myth, then how do we explain the sightings of the creature and the witness accounts from reliable persons like businessmen, police officers and public officials? They are not easy to dismiss as hearsay or the result of heavy drinking. Could the Jersey Devil have been real after all? And if so, is it still out there somewhere in the remote regions of the Pine Barrens - just waiting to be found?

METAL BOLTS

MOTHMAN ENCOUNTERS AND THE SILVER BRIDGE

On December 15, 1967, the so-called "Silver Bridge," which crossed the Ohio River between Point Pleasant, West Virginia, and Gallipolis, Ohio, collapsed during heavy rush hour traffic and plunged into the river below. It carried with it dozens of cars, thousands of pounds of twisted metal and scores of people returning from work and holiday shopping. Forty-six people were killed in the disaster and two of the victims were never found.

An investigation of the eye-bar chain suspension bridge, dubbed the "Silver Bridge" due to the color of its aluminum paint, revealed that the collapse was caused by the failure of a single point in a suspension chain: a crack that was less than one-tenth of an inch deep. The bridge was carrying heavier loads than it had been designed for back when it was erected in 1928, investigators said, and it had been poorly maintained.

That was the logical explanation for the bridge's collapse, but rumor and legend told other, much darker tales. It was said that a mysterious figure was seen near the bridge just before the disaster: a sort of "portent of doom" that had been plaguing Point Pleasant for the previous thirteen months. The bridge collapse marked the last time that the figure was seen in the area. What was it? To this day, no one knows for sure, but locals began calling the man-like creature the "Mothman" because of its unusual appearance.

To this day, the Mothman remains one of the strangest enigmas in the annals of the unexplained in American history.

The weird events connected to the creature that became known as the "Mothman" began on November 12, 1966, near Clendenin, West Virginia. Five men were in the local cemetery that day, preparing a grave for a burial, when something that looked like a "brown human being" lifted off from some nearby trees and flew over their heads. The men were baffled. It did not appear to be a bird, but more like a man with wings. A few days later, more sightings would take place, electrifying the entire region.

Late in the evening of November 15, two young married couples had a very strange encounter as they drove past an abandoned explosives plant near Point Pleasant, West Virginia. Standing in the doorway of one of the abandoned bunkers, the couples spotted two large eyes that were attached to something that was "shaped like a man, but bigger, maybe six or seven feet tall. And it had big wings folded against its back." When the creature moved toward the door, the couples panicked and sped away. Moments later, they saw the same creature on a hillside near the road. It spread its wings and rose into the air, following their car, which by now was traveling at over 100 miles per hour. "That bird kept right up with us," said one of the members of the group. They told Deputy Sheriff Millard Halstead that it followed them down Highway 62 to the Point Pleasant city limits. The two young couples would not be the only ones to report the creature that night. Another group of four witnesses claimed to see the "bird" three different times.

Another sighting had more bizarre results. At about 10:30 p.m. on that same evening, Newell Partridge, a local building contractor who lived in Salem, about ninety miles from Point Pleasant, was watching television when the screen suddenly went dark. He stated that a weird pattern filled the screen and then he heard a loud, whining sound from outside that raised in pitch and then ceased. "It sounded like a generator winding up," he later stated. Partridge's dog, Bandit, began to howl out on the front porch and Newell went to see what was going on.

When he walked outside, he saw Bandit facing the hay barn, about one hundred and fifty yards from the house. Puzzled, Partridge turned a flashlight in that direction and spotted two red circles that looked like eyes or "bicycle reflectors." The moving red orbs were certainly not an animal's eyes, he believed, and the sight of them frightened him. Bandit, an experienced hunting dog and protective of his territory, shot off across the yard in pursuit of the glowing eyes. Partridge called for him to stop, but the animal paid no attention. His owner turned and went back into the house for his gun, but then was too scared to go back outside again. He slept that night with his gun propped up next to the bed. The next morning, he realized that Bandit had disappeared. The dog had still not shown up two days later when Partridge read in the newspaper about the sightings in Point Pleasant that same night.

One statement that he read in the newspaper chilled him to the bone. Roger Scarberry, a member of the group who spotted the strange "bird" at the TNT plant, said that as they entered the city limits of Point Pleasant, they saw the body of a large dog lying on the side of the road. A few minutes later, on the way back out of town, the dog was gone. They even stopped to look for the body, knowing they had passed it just a few minutes before. Newell Partridge immediately thought of Bandit, who was never seen again.

On November 16, a press conference was held in the county courthouse and the couples from the TNT plant sighting repeated their story. Deputy Halstead, who had known the four young people all of their lives, took them very seriously. "They've never been in any trouble," he told investigators and he had no reason to doubt their stories. Many of the reporters who were present for the weird recounting felt the same way. The news of the strange sightings spread around the world. The press dubbed the odd flying creature "Mothman," after a character from the popular *Batman* television series of the day.

The remote and abandoned TNT plant became the lair of the Mothman in the months ahead, and it could not have picked a better place in which to hide. The area was made up of several hundred acres of woods and large concrete domes where high explosives were stored during World War II. A network of tunnels honeycombed the area, making it possible for the creature to move about without being seen. In addition to the manmade labyrinth, the area was also comprised of the McClintic Wildlife Station, a heavily forested animal preserve filled with woods, artificial ponds and steep ridges and hills. Much of the property was almost inaccessible and without a doubt, Mothman could have hidden there for weeks or months and remained totally unseen. The only people who ever wandered there were hunters and fishermen and the local teenagers, who used the rutted dirt roads of the preserve as lovers' lanes.

Very few homes could be found in the region, but one dwelling belonged to the Ralph Thomas family. On November 16, they spotted a "funny red light" in the sky that moved and hovered above the TNT plant. "It wasn't an airplane," Mrs. Marcella Bennett (a friend of the Thomas family) said, "but we couldn't figure out what it was." Mrs. Bennett drove to the Thomas house a few minutes later and got out of the car with her baby. Suddenly, a figure stirred near the automobile. "It seemed as though it had been lying down," she later recalled. "It rose up slowly from the ground... a big gray thing... bigger than a man with terrible glowing eyes."

Mrs. Bennett was so horrified that she dropped her little girl. She quickly recovered, picked up the child, and ran to the house. The family locked everyone inside but hysteria gripped them as the creature shuffled onto the porch and peered into the windows. The police were summoned, but Mothman had vanished by the time the authorities had arrived.

Mrs. Bennett would not recover from the incident for months, and was so distraught that she sought medical attention to deal with her anxiety. She was tormented by frightening dreams and she later told investigators that she believed the creature had visited her own home too. She said that she often heard keening sounds --- like a woman screaming-- near her isolated home on the edge of Point Pleasant.

Many would come to believe that the sightings of Mothman, as well as UFO sightings and encounters with "men in black" in the area, which occurred over the course of the months that followed, were all related. For over a year, strange happenings continued in the area. Researchers, investigators and "monster hunters" descended on the area, but none of them became as famous John Keel, an author on anomalies who went on to write extensively about Mothman, strange creatures and other unexplained events. His later writings about UFOs caused great controversy in the mainstream UFO movement because he dismissed the standard extraterrestrial theories. According to Keel, man has had a long history of interaction with the supernatural. He believed that the intervention of mysterious strangers in the lives of historic personages like Thomas Jefferson and Malcolm X provided evidence of the continuing presence of the "gods of old." The manifestation of these elder gods came in the form of UFOs and aliens, monsters, demons, angels and even ghosts. During his lifetime, he was a colorful character but remained a respected figure in the field, thanks to his research and writings. It would be the Mothman case that really started his career.

Keel became the major chronicler of the Mothman investigation and wrote that at least one hundred people personally witnessed the creature between November 1966 and November 1967. According to their reports, the creature stood between five and seven feet tall, was wider than a man and shuffled on human-like legs. Its eyes were set near the top of its shoulders and it had bat-like wings that caused it to glide, rather than flap, when it flew. Strangely, it was able to ascend straight up "like a helicopter." Witnesses described its murky skin as being either gray or brown and it was said to emit a humming sound when it flew. The Mothman was apparently incapable of speech and gave off a screeching sound.

John Keel arrived in Point Pleasant in December 1966 and immediately began collecting reports of Mothman sightings and even UFO reports that occurred before the creature was seen. He also compiled evidence that suggested a problem with televisions and phones that began in the fall of 1966. Lights had been seen in the skies, particularly around the TNT plant, and cars that passed along the nearby road sometimes stalled without explanation. He and his fellow researchers also uncovered a number of short-lived poltergeist cases in the Ohio Valley area. Locked doors opened and closed by themselves, strange thumps were heard inside and outside of homes and often, inexplicable voices were heard. The James Lilley family, who lived just south of the TNT plant, were so bothered by the bizarre events that they sold their home and moved to another neighborhood. Keel was convinced that the intense period of activity was all connected.

And stranger things took place.....

A reporter named Mary Hyre, who was the Point Pleasant correspondent for the Athens, Ohio, newspaper the *Messenger*, also wrote extensively about the local sightings. After one very active weekend, she was deluged with over five hundred phone calls from people who reported seeing strange lights in the skies. One night in January 1967, she was working late in her office in the county courthouse when a man walked in the door. He was very short and had strange eyes that were covered with thick glasses. He had long, black hair that was cut squarely "like a bowl haircut." Hyre said that he spoke in a low, halting voice as he asked for directions to Welsh, West Virginia. She thought that he had some sort of speech impediment and for some reason, he terrified her. "He kept getting closer and closer to me," she said, "and his funny eyes were staring at me almost hypnotically."

Alarmed, she summoned the newspaper's circulation manager to her office and together, they spoke to the strange little man. She said that at one point in the discussion, she answered the telephone when it rang and she noticed the little man pick up a pen from her desk. He looked at it in amazement, "as if he had never seen a pen before." Then, he grabbed the pen, laughed loudly and ran out of the building.

Several weeks later, Hyre was crossing the street near her office when she saw the same man on the street. He appeared to be startled when he realized that she was watching him, and turned away and ran for a large, black car that suddenly came around the corner. The little man climbed in and it quickly drove away.

By late fall 1967, the Mothman was being reported less and less, but it seems that it had one last appearance to make. Around 5:00 p.m. on December 15, 1967, the Silver Bridge suddenly collapsed as thirty-seven vehicles were crossing it, sending forty-six people to their deaths. Another nine people were seriously injured. Along with the fatalities and injuries, a major transportation route connecting West Virginia and Ohio was destroyed, disrupting the lives of many and causing fear about other bridges across the nation.

The bridge had been constructed in 1928, a time when the typical family automobile was the Ford Model T, which weighed about 1,500 pounds. By contrast, at the time of the collapse, a typical car weighed about 4,000 pounds, and this weight did not include the numerous trucks that crossed the Silver Bridge every day. Bumper-to-bumper traffic jams on the bridge were common, occurring several times a day, five days each week, thus causing more stress to the bridge.

The bridge was dubbed the "Silver Bridge" because it was the country's first aluminum-painted bridge. It was designed with a twenty-two foot roadway and one five-foot sidewalk. Some unique engineering techniques were featured on the Silver Bridge such as "High Tension" eye-bar chains, a unique anchorage system, and 'Rocker" towers. The Silver Bridge was the first eye-bar suspension bridge of its type to be constructed in the United States. The bridge's eye-bars were linked together in pairs like a chain. A huge pin passed through the eye and linked each piece to the next. The length of each chain varied depending upon its location on the bridge. It would be a crack in one of the eye-bars that would cause the bridge to collapse. It all happened in one terrible second.

On the evening of December 15, many people were out buying Christmas trees and enjoying the holiday season, unaware of the disaster, until they heard the sound. Some individuals said, "the sound of the collapse was like that of a shotgun." For those who saw the bridge collapse, they said, "it looked like the bridge fell like a card deck." When the structure fell, horror captivated the area and lives were changed forever.

Many heroic eyewitnesses tried to help the victims who fell in the water. Rescue crews were at the disaster scene within minutes, and were able to save some of the victims from drowning in the Ohio River. Witnesses said that many of the vehicles were floating downstream while passengers were beating wildly on the windows, trying to escape. One eyewitness described seeing a truck driver standing on the top of his truck cab yelling for help as his vehicle slowly floated downstream in the cold water. William Needham, a truck driver from Kernersville, North Carolina, barely escaped death. He was in the cab of his truck driving across the bridge, when the collapse occurred. He managed to survive, but his partner, who had been asleep in the rear of the cab, was unable to escape. As the truck sank to the river bottom, Needham made it out by breaking a window and swimming for the surface.

Another survivor, Howard Boggs, of Gallipolis, Ohio, lost his family in the collapse. His wife, Marjorie, and seventeen-month-old daughter were in their vehicle when the disaster occurred. He claimed that Marjorie noticed that the bridge was "quivering" as they became stalled on the bridge in the heavy traffic. She then asked, "What will we do if this thing breaks?" The next thing Boggs remembered was scrambling for his life by breaking out his car window. Tragically, his wife and child never made it out of the car.

On the same night that the bridge collapsed, the James Lilley family (who still lived near the TNT plant at that time) counted more than twelve eerie lights that flashed above their home and vanished into the forest.

The collapse of the Silver Bridge made headlines all over the country. The local citizens were stunned with horror and disbelief and for many, the tragedy is still being felt today. An investigation later determined that a tiny crack in one of the eye-bar links, combined with the weight of cars and trucks that the bridge had not been designed to hold, caused the disaster to occur. But not everyone believed this. Rumors would soon spread that there were other, much stranger, causes for the disaster.

There were many people - perhaps most people in the area - who believed that the Mothman sightings, the bizarre events and the reports of strange lights were somehow connected to the bridge collapse. Some saw the earlier events as a warning, or premonition, of the deadly accident to come. Others believed that the Mothman was directly responsible for the horror. A few even insisted that the creature was seen near the bridge just minutes before the collapse occurred.

So, who - or what - was the Mothman and what was behind the strange events in Point Pleasant?

Whatever the creature may have been, it seems clear that Mothman was no hoax. There were simply too many credible witnesses who saw "something." It was suggested at the time that the creature might have been a sand hill crane, which while they are not native to the area, could have migrated south from Canada. That was one explanation anyway, although it was one that was rejected by Mothman witnesses, who stated that what they saw looked nothing like a crane.

But there could have been a logical explanation for some of the sightings. Even John Keel (who believed the creature was genuine) suspected that a few of the cases involved people who were spooked by recent reports of a strange flying creature and panicked when they saw owls flying along deserted roads at night. Even so, Mothman remains hard to easily dismiss. The case is filled with an impressive number of multiple-witness sightings by individuals that were deemed reliable, among them law enforcement officials.

But if Mothman was real --- and he truly was some unidentified creature that cannot be explained -- what was behind the UFO sightings, the poltergeist reports, the strange lights, sounds, the "men in black" and most horrifying, the collapse of the Silver Bridge?

John Keel believed that Point Pleasant was a "window" area, a place that was marked by long periods of strange sightings, monster reports and the coming and going of unusual persons. He stated that it may be wrong to blame the collapse of the bridge on the local UFO sightings, but the intense activity in the area at the time did suggest some sort of connection.

One thing was sure, though, the Point Pleasant area was no stranger to weird events. It had been marked by a long history of tragedy and disaster, which some claimed dated back to the 1770s, when the legendary "Cornstalk Curse" was placed on the region. Could such a "curse" explain the bizarre events of the 1960s?

In 1774, the Battle of Point Pleasant took place between an army made up of white settlers and a large portion of the Native American population of the region. The commander of the Indian war party was Chief Cornstalk, a well-respected and intelligent leader. During the battle, Cornstalk could see that defeat was imminent for his forces. He therefore let his troops make a crucial decision: either to fight to the death or surrender. The Indian warriors chose to surrender. With the surrender, Chief Cornstalk signed the Treaty of Camp Charlotte. Cornstalk and his son were later captured and murdered at Fort Randolph. Legend states that in his dying words Chief Cornstalk, still upset over his troops' defeat, placed a curse of death and destruction upon the entire region.

In 1794, the town of Point Pleasant was established near the site of the old fort. For many years after, Chief Cornstalk's grave lay undisturbed, but in 1840 his bones were removed to the grounds of the Mason County Court House where, in 1899, a monument was erected in his memory. In the late 1950s, a new court house was built in Point Pleasant and the chief's remains (which now consisted of three teeth and about fifteen pieces of bone) were placed in an aluminum box and reinterred in a corner of the town's Tu-Endie-Wei Park, next to the grave of a Virginia frontiersman that Cornstalk once fought and later befriended.

Some believe that the original disturbance of Cornstalk's remains ignited the curse that he had once placed on the area. Many tragedies and disasters were blamed on the curse, including a 1907 mine disaster that killed more than three hundred miners; a 1944 tornado that killed one hundred and fifty people in the region; the collapse of the Silver Bridge in 1967; an airline crash in 1968 that killed thirty-five people; a 1970 airline disaster that killed all seventy-five passengers on board; a flash flood that occurred in 1972 that wiped out several towns and killed one hundred and twenty people; a January 1978 train derailment that dumped thousands of gallons of toxic chemicals into Point Pleasant's water supply; an April 1978 tragedy that took place when fifty-one men working on the Willow Island power plant were killed when a construction scaffolding collapsed, and even an explosion at the Mason County Jail in Point Pleasant that occurred in 1976. Housed in the jail was a woman named Harriet Sisk, who had been arrested for the murder of her infant daughter. On March 2, her husband came to the jail with a suitcase full of explosives to kill himself and his wife and to destroy the building. Both of the Sisks were killed, along with three law enforcement officers.

And there have been many other strange occurrences, fires and floods. Most would say, however, that floods are a natural part of living on the river, although floodwaters nearly obliterated Point Pleasant in 1913 and 1937. It might be hard to tie such natural occurrences to a curse, but what about the barge explosion that killed six men from town just before Christmas 1953? Or the fire that destroyed an entire downtown city block in the late 1880s? Some have even gone as far as to blame the curse for the death of Point Pleasant's local economy, an event linked to the passing of river travel and commerce. Largely, the curse has been forgotten over time and today, Point Pleasant is better known for its connection to otherworldly visitors like Mothman than for Indian curses and bloody frontier battles.

But how real was the curse? Was it simply a string of bloody and tragic coincidences, culled from two centuries of sad but natural events in the region? Could it be used to explain why the area seems to attract strange happenings and eerie tales? Or is the area somehow blighted, separate from any curse, and attractive to the strangeness that seems to lurk in the shadowy corners of America?

ROCK PAINTING

The Mississippi River Piasa Bird

As visitors leave the city of Alton, Illinois, and drive north along the Mississippi River, they are often surprised to see a rock painting on the side of a bluff that portrays a vicious-looking winged creature. Years ago, this rock painting was actually a petroglyph that showed two such creatures. These monsters, like the modern rendering of the paintings, were called the "Piasa" by the Illiniwek Indians. The original painting existed near this location for hundreds of years and was first described in the journals of Pere Marquette in 1673 as he was exploring the Mississippi River. The original site of the painting is now long gone, but Marquette described the creatures portrayed there in this manner:

While skirting some rocks, which by their height and length inspired awe, we saw upon one of them two painted monsters which at first made us afraid, and upon which the boldest savages dare not long rest their eyes. They are as large as a calf; they have horns on their heads like those of a deer, a horrible look, red eyes, a beard like a tiger's, a face somewhat like a man's, a body covered with scales, and so long a tail that winds all around the body, passing above the head and going back between the legs, ending in a fish's tail. Green, red and black are the colors composing the picture. Moreover, these two monsters are so well painted that we cannot believe any savage is their author; for good painters in France would find it difficult to reach that place conveniently to paint them.

Marquette added a drawing of the creatures to his journal account but the drawing was unfortunately lost a short time later when his canoe capsized. In 1678, though, a map that was drawn by the French map-maker Jean-Baptiste Louis Franquelin included a picture of the fierce Piasa, based on Marquette's writings.

Father Hennepin, another early explorer of the West, published a book in 1698 called *A New Discovery of a Vast Country in America*. He also wrote about seeing the paintings of the Piasa, which incidentally, were first incised and cut into the bluff and then painted over. Unlike Father Marquette, Hennepin included the description that the Piasa had wings, making it a fearsome bird rather than simply an Indian monster. The mystery as to why he portrayed the monster in such a way was solved many years later.

In 1812, the first use of the word "Piasa" appeared in print. Major Amos Stoddard, who had earlier been appointed by President Thomas Jefferson as commander of the northern portion of the Louisiana Purchase, wrote "What they call 'painted monsters' on the side of a high perpendicular rock, apparently inaccessible to man, located between the Missouri and Illinois Rivers and known to moderns by the name of Piasa, still remains to a good degree of preservation."

In 1820, Captain Gideon Spencer came up the Mississippi and got a glimpse of the Piasa. By this time, only one of the paintings remained. The fate of the second creature is unknown but it's likely that it was destroyed by weather and falling rock, as the bluffs near Alton can be dangerously unstable at times. Spencer asked the Indians what the strange painting was and they told him that it was a "Storm Bird" or a "Thunder Bird" and that it had been placed there long ago. The Indians would fire their guns at it and some would offer it tobacco by puffing on their pipes and blowing smoke in the direction of the image.

The Piasa painting was located immediately below where the first Illinois state prison was located in Alton. The painting was partially destroyed in the 1840s when quarrying was done on the bluff by convicts from the prison, and further work done in the 1860s, when the abandoned prison was used as a Confederate penitentiary during the Civil War, ruined what was left of it.

The painting was later described by a Professor William McAdams, an Illinois State Geologist, who drew an illustration of the bird in the 1880s. It is from his drawing that all of the modern-day renditions of the Piasa Bird come. McAdams also seems to be the person responsible for creating the mythology of a single bird-like creature, instead of two monsters, as the Indians originally passed along the story. In McAdams' day, the original painting no longer existed. A quarry had purchased the property and they had blasted away the wall on which it could be found some time around 1847. The drawing that McAdams made was based on the testimony of five men who recalled seeing the painting before it was destroyed. It was later featured in the *Literary Digest* and it is believed to be the most accurate depiction of the Piasa.

Some have criticized McAdams, claiming that he created the mythology that the Piasa was a bird instead of simply a monster. The evidence they cite is that the Piasa had never been written about or drawn with wings prior to McAdams' version in *Literary Digest*, but this is not the case. Another painting that was done of the Piasa at roughly this same time was created by a man named Ladd, a former mayor of White Hall, Illinois. According to Ladd, he based his picture on a recollection of the original image that had been given to him by "Spencer Russell of Bluffdale, who had been nearer to the Piasa than any person now living." He spoke to the man, who told him this:

I used to climb the rocks to look at it when I was a boy. I have been within sixty feet of it. I once pointed it out from the deck of an English steamer to a lady and she looked at it through a field glass. No wings showed that day for the weather was dry. The colors were always affected by dampness, and it stood out distinctly after rain. Father Marquette evidently saw the Piasa on a dry day for he pictured it without wings.

Some have also claimed that the word "Piasa" was never a part of the language of the Illinois Indians, but this does not seem to be the case either. In 1883, the Bureau of Ethnology described the word as an Illinois Indian name denoting - disturbingly -- "a bird that devours men." Even among the Sauk Indians, relatives of the Illinois, the name was known and the famous Black Hawk's father was himself called "Pyesa."

Who created the original painting? No one will ever know for sure, but it must have existed for some time as part of the culture of the local Native Americans. It was said that on a flat ledge below the painting were hundreds of arrow heads and spear points. It is believed that the Indians who passed the Piasa on the river would "attack" the creature by firing an arrow at it. It apparently became a custom when floating past the future site of Alton. The Piasa Bird is considered one of the most enduring legends of the region: a tall tale and an Indian myth that's now used to entertain children and tourists.

But what if it wasn't merely a myth? What if there was more to the legend that meets the eye?

The legend of the Piasa Bird dates back to long before the white man came to region. It has been traced to a band of Illiniwek Indians who lived along the Mississippi in the vicinity north of present-day Alton. This tribe, led by a chief named Owatoga, hunted and fished the valley and the river and lived a contented life until the "great beast" came.

One morning, Owatoga's son, Utim, and a friend were fishing when they heard a terrible scream. They looked in the direction of the scream and saw a huge bird rising from the edge of the river. The legend states that the bird was so enormous that it could carry away a full-grown deer in its talons, and that once it obtained a taste for human flesh, it would eat nothing else. The creature the two men saw had a young man gripped in its claws and it carried him away and out of sight. Quickly, the two young men returned to their village and found their people very frightened. They waited all day for the young man to escape from the bird and return, but he did not.

After that, nearly every morning, the great bird would appear in the sky and carry away a member of the tribe: a man, woman or a child. Those who were carried off were never seen again. The people began to call the bird the "Piasa," which meant "the bird which devours men." Owatoga realized that they were powerless against this beast and he retreated to his lodge to fast and to pray for guidance. He emerged the next day with a daring plan that had been revealed to him in a vision.

According to his vision, Owatoga was to take six of his finest braves and climb to the top of one of the highest bluffs. The young men were to carry with them only their bows and a quiver of poisoned arrows. They were to hide themselves while Owatoga stood on the edge of the bluff and waited for the Piasa to appear. When the monster came, the chief was to throw himself down on the rocks and hold on while the bird attempted to carry him away. As it did so, the braves would appear with their bows and slay the beast.

Of course, all of the men in the tribe offered to help kill the Piasa, but Owatoga chose only young, unmarried men, his own son among them. The arrows were duly sharpened and poisoned and the group climbed to the top of the bluff. The six young men hid themselves beneath a rock ledge and Owatoga stepped out to the edge of the cliff. He folded his arms and waited for the creature to appear. Suddenly, the sky darkened overhead and the bird's massive wings were heard. The Piasa swooped down toward Owatoga. Just as the tip of the creature's sharp talon sunk into this shoulder, Owatoga threw himself flat upon the rocks. His hands curled around the roots of a tree and he clung desperately to them. The Piasa roared in frustration and its wings beat furiously, trying to lift the Indian from the rocks.

The wings unfolded once more and as it exposed itself, the young men burst from their hiding place and fired their arrows at the beast. The arrows found their mark but the Piasa continued to fight, trying over and over to lift Owatoga from the rocks. Then, with a howl of agony, the creature released him and collapsed backward, crashing over the edge of the bluff. It spiraled down out of sight and plunged beneath the waters of the Mississippi. The terrible creature was never seen again.

Despite his wounds, Owatoga joined in the celebration over the death of the Piasa. They ate, danced and celebrated into the night. The next day, they painted a colorful tribute to the Piasa bird on the stone face of the bluff where it had been destroyed. From that time on, any Indian who went up or down the river fired an arrow at the image of the Piasa Bird in memory of their deliverance from the monster.

When the white men settled this region and heard the tales of the Piasa, they assumed that the creature was just a myth. But the Indians who still lived along the river believed the monster had been real. They took great pleasure in loosing arrows at the creature as they passed on the river and later fired their rifles at it as well.

In July 1836, a Professor John Russell discovered something very unusual concerning the legend of the Piasa Bird. Russell was a professor at Shurtleff

College in Alton and had enough interest in the local legend to do a little exploring and research into the story of the creature. His adventures were later recounted in a magazine article in 1848 and in *Records of Ancient Races in the Mississippi Valley* by William McAdams, published in 1887. Here is his chilling story, written in his own words:

Near the close of March of the present year, I was induced to visit the bluffs below the mouth of the Illinois River, above that of the Piasa. My curiosity was principally directed to the examination of a cave, connected with the above tradition as one of those to which the bird had carried his human victims.

Preceded by an intelligent guide, who carried a spade, I set out on my excursion. The cave was extremely difficult of access, and at one point in our progress I stood at an elevation of one hundred fifty feet on the perpendicular face of the bluff, with barely room to sustain one foot. The unbroken wall towered above me, while below me was the river.

After a long and perilous climb, we reached the cave, which was about fifty feet above the surface of the river....The roof of the cavern was vaulted, and the top was hardly less than twenty feet high. The shape of the cavern was irregular; but, so far as I could judge, the bottom would average twenty by thirty feet.

The floor of the cavern throughout its whole extent was one mass of human bones. Skulls and other bones were mingled in the utmost confusion. To what depth they extended I was unable to decide; but we dug to a depth of 3 or 4 feet in every part of the cavern, and still we found only bones. The remains of thousands must have been deposited here. How, and by whom, and for what purpose, it is impossible to conjecture.

In 1873, Martin Beem authored an article on the Piasa Legend for the *Illinois State Journal* of Springfield, Illinois. The legend he describes is similar to that recounted by Professor Russell and he also described the bones that were found in the cave. With the publication of these articles, the story grew and was told and re-told countless times. In 1875, author A.D. Jones also wrote about the paintings, and not long after, Edmund Flagg, on a tour of the western country, claimed that he also saw the bone-filled cave and corroborated Russell's story,

Was this cave really the lair of the Piasa Bird? Did this bird, always thought to be merely a mythological creature, actually exist? Did the monster really carry off and slay a large number of the Native Americans who once lived in this region? Could such a giant bird actually exist?

As a simple answer to a number of complex questions: no one really knows. The mystery of the Piasa Bird remains unsolved, and while many have gone in search of this elusive cave over the years, none have yet been able to find it. This is not as strange as you might think, though. There are many remote areas in this immediate region, overgrown by forests, lost among the bluffs and simply forgotten. Homes, buildings, churches and cemeteries have all been abandoned by time and so it's very possible that the same thing could happen with natural formations like caves, hundreds of which are scattered through the bluffs along the river. Stories are still told of caves, untouched for generations, which are discovered among the bluffs that contain Indian drawings and artifacts. One report even recalled a cave that contained an ancient rendition of the Piasa above the Illinois River beyond Grafton, Illinois. This petroglyph has proven to be as elusive as the bone cave of the Piasa Bird, but who knows what future searches might reveal?

Strangely, the small river town of Alton has been the scene of reports of other giant birds in the modern era. American Indian lore is filled with stories of strange, monster birds with enormous wingspans and the propensity to carry away human victims. They called these creatures "Thunderbirds" because the legends claimed that their flapping wings made a sound like rolling thunder. The birds were described as having wingspans of twenty feet or more, hooked talons and razor-sharp beaks. But not all of these stories and accounts date back to the times of the early Americans.

A more modern day rash of Thunderbird sightings began in Alton in 1948. On April 4, a former Army Colonel named Walter F. Siegmund revealed that he had seen a gigantic bird in the sky above Alton. He had been talking with a local farmer and Colonel Ralph Jackson, the head of the Western Military Academy, at the time. "I thought there was something wrong with my eyesight," he said, "but it was definitely a bird and not a glider or a jet plane. It appeared to be flying northeast... from the movements of the object and its size, I figured it could only be a bird of tremendous size."

A few days later, a farmer named Robert Price from Caledonia would see the same, or a similar, bird. He called it a "monster bird... bigger than an airplane." On April 10, another sighting took place and in Overland, Illinois. Mr. and Mrs. Clyde Smith and Les Bacon spotted a huge bird. They said they thought the creature was an airplane until it started to flap its wings furiously.

On April 24, the bird was back in Alton. It was sighted by E.M. Coleman and his son, James. "It was an enormous, incredible thing with a body that looked like a naval torpedo," Coleman recalled later. "It was flying at about 500 feet and cast a shadow the same size as a Piper Cub at that height."

Then, on May 5, the bird was sighted for the last time in Alton. A man named Arthur Davidson called the police that evening to report the bird flying above the city. Later on that same night, Mrs. William Stallings of St. Louis informed the authorities that she had also seen it. "It was bright, about as big as a house," she said. A number of sightings then followed in the St. Louis area, but just when the public excitement over the bird reached its peak, the sightings came to an end.

But this was not the last time that giant birds took to the skies over Illinois.

A LOCK OF WHITE HAIR
The Marlon Lowe Attack and the 1977
Illinois Thunderbirds

For as long as I can remember, I have been fascinated with the idea of giant birds that swoop across the sky, frightening the unsuspecting, and then vanishing into the clouds. There is no way that I can explain my interest, for I have never seen one of these strange flying beasts, other than to say that I was born and raised in Illinois. This is a state that seems to have an inordinate number of such sightings and encounters, including the legendary Piasa and the infamous "Lawndale Thunderbird Attack." Such accounts were certainly enough to have us watching the skies when we were growing up among the woods and fields of Illinois.

And the stories today are still a part of the larger history of the unexplained in America.

As mentioned in the previous chapter, the American Indians had plenty of lore about "Thunderbirds," flying monsters with wings that made a sound like rolling thunder, and which carried fully-grown adults away in their talons. Aside from Indian legends, there are modern accounts of Thunderbirds and winged creatures attacking and carrying off people. Logically speaking, such accounts should not exist -- and yet they do.

One of the earliest reports I could find of someone being attacked by a giant bird took place in Tippah County, Missouri, in 1868. According to the report, an eight-year-old boy was actually carried off by what his teacher described as an "eagle." It happened one day during school. The teacher's account states that "a sad tragedy occurred at my school a few days ago." He wrote that "eagles" had been very troublesome in the neighborhood, carrying off small pigs and lambs. No one thought that they would ever bother the local children until one afternoon, when one of the birds swooped down and picked up a boy named

Jemmie Kenney and flew off with him. The other children called out, but by the time the teacher ran outside to see what was going on, he could only hear the child's screams as he vanished into the sky. The teacher and the children on the playground began to cry out to raise the alarm in town and apparently, the noise frightened the bird and it dropped the boy. "But his talons had been buried in him so deeply, and the fall was so great, that he was killed."

What could this creature have really been? Could it have actually been an eagle? If so, it must have been a monstrous one because according to renowned zoologist Dr. Bernard Heuvelmans, even the most powerful eagle cannot lift more than a rabbit or a lamb. Most experts insist that even the strongest birds cannot carry off a small child -- so what occurred in Missouri in 1868?

Sightings and encounters with giant birds have been reported all over the country, but perhaps one of the most exciting - and frightening - rash of events began in 1977 in Lawndale, Illinois, when a young boy was actually picked up and nearly carried off by some sort of giant bird in front of several startled witnesses.

On the evening of July 25, two giant birds appeared in the sky above Lawndale. It was a warm, humid evening and three boys were playing hide and seek in the backyard of Ruth and Jake Lowe. The boys --Travis Goodwin, Michael Thompson and ten-year-old Marlon Lowe -- were in the yard at about 8:30 p.m. when the two birds approached them from the south. Marlon Lowe later told newspapers that the three boys first saw the birds swoop toward Travis Goodwin, who ran away and jumped into a small, plastic swimming pool that was in the yard. The birds then swerved and headed toward Marlon. One of the birds grasped the boy's sleeveless shirt, snagging its talons into the cloth. The boy tried in vain to fight the bird off, and then cried loudly for help.

The cries from all three boys brought Marlon's mother, as well as Jake Lowe and Betty and Jim Daniels, two friends from nearby Lincoln, Illinois, running to see what was going on. They had been cleaning inside a camper parked in the Lowes' driveway at the time. As Marlon screamed for his mother, Mrs. Lowe appeared in time to see the bird actually lift the child from the ground and into the air. She screamed but the bird may not have released him if Marlon had not hammered at it with his fists. The bird had carried him, at a height of about three feet, for a distance of about thirty-five feet by the time Mrs. Lowe had reached the backyard. She was sure that if she had not come outside, the bird was capable of carrying the boy away. She later stated that the bird had been bending down, trying to peck at the boy as it carried him off. Luckily, although scratched and badly frightened, Marlon was not seriously injured.

According to Ruth Lowe, "The birds just cleared the top of the camper, went beneath some telephone wires and flapped their wings, very gracefully, one more time."

The other three adults appeared on the scene within seconds of the attack. They described the birds as being black in color, with bands of white around their necks. They had long, curved beaks and a wingspan of at least ten feet. The two birds were last seen flying toward some trees near Kickapoo Creek.

Following his release from the bird's talons, Marlon ran into the camper that was parked in the driveway and refused to come out for a long time. He had not been badly injured by the experience but his shirt was tattered and torn. His mother reported afterward that he was unable to sleep that night - or for many nights to come. "He kept fighting those birds all night long," she said, referring to the nightmares that followed.

On the evening of the attack, Mrs. Lowe called the police and a game warden to report what had occurred. She said she decided to call them because of her concern for other children who lived nearby, especially those who swam and fished in Kickapoo Creek, which was located in the direction the birds were flying after the attack. Deputies from the Logan County Sheriff's Department searched the area around the creek on July 25 and 26 but found no evidence of the birds.

Investigator Jerry Coleman, who lived in Decatur at the time, was able to interview the Lowe family, and the other witnesses, within hours of the incident and detailed the event. He returned to Lawndale two years later to speak to the family again and discovered that they had been harassed and bothered by media attention during that time, and by locals in the community. It was not uncommon to find dead birds on their doorstep in the morning, placed there by mean-spirited pranksters.

Marlon Lowe also had trouble dealing with the frightening encounter. The shock of the incident took years to wear off. Nightmares about it plagued him for a long time, and in the days that followed the attack, a portion of his hair actually turned white from worry and stress.

Ruth Lowe also had vivid memories of the event, and spent years trying to identify the huge winged creatures that had almost taken her son. She spent long hours looking through books, certain that the creature had not been a turkey vulture, as an area game warden tried to convince her that it was. "I was standing at the door," she told the investigators, "and all I saw was Marlon's feet dangling in the air. There aren't any birds around here that can lift him up like that."

After hours and hours spent looking at photographs and illustrations of large birds, Ruth Lowe said that the closest that she could find to the birds that attacked her son were California Condors. Marlon Lowe agreed that these birds were the most similar to what they had seen. Michael Thompson, who had also been present in the yard that day, also picked out the condors as the offending birds --- or at least they looked like them.

Interestingly, though, California Condors are nearly extinct creatures that, until 1987, could only be found in the wild living in the deserts of southern California. Their coloring does not match the birds reported in Lawndale, nor does their size, and they are not capable of picking up a small child. Out of all of the known birds, however, they looked most like the Thunderbirds seen in Illinois. But what if those creatures were not a "known bird?"

This was just one of the many problems that caused the negative public reaction toward the Lowes. Because the reports were so strange -- and seemingly could not have happened -- local wildlife officials immediately denied that the attack could have taken place. A Logan County conservation officer named A. A. Mervar was quoted as saying, "I don't think the child was picked up." Vern Wright, a biologist with the Illinois Department of Conservation in Springfield told the press that the flying creature definitely did not pick up the boy. Many Illinois newspapers were not kind either. One Chicago paper ran a headline that read: "Expert: 'Attack' Tale is for the Birds." The first paragraph of the article consisted of only two words --- "Thoroughly Ridiculous!"

But not all of the media outlets, or the general public, were so skeptical. Many newspapers picked up the story in the days following the attack and continued to update readers over the next few months as the two birds - or at least two that looked an awful lot like them -- continued their journey across Illinois. Ruth Lowe was interviewed by dozens of newspapers and received scores of telephone calls that promised support. "Some people did call to say that they believed me," Ruth Lowe later recalled. Could some of those people have seen the same birds?

The Lawndale Attack of July 1977 was just the start of Thunderbird sightings in Illinois.

The ridicule that was suffered by the Lowes following their public report of the attack did not keep other people from calling newspapers and law enforcement authorities to report their own giant bird sightings over the days and weeks that followed. The giant birds seemed to be on the move, and as they traveled, they wreaked havoc across the state.

Three days after the attack, on July 28, Janet Brandt of Armington was driving home on the road between Minier and Armington when she spotted a bird that was larger than the hood of her car. It was at about 5:30 p.m. and she saw it flying from east to west in the late afternoon light. She only saw it for a few moments, flying about thirty feet off the ground, but she did notice that it seemed to have a ring of white around its neck.

Later that same day, at around 8:00 p.m., a McLean County farmer named Stanley Thompson saw a bird of the same size and description flying over his farm. He, his wife, and several friends were watching radio-controlled airplanes when the bird flew close to the models. He claimed the bird had a wingspan of at least ten feet. It dwarfed the small planes that buzzed close to it. He later told McLean County Sheriff's Sergeant Robert Boyd that the bird had about a six-foot body and easily a wingspan of nine feet. Boyd commented that Thompson was a "credible witness." He had lived in the area for a long time and had no reason to make up stories. He questioned the original reports that came in, but after speaking with Thompson, he had decided to investigate.

On July 28, Lisa Montgomery of Tremont was washing her car when she looked up and saw a giant bird crossing the sky overhead, soaring slowly over a nearby cornfield. She estimated that it had a seven-foot wingspan and was black with a low tail. She said that it disappeared into the sky towards Pekin.

The next sighting took place near Bloomington on July 29 when a mail truck driver named James Majors spotted two giant birds. He was driving from Armington to Delevan at 5:30 a.m. when he saw them alongside of the highway. He was just passing by a Hampshire hog farm when he spotted the birds overhead. One of the creatures dropped down into a field and extended its claws more than two feet from its body. Suddenly, it snatched up a small animal that Majors believed was a baby pig, which he guessed weighed between forty and sixty pounds. The bird then flapped its wings and soared back into the sky to rejoin its companion. Both birds flew away to the north. Majors was unable to identify the birds, but he had seen condors in California and stated that these birds were larger. Majors quickly drove to the next town and then jumped out of the truck and chain-smoked four cigarettes to regain his composure.

At 2:00 a.m. on Saturday, July 30, Dennis Turner and several friends from Downs, Illinois, reported a monstrous bird perched on a telephone pole. Turner claimed that the bird dropped something near the base of the pole. When police officers investigated the sighting, they found a huge rat near the spot. Several residents of Waynesville reported seeing a black bird with an eight-foot wingspan later on that same day.

Reports of giant birds continued to come in from Bloomington and the north-central Illinois area, then from farther south, from Decatur to Macon and Sullivan. On July 30, the same day the birds were reported near Bloomington, a writer and construction worker named "Texas John" (now known as "Chief A.J.") Huffer filmed two large birds while fishing at Lake Shelbyville, about two hours to the south.

Huffer was a resident of Tuscola and was spending the day with his son when they both spotted the birds roosting in a tree. Huffer frightened the birds with his boat horn and when they took flight, he managed to shoot 100 feet of color film. Huffer had experience as a combat photographer with the Marines and as an avid outdoorsman, usually kept his 16mm motion picture camera with him on outings. As he grabbed the camera, he noted that the birds were black and made a kind of "clacking" sound that he described as "primeval." Huffer stated recently that he believed the largest bird had a wingspan of eighteen to twenty feet.

Huffer sold a portion of the footage to the CBS television affiliate in Champaign, and it aired later that night during a newscast. After the footage aired, experts were quick to dismiss Huffer's claims, along with the accounts of everyone else who had been reporting huge birds around this time. Officials from the Department of Conservation insisted the birds were merely turkey vultures and were nothing out of the ordinary. These claims were refuted by wildlife experts, who stated that no turkey vultures were of the size reported by witnesses.

Unfortunately, no real proof of anything can be obtained from Huffer's footage. Biologists, and several wildlife experts, who have seen the film state that it's impossible to tell the size of the birds from the footage that Huffer has produced. Although by no means an expert on birds, I would have to agree.

Because much of the footage films the birds with only the sky as the background, it's hard to see if the birds are actually as large as Huffer's recollection of them. Even the footage shot with trees as a backdrop is too far away from the subjects to be sure of the birds' size. It is interesting footage -- there's no doubt about that -- but the question remains as to what kind of birds it actually captured.

The bird sightings continued. On July 31, Mrs. Albert Dunham of rural Bloomington was on the second floor of her house when she noticed a large, dark shadow passing by her window. She quickly realized that it was a giant bird and got a good look at it. Her description was almost identical to others reported at the same time, including the white ring around its neck. Her son chased the bird to a nearby landfill, but it had vanished before a local newspaper photographer could get a photo of it.

On August 11, John and Wanda Chappell saw a giant bird land in a tree near their home in Odin, Illinois. According to the witnesses, it was gray-black in color with about a twelve-foot wingspan. John Chappell stated that it looked like a "prehistoric bird" and that it was likely big enough to have carried away his small daughter if it had wanted to. The huge bird had circled above the Chappell's pond before coming to rest in the tree. John Chappell said that he thought the bird was "so big it had a hard time finding a limb big enough to land on." Wanda Chappell said she knew the bird had to be heavy because "when it settled in the tree, the tree settled quite a bit." She and her husband had been having coffee in the kitchen and saw the bird through a sliding glass door. They opened the door carefully, so as to not scare the creature, and called their son to come and look. It stayed in the tree for about five to ten minutes and then flew off without a sound toward Raccoon Lake and the town of Centralia. Wanda Chappell said that she and her husband almost didn't report the sighting because they were afraid that people would think they were crazy.

And it's not surprising that they felt this way. The bird sightings of 1977 vanished from the press after the Odin, Illinois, report from John and Wanda Chappell. As the notion appeared in many people's heads that these massive birds could be "turkey vultures," interest in the accounts began to fade and many were hesitant to report further sightings for fear of being laughed at, as the Lowe family in Lawndale were. The stories continued to spread of further sightings, though, and have not been forgotten more than three decades later.

On August 15, 1977, a witness who lived near Herrick reported seeing two giant birds in a section of forest outside of town. He estimated the wingspans of the creatures to have been at least ten feet. He followed their flight path to an abandoned barn at the edge of a field where they landed for about five minutes. After that, they vanished into the sky towards Taylorville.

On August 20, Paul Harrold reported seeing a giant bird in the sky near Fairfield. He told me that the bird landed in a field not far from his car and remained there for a few moments before flying off again. According to his report, its wingspan was at least twelve feet in width. Harrold also stated that he was sure the bird was no vulture or buzzard, which are common in Illinois.

Having lived out West for several years, he was familiar with large birds but said that he had never seen anything this big.

Another witness contacted me after seeing accounts of some Illinois big bird sightings in one of my books, and said that she had also seen a huge winged creature in 1977. On November 1, she looked out the window of her home near Chester and had seen a huge bird resting in the top of a tall tree in her backyard. The bird seemed massive, much larger than anything else she had ever seen before, and had huge wings that it folded around itself. A few minutes later, it opened its wings and took off into the sky, gliding towards the Mississippi River. Its wingspan, she guessed, was at least ten or fifteen feet. After that, the 1977 Illinois thunderbird sightings came to an end.

So, what were these creatures? Some will try and convince you that the giant birds were nothing more than turkey vultures or condors. In many cases, though, the birds were spotted by people who would have recognized these commonly-known birds. But even if they had never seen one of those types of birds, the descriptions they gave would have only dismissed a small percentage of the anomalous reports. Some researchers believe that the reported Thunderbirds might be "Teratorns," from the Greek "monster bird," a supposedly extinct bird of prey that once roamed North and South America. If these prehistoric survivors somehow survived into the modern era, they could certainly account for the reports of the giant birds.

But could some of these winged creatures be something else altogether? In Texas in 1976, witnesses who spotted giant birds were able to use a guide to prehistoric animals to identify the birds they saw as pteranodons, which seems impossible, and yet they were sure of what they had seen.

We have to be puzzled as we read such tales and wonder about the validity of the strange sightings, for the reports certainly did not end in 1977. Are these mysterious flying creatures actually real? Do they fill the skies of anything other than our imaginations? If so, then what have so many people seen over the years? At this point, such creatures remain a mystery but one thing is sure: the sightings have continued over the years, and occasionally an unusual report still trickles in from somewhere across the country. So keep that in mind the next time that you are standing in an open field and a large, dark shadow suddenly fills the sky overhead. Was that just a cloud passing in front of the sun - or something else?

TOMBSTONE THUNDERBIRD PHOTOGRAPH
TRUTH OR FICTION?

As I stated at the beginning of this book, I grew up with a rabid interest in the unknown and the unexplained. I went out of my way to track down every book and every story that I could find on every kind of assorted American weirdness. One of the stories that fascinated me the most was the story of the infamous Tombstone, Arizona "thunderbird" photograph. I was not alone in my obsession about this mysterious flying creature, or about the photograph that was allegedly taken of it. As a child, I read the original story about the creature and remember being amazed. How, I asked myself, could what seemed to be a prehistoric creature like a pterodactyl have been shot by cowboys in the 1800s? Such a thing seemed impossible, but evidence existed in the form of many stories and references to the event and of course, proof existed in the form of a photograph. That was the really exciting part: that photograph! I still remember what it looked like today. Or do I?

You see, in more recent years, an even greater mystery has developed than whether or not a group of cowpokes shot down a "flying monster" in the Arizona desert. That mystery surrounds the elusive photograph that was taken of the incident and which many of us (myself included) believe that we saw. But if we did, where is the photo now?

For many years, the story of the Tombstone Thunderbird photograph began with the April 26, 1890 edition of the *Tombstone Epitaph* newspaper. Legend had it that the photograph accompanied the article. But as it turns out, the original account of the monster was several years older and it allegedly made an appearance in California before it ever made its way to Arizona.

One of the first accounts written of the Thunderbird was in the book *On the Old West Coast* by Major Horace Bell. I was able to track down a copy of this long-out-of-print title and found it to be a very readable and entertaining account of Bell's adventures in California in the late 1800s. *On the Old West Coast* was published in 1930 and edited by Lanier Bartlett.

Horace Bell had previously written a book called *Reminiscences of a Ranger* about his life and journeys throughout California, Texas, Mexico and Central America. Bell had lived an exciting life, having been a miner, a Texas Ranger who pursued Joaquin Murrieta, a soldier of fortune in the forces of Benito Juarez in Mexico, an aide to General William Walker in Nicaragua, a Union officer in the Civil War and on the Texas border and finally, a newspaper editor in Los Angeles. He was considered to be a history writer, and while he admitted to often writing stories that were tongue in cheek, he declared that he was a truthful history writer, chronicling events as they happened. This is why the events that he wrote about in the Lake Elizabeth area -- and by extension, Tombstone -- are so strange to read about today.

The account in Bell's book, in a chapter entitled "Spit in the Mouth of Hell," does not start out to be about the creature that was killed in Tombstone. Bell believed that the creature had its origins in California instead.

In October 1886, a Los Angeles newspaper reported on some strange events that had been occurring for years around nearby Lake Elizabeth. According to early stories from the days of the Spanish occupation of the region, the lake had long been considered a haunted place, plagued by frightening voices, shrieks, screams and groans that apparently emanated from the waters of the lake itself. After the Spanish left, the Mexican settlers refused to live near the lake. They called it *"La Laguna del Diablo"*: the Devil's Lake.

In the middle 1830s, Don Pedro Carrillo purchased the land around the lake and built a hacienda, barn and corral. He disregarded the superstitions about the place but just three months after construction on his ranch was completed, he abandoned the place. He stated that there were supernatural beings nearby and refused to live there. The land remained idle for the next two decades. Even after the Americans came to the region, the lake was shunned as a cursed spot.

Some years later, Don Chico Lopez settled on the property and what occurred next was told in a manuscript by Don Guillermo Embustero y Mentiroso, who was a guest at the Lopez ranch. According to Don Guillermo, a great agitation took place during his visit. Around noon one day, Lopez's foreman, Chico Vasquez, rode up to the hacienda in a state of agitation. He told of strange happenings at the lake and everyone saddled their horses and rode out to have a look. They arrived to find the water calm and quiet, and nothing out of the ordinary going on. Lopez began berating his foreman for sending them tearing out there over nothing, but then stopped as a terrifying scream burst forth from some brush at the edge of the lake. The plants whipped back and forth and Don Guillermo's account stated that they were so close to whatever was lurking in the brush that they could smell its foul breath. The men were even more startled when their horses reared up and began running in fright.

As they brought their horses back under control, the men turned and looked back to the lake. Silhouetted against the sky was a large creature with enormous wings. The creature flapped its wings over and over again as it struggled to rise from the mud. It roared and screamed and churned up the water around it. The horses and men fled in a panic. The next morning, all of the vaqueros on the ranch were mustered, armed, and sent down to the lake to investigate. There was no sign of the winged monster but it was said that the stench of it still lingered in the air.

In 1883, the Lopez horses and cattle began to vanish. At first, bears or wolves were thought to be the culprits, but then one night, there was a terrible uproar in the corral. When the vaqueros came running, they found that ten mares and foals had been slaughtered. Outlined against the sky, they saw the huge flying creature flapping away into the darkness. Lopez promptly sold the property and moved away from the area.

Then in 1886, the newspaper reported more strange happenings at Lake Elizabeth. The reports stated that a creature had been feeding on cattle, horses, sheep and chickens and had caused terror and excitement among the local inhabitants. On one occasion, the beast had tried to devour a large steer but as the animal bellowed and kicked, the sound attracted the attention of its owner, Don Felipe Rivera. The steer put up a fierce fight and managed to free itself. The angry creature then retreated, but not before Rivera got a good look at it. He said that it was at least forty-five feet long and had wings that laid flat on its back when not expanded. He pursued the monster as it started towards the lake and fired at it with his Colt revolver. Rivera said that when the bullets struck the monster's side, it sounded as if they were hitting a "great iron kettle."

Don Felipe was nothing if not enterprising and he made immediate plans to try and capture the creature and sell it to the circus. He even signed a contract with Sells Brothers, who agreed to pay him $20,000 if he could deliver the beast alive. Don Felipe never managed to capture the creature, although it was reportedly seen several times in 1886. It was last seen, according to Horace Bell, winging away to the east.

"Since then," he wrote, "it has never been seen in its native valley because it was found and killed 800 miles from Lake Elizabeth, as is proved by the article that appeared in the *Epitaph*, Tombstone, Arizona." Bell then goes on to quote from the article, which he apparently saw, and provides details to the story. However, he does not say that the event occurred in 1886, as many believe. He provides a follow-up story about the Tombstone article, which appeared in a Los Angeles newspaper in 1890. For this reason, it's safe to assume that the Thunderbird (if it really existed) was killed at some point between 1886 and 1890.

For many years, it was claimed that the Thunderbird story never actually ran in the *Epitaph*. A number of researchers stated that they had been through entire runs of the newspaper and did not see anything about the creature - but this is not the case. In clear type, on April 26, 1890, an *Epitaph* headline appears that reads: "Found in the Desert - A Strange Winged Monster Discovered and Killed in the Huachuca Desert."

And while there was no photograph published with the article, it did state that two ranchers sighted an enormous flying creature in the desert between Whetstone, Arizona, and the Huachuca Mountains. The beast resembled a huge alligator with an extremely elongated tail and an immense pair of wings. According to their story, the creature was seemed to be exhausted and was only able to fly a short distance at a time. The men, who were on horseback and armed with Winchester rifles, pursued the creature for several miles before getting close enough to open fire on it and wound it. It then turned on the cowboys, but due to its exhaustion, they were able to keep far enough away from it until a few more shots could kill it.

An examination of the creature showed that it measured ninety-two feet in length and that its greatest diameter was about fifty inches. It had only two feet, situated a short distance in front of where the wings joined the body. The beak, as near as they could judge, was about eight feet long and its jaws were set with strong, sharp teeth. They experienced some difficulty trying to measure the wings, as they had folded up underneath the body as the monster had fallen, but they eventually unrolled one of them. It was an incredible seventy-eight feet in length, giving the beast a wingspan of about one hundred and sixty feet. The wings were of a thick, nearly transparent membrane that had no feathers or hair. Its flesh was relatively smooth and had been easily penetrated by their bullets.

The ranchers cut off a portion of the wing and took it with them, perhaps as proof of what they had seen. After arriving in Tombstone, they spread the word about the creature and made plans to return to the site where it had fallen in order to skin it. They planned, the article stated, to offer the hide to eminent scientists for examination. They returned to the site to bring the creature back to town and here, the article ends. There are no details of the body being retrieved, and no mention whatsoever of any photograph being taken.

The story of the Thunderbird was relegated to the ranks of mythical creatures like the "jackalope" until 1963, when the story was revived. In the May 1963 issue of *Saga*, a men's magazine of the day, writer Jack Pearl published an article called "Monster Bird that Carries off Human Beings!" Pearl recounted the story of the Tombstone Thunderbird, but gives the date of the *Epitaph* article as 1886 rather than 1890. The writer not only told the story, but he went one step further and claimed that the *Tombstone Epitaph* had "published a photograph of a huge bird nailed to a wall. The newspaper said that it had been shot by two prospectors and hauled into town by wagon. Lined up in front of the bird were six grown men with their arms outstretched, fingertip to fingertip. The creature measured about 36 feet from wingtip to wingtip."

While this is a different variation of the story (and size of the creature), it seems to be referring to the same incident. Most importantly, though, is that this is the first time that the Thunderbird photo was mentioned in print. With no earlier printed mention, this article may be the source of the Thunderbird photo legend with respect to its emergence into the public consciousness. It's even possible that "Jack Pearl" (whoever he may have been, no records exist) made up the story about the article. If there really is no photograph, that is.

There are only two possibilities: Pearl either made up the story of the photograph or he had a source. If he had a source, then there is some evidence of knowledge of the photo that predates Pearl's article.

Many young men of the era undoubtedly read Pearl's description of the photo in *Saga*. It was a popular magazine of the day, along with *Argosy, True, Male* and so on. Did Pearl's description of the image become implanted in their memories, causing them to believe that they saw the photo itself years later? And has reading about the photo continued this problem with people like myself, who became interested long after that article was published? It's possible, but may not be the case.

Pearl's article may have been the first mention of the photo's description, but this may have been more by chance than design. When reading the article, it becomes clear that Pearl was not just spinning yarns when he wrote the story. He was actually cobbling together letters and clippings from a "thunderbird file" that had most likely been collected over time by *Saga* editors. Pearl was not a folklorist or researcher of the unexplained. He was just a writer, working on an assignment.

Pearl may have been responsible for introducing the notion of the Thunderbird photo to the public, but it seems from the article that he got the information from somewhere else, just like the other giant bird stories included in his piece. But where did he get it? The answer to that question may have been answered a short time later, in another magazine.

In the September 1963 issue of *FATE Magazine*, a correspondent named H.M Cranmer of Hammersley Fork, Pennsylvania, also wrote about the Thunderbird photograph. Cranmer was the author of a series of letters to *FATE* about thunderbirds, which began in December 1950. In the September 1963 issue, just four months after Pearl's article, Cranmer addressed the question of the photograph. There are many clues to suggest that Cranmer was Pearl's source. In his article, Pearl said that some thunderbird reports were received by *Saga* magazine "from a Pennsylvania resident." We know that Cranmer lived in Pennsylvania and that he was sending thunderbird reports to magazine editors in the 1950s and 1960s. Pearl then goes on to quote his unnamed source, describing three thunderbird sightings in Pennsylvania - the same first-person accounts that Cranmer described to *FATE* in the 1963 letter.

It's likely that Cranmer sent letters to *Saga* and *FATE* around the same time and that both letters were used in different ways by the two magazines. The letter that was printed in *FATE* was likely the exact letter that supplied Pearl with the Thunderbird photo description that he used in the *Saga* article. In the letter published by *FATE*, Cranmer wrote:

Sometime about the year 1900, two prospectors shot and carried into Tombstone, Ariz., on a burro one of these birds. When nailed against the wall of the Tombstone *Epitaph* its wingspread measured 36 feet. A picture showed six men, with outstretched arms touching, standing under the bird. Later, a group of actors dressed as professors were photographed under the bird, with one of them saying, "Shucks, there is no such bird, never was, never will be."

Cranmer then goes on to describe his April 1922, March 1957 and July 1962 sightings of giant birds. By including detail like the caption on the photograph, Cranmer gives the impression that he has seen the photo, but makes no mention of having a copy. He uses the past tense when referring to the photo, which we would not expect if he owned one. In a later, March 1966 letter to *FATE* on the subject, Cranmer also discusses the photograph, but once again he makes no claim to having a copy of it. In fact, he even states that he heard about the photograph from a "lady in Tombstone."

And the issue becomes even more confusing. Cranmer, who died in a tragic house fire, was described as a regional storyteller, whose tall tales appeared in a collection of Pennsylvania folk tales in 1966. In addition to multiple giant bird sightings, Cranmer also claimed that he had seen a good number of UFOs hovering around oil and gas rigs in Hammersley Fork in 1950 and 1954. Needless to say, this doesn't help his credibility very much.

However, there was one source, Robert Ray Lyman, Jr. (also deceased), who claimed that Cranmer had some sort of Thunderbird photo or picture hanging in his living room. Whatever this photo was, it was destroyed in the fire that killed Cranmer. Was it the mysterious Thunderbird photo? This seems unlikely. If Cranmer had the Thunderbird photo, or a copy of it, he would have surely sent a copy to *FATE* and *Saga* to support the material that he was presenting in his letters. Also, Cranmer's letters don't make it sound as though he had a copy of the photo. If he had, he almost certainly would have mentioned it. And then, of course, in his follow-up 1966 letter, he "heard about" the photo, which turns the entire thing into a sort-of friend-of-a-friend "urban legend."

Did Cranmer's letters give birth to the legend of a Thunderbird photo? If so, then why are so many people convinced they have seen it? Eminent cryptozoologist and paranormal researcher Ivan T. Sanderson remembered seeing the photo. In fact, he even claimed to have once had a photocopy of it that he loaned to two associates, who subsequently lost it. The editors of *FATE* even came to believe that they may have published the photo in an earlier issue of the magazine, but a search through back issues failed to reveal it. Meanwhile, the original *Epitaph* story, which again mentions no photograph, was revived in a 1969 issue of *Old West* magazine, further confusing the issue as to whether the photo existed or not.

The *Epitaph*, however, stated that it did not exist, or if it did, it had not been published in their newspaper. Responding to numerous inquiries, employees of the paper made a thorough search of back issues and files. They could find no such photo, and an extended search of other Arizona and California newspapers of the period produced no results. A number of articles that appeared in *Pursuit*, the journal for the Society for the Investigation of the Unexplained prompted a memory from Canadian researcher W. Ritchie Benedict, who recalled seeing Ivan Sanderson display a copy of the photo on Canadian television's *The Pierre Benton Show*. Unfortunately, no copies of the show have ever been found.

So, was the photo real? And if not, then why do so many of us with an interest in the unusual claim to remember seeing it? Who knows? In the late 1990s, author John Keel insisted that, "I know I saw it! And not only that -- I compared notes with a lot of other people who saw it." Like many of us, Keel believes that he saw it in one of the men's magazines (like *Saga* or *True*) that were popular in the 1960s. Many of these magazines featured articles that dealt with amazing subject matter like Bigfoot, ghosts and more. Keel also remembers the photo in the same way that most of us do: with men wearing cowboy clothing and the bird looking like a pterodactyl or some prehistoric, winged creature.

During the 1990s, the search for the "Thunderbird Photo" reached a point of obsession for those interested in the subject. A discussion of the matter stretched over several issues of Mark Chorvinsky's *Strange* magazine and readers who believed they had seen the photo cited sources that ranged from old books to Western photograph collections, men's magazines, *National Geographic* and beyond. As for myself, I combed through literally hundreds of issues of dusty copies of *True* and *Saga* but could find nothing more than the previously mentioned article by Jack Pearl. If the photo exists, I certainly don't have it in my own collection.

In the early 2000s, a fictional television show called *Freakylinks*, which featured young people in pursuit of the unknown, created a fake Thunderbird photo for their website. Soon, unknowing internet surfers began deluging researchers (myself included) with the photo, believing that they had found the elusive image. Other fakes followed. Some used cowboys, others used Civil War soldiers and one innovative hoaxer even doctored a real photo of a murdered outlaw with a posse standing around him by removing the corpse and putting a pterodactyl in its place. To date, the "authentic" photo has not been found in the dark corners of the internet.

So, how do we explain this weird phenomenon of a photograph that so many people remember seeing and yet no one can seem to find? Author Mark Hall believes that the description of the photo creates such a vivid image in our minds that many of us who have knowledge and interest in curious and eclectic things begin to think the photo is familiar. It literally creates a "shared memory" of something that does not exist. We think we have seen it, but we actually haven't.

Could this be the answer? Maybe - or maybe not. What if the photo does exist and it's out there, just waiting to be discovered in some dusty garage, overflowing file cabinet or musty basement. I, for one, haven't given up quite yet, and I have a feeling that I am not the only one who is still out there looking.

WEREWOLF T-SHIRT
The Strange Story of the Beast of Bray Road

The belief in werewolves has been with us for centuries. Many historians and folklorists have pondered the origins of the belief in lycanthropy, which is really the human ability to change into not only wolves but bears, big cats and other dangerous creatures. Of all of these transformations that of man into wolf is the best-known. This is largely due to the Old World traditions of wolves being feared as predators by the Europeans. There are many historical accounts of wolves preying on human beings during wars and hard winters, although not all of these accounts can be taken as fact. However, the true accounts were prevalent enough that the French had a word for the wolf that has acquired a taste for human flesh, the "werewolf" or the *loup-garou*.

Although modern naturalists and wildlife experts would agree that the wolf has gained an unfair reputation over the years, centuries of stories and links to the dark side have maintained most people's fears about these creatures. In northern Europe, wolf men or berserkers -- which were warriors clad in animal skins -- were greatly and justifiably feared for their slaughtering of other warriors and innocents alike. In the Baltic and Slavic regions of Europe, people worshipped a wolf deity that could be benevolent or turn deadly without warning.

In the eighteenth century, the legendary Beast of Gévaudan wreaked havoc in France, bringing further infamy to the wolf. The Beast was a man-eating, wolf-like animal that terrorized the province of Gévaudan in south-central France between 1764 and 1767. The monster, said to be larger than a wolf, was said to have been wounded many times without dying. Victims were often killed by having their throats torn out. The French government used a considerable amount of manpower and money to hunt the animal, including the resources of several nobles, the army, civilians, and a number of royal huntsmen. After more than two hundred attacks, one hundred and thirteen people were killed and another forty-nine were injured. Ninety-eight of the victims were partially eaten.

The Beast of Gévaudan carried out its first recorded attack in the early summer of 1764. A young woman, who was tending cattle, saw the creature coming toward her. She was only saved by the bulls in her herd, which kept the Beast at bay. Shortly afterwards the first official victim of the Beast was recorded when fourteen-year-old Janne Boulet was killed near the village of Les Hubacs, near the town of Langogne.

In late 1764, more attacks were reported throughout the region. Terror gripped the populace because the Beast was repeatedly preying on lone men, women and children as they tended livestock in the forests around Gévaudan. Reports noted that the Beast seemed to only target the victim's head or neck regions and not the arms or legs, the usual body parts favored by wolves. Rumors spread that the Beast was something more than an ordinary wolf.

Descriptions of the time vary, but generally the Beast was said to look like a wolf but was about as big as a cow. It had a large, dog-like head with small, straight ears, a wide chest, and a wide mouth, which exposed very large teeth. The claws on its feet were as sharp as razors. The Beast's fur was said to be primarily red in color but its back was streaked with black. Survivors of its attacks said that it gave off a terrible odor.

On January 12, 1765, Jacques Portefaix and seven friends were attacked by the Beast. After several attacks, they drove it away by staying grouped together. The encounter eventually came to the attention of Louis XV who awarded 300 livres to Portefaix and another 350 livres to be shared among his companions. The king also directed that Portefaix be educated at the state's expense. He then decreed that the French government would help find and kill the Beast.

Three weeks later, Louis XV sent two professional wolf-hunters, Jean Charles Marc Antoine Vaumesle d'Enneval and his son Jean-François, to Gévaudan. They arrived in Clermont-Ferrand on February 17 and brought along eight bloodhounds that had been train to hunt wolves. They were convinced that the man-eating Beast was a Eurasian wolf and over the next four months, they hunted these animals in the forests - but attacks by the Beast continued. In June, they were replaced by François Antoine, the king's Lieutenant of the Hunt.

By September 1767, Antoine had killed his third large grey wolf. This one was of massive size, measuring nearly six feet long and weighing more than one hundred and thirty pounds. He promptly decided that this animal had been the Beast. His official statement read: "We declare by the present report signed from our hand, we never saw a big wolf that could be compared to this one. Which is why we estimate this could be the fearsome beast that caused so much damage." He managed to get several survivors to identify scars on the wolf that they had placed there while defending themselves against it. The fact that this wolf did not match the descriptions of the Beast given by these same witnesses was ignored. The wolf was stuffed and sent to Versailles where Antoine was hailed as a hero, receiving a large sum of money, titles and awards.

Then, on December 2, 1767, the real Beast severely injured two men. A dozen more deaths followed these attacks. They were largely ignored by the government.

The killing of the Beast, finally ending the attacks, is credited to a local hunter named Jean Chastel. He is said to have killed the Beast at Sogne d'Auvers on June 19, 1770. The final battle has become the stuff of legend. The story goes that Chastel was part of a larger hunting party and sat down to read his Bible and rest. While he was praying, the creature came into sight, staring at Chastel, who nonchalantly finished his prayer before shooting the Beast. Since the monster usually attacked on sight, this seems like bizarre behavior, which leads some theorists to believe that perhaps Chastel had actually trained the animal and finally felt the pressure to dispose of it. However, the story of the prayer may simply have been invented out of religious or romantic motives. Writers later introduced the idea that Chastel shot the creature with a blessed silver bullet of his own manufacture and upon being cut open, the animal's stomach was discovered to be filled with human remains.

What was the Beast of Gévaudan? Since the late eighteenth century, there have been numerous theories about the identity and origin of the creature. They range from a freakishly large wolf, a werewolf, a wolf-dog hybrid, a hyena, and even a red-colored mastiff that was bred by Jean Chastel and was able to resist bullets by wearing the armored hide of a young boar. This would also explain its reddish color. In the 2001 film, *Le Pacte des Loups* (*Brotherhood of the Wolf*), the Beast was an African lion that was armored and trained to attack the people of the region in an effort to embarrass the French government.

To this day, the Beast remains a mystery but it certainly cemented the fact that the wolf was a creature to be feared. As the pagans once worshipped the wolf, the Church worked hard to tarnish the animal's image. As Christianity rose to power, the Church turned the wolf into a symbol of evil. Legends and folktales told of men who could change into wolves, but religious authorities assured the people that Satan merely caused witnesses to be deluded into thinking a man had changed into a wolf.

For those who claimed such powers, their delusions were frighteningly real. Many people who believed themselves to be werewolves testified, under torture and otherwise, of murdering both people and animals while in their transformed state. For this reason, many researchers today have associated being a "werewolf" with those we would deem to be murderously mentally ill. Among these were serial killers like Stubbe Peeter, who was tried in Germany in 1589 for a twenty-five-year crime spree. During that time, he murdered adults and children (including his own son), committed cannibalism and incest and attacked animals. Peeter claimed to have made a pact with Satan, who had given him an animal pelt that would change him into a wolf.

In 1598, French authorities arrested Jacques Roulet after he was found hiding in some brush, covered with the blood of a mutilated teenaged boy. Roulet claimed that he had killed the boy while transformed into a werewolf.

With tales such of this, lycanthropy has been deemed as a serious mental disorder. But can we really place all accounts of werewolves into a category of mental dysfunction? There are sightings and accounts that do exist, although few of them are such that cause researchers to ponder whether or not man-wolves can actually be real. In reality, these creatures should not exist, but so much of our understanding of these creatures comes from anthropologists and folklorists (not to mention the movies), and since these sensible people would never believe that a werewolf could possibly be seen they naturally dismiss any true accounts that might surface.

This is not to say that werewolves are real -- I leave such decisions for the reader to judge -- but there are some accounts out there that just might have you thinking twice. Remember that werewolves are only slightly less implausible than many other creatures that people claim to see (from Bigfoot to giant winged creatures) but most of us have a lot less trouble believing in the other assorted monsters said to wander the land. With the stories that follow, I'm not trying to convince you that werewolves are real and prowling the dark back roads of America - but they might leave you wondering.

1938: Paris, Michigan
Robert Fortney was fishing on the banks of the Muskegon River when a pack of what appeared to be wild dogs emerged from the forest. The dogs began to snap at him and in fear for his life, he fired a shot. All but one of the animals ran away. His fear turned to terror when the huge, black-furred animal reared up on its hind legs and stared at Fortney with "slanted, evil eyes and a hint of a grin." The standoff ended with a mutual retreat, but Fortney never forgot the encounter. Fifty years later, he recalled, "It scared the devil out of me."

1981: Atoka, Oklahoma
On a clear, autumn night on the road between Atoka and Antlers, Oklahoma, two men were driving toward Stillwater on a rural stretch of highway. They were about five miles from the Muddy Boggy Creek Bridge when the headlights of the car revealed a figure standing on the side of the road. At first they thought it was a tall, athletic-looking man, about seven feet in height, but as they got closer, they realized that it was covered in black fur and had ears "like a wolf's, but smaller" and a muzzle like a dog's.

The men had just realized they were seeing what appeared to be a dog walking upright, when the creature made a surprising move. It suddenly turned directly in front of the car and tore straight across the road without breaking stride. When it reached the open field on the other side, it dropped onto all fours and vanished into the darkness. One of the witnesses later stated that the ease at which the beast changed from two legs to four unnerved the two men. He noted, "Fear verging on terror was the immediate aftermath."

Worried that the creature might chase after their car, he immediately accelerated and kept going. His friend urged him to go even faster. They were completely sober at the time, he said, and neither man ever traveled that stretch of road again after dark.

2004: Elkton, Maryland

A couple driving on a rural road near Elkton, in the northeast corner of Maryland, got a frightening surprise one night as they were on their way home from an evening out. It was near midnight and they were driving along a wooded stretch of roadway when they saw a pair of yellow-green eyes reflecting their headlights on the side of the road. The eyes were far enough above the ground that they thought they must belong to a deer, but as they get closer, they saw the eyes belonged to something canine: a creature that stood hunched over on its hind legs, upright like a man. It looked at them as they slowed the car.

The creature was covered in dark brown, "scruffy and mangy" fur, with a thick patch of heavy fur on the back of its neck. Its face had the snout of a dog and pointed ears. It was sitting next to a mailbox that was tall, so that it could be accessed by a rural mail delivery truck, and even on its haunches, the creature would have been taller than the mailbox: at least six feet tall when standing. According one of the witnesses, she worked professionally with all breeds of dogs and this creature was not a dog.

That realization made her speed up the car in fright, even though the creature never moved. Her husband saw exactly the same thing as she did, and since they saw the beast only a half-mile from where they lived, they closed the garage door quickly in case the thing had followed them home.

The encounter might be written off as a trick of the light, intensified by active imaginations, had a family friend not seen the creature a year later on the same road. The friend first saw it with its back toward her but as it turned to show its dog-like face, she knew something was wrong. This time it was standing and ran away on its hind legs with the same "hunched" posture that the couple had observed. They had never told the friend about their own experience, but her description matched their own almost perfectly.

That meant that it was still in the neighborhood, but thankfully, they never saw it again.

2007: Selma, Alabama

A fisherman was in a shallow boat one summer night on the Alabama River with his pit bull as a companion when he realized that "something" was nearby on the bank. Whatever it was, it ran down the bank and rushed toward the fisherman and his dog. The creature was then revealed to be a huge canine-looking beast that stood between six and seven feet tall, running on its hind legs. It was covered in reddish-brown fur and the witness could clearly see male genitalia. It had a long snout, fully bared teeth, pointed ears that were laid back atop a "human-like" forehead and yellowish eyes. Even from a distance, the witness noticed a "rancid" stench.

According to the fisherman, the creature waded out into the river and was standing about ten feet away from the boat when the he fired up the boat motor, threw it into reverse and grabbed his pistol, all at the same time. He turned to see the creature advancing on his dog, who stood menacingly in the bow of the boat, but it stopped when the boat's engine roared to life. It turned back to shore and was standing there, still on its hind legs, when the witness pointed his gun and emptied a nine-round clip at it. The creature did not seem to be hit, and vanished into the trees.

The fisherman fled the area and never returned. He was not sure what the creature could be, but was sure that it was not a bear or anything else he recognized.

And those are just a sampling. Some states seem to have more werewolf stories than others, like Texas, for example. My friend April Slaughter, who wrote the book *Ghosthunting Texas,* was the first to pass on to me some of the weird stales of the Lone Star State.

Some of the accounts of Texas werewolves and wolf-like beasts date back to the earliest days of the region's settlement. One of the strangest involved "La Chica Lobo del Rio Diablo," a mysterious girl who was seen living with a pack of wolves in 1845. A young boy who lived at San Felipe Springs first reported the girl when he witnessed the wolves attack a herd of ghosts. He said that she was naked and running with the pack. His story was ridiculed but it spread among the settlements in the area.

About a year later, a Mexican woman in San Felipe Springs also reported seeing the girl. She said that she had seen two large wolves and a naked girl eating a freshly killed goat. She got close to them before they saw her, but when they looked up, they ran off. The girl at first ran on all fours but then rose up and ran on two feet, keeping in time with the wolves. The woman was sure about what she had seen, and soon people in the area began keeping a lookout for the weird girl. Local Indians reported finding wolf and human tracks in sandy spots along the river and told the locals about them. Stories spread that the girl might be a baby that went missing from a settler's cabin years before. The homesteaders had been massacred by Indians, but when the scene was investigated, there were allegedly large wolf tracks found in the ruins of their burned-out cabin.

A hunt was organized to capture the "Wolf Girl of the Devil's River," as they came to call her. A number of riders came together and set off along the stark, isolated border region to look for her. On the third day of the hunt, two of the riders jumped the girl in a side canyon. She was with a large wolf that cut off from her when she dodged into a crevice in the canyon wall. She cowered at first but when the men came close to her, she spat and then clawed and bit at them like a wild animal. As they tried to tie her up with ropes, the wild girl began to howl and cry with a sound that resembled both the scream of a girl and the baying of a wolf. As she let out this awful scream, the huge wolf that she had been running with suddenly rushed at her captors. With a roar, the animal sprang at them but one of the men saw it coming, drew his pistol and shot it down. As the animal collapsed into the sand, the girl fainted dead away.

The captured creature, now securely tied, was examined more closely by the men. She was excessively hairy but had small breasts that were just starting to form and other features that showed that she was a normally developed, young female. Her hands, arms and legs were unusually muscular but not abnormal in any way.

The hunters carried the girl to a horse and after reviving, she watched them warily as she was taken to a nearby ranch for the night. There, she was untied and placed in an isolated room. The rancher's wife offered her food, water and some clothing to cover herself with but the girl cowered away from her. Snarling, she pressed herself into the darkest corner of the room. The door to the room was locked and a small window, the only other exit, was nailed shut. As soon as the door was closed, the girl began to howl frantically - terrifying howls that were soon answered by animals outside. The cries came from all sides of the ranch. The men inside the house, cowboys who had lived in the region all of their lives, had never heard anything like it before, either in the sheer number of wolves assembling or in the quality of their long, deep howling.

As the girl in the room continued to cry, the men yelled at her and tried to quiet her down. The rancher's wife spoke to her soothingly. Nothing seemed to help, though, and she wailed louder and louder. The horde of wolves outside gathered close to the ranch, howling in unison. They bellowed and then paused and waited for the wild girl to answer back with her unearthly howling scream.

After a time, the pack made a rush for the corral and the barns, attacking goats, milk cows and the saddle horses. The screams and neighs of the domestic animals, accompanied by the thudding sounds of the kicking horses on the wooden stalls, brought the men out of the house and to the rescue. The wolves attacked. The men kept close together as they ran into the yard, shooting into the darkness and yelling as they advanced. Only the onslaught of the guns made the wolves retreat.

Once the men ran out of the house, the wolf girl somehow wrenched loose the plank that had been nailed over the window and disappeared into the night. It was assumed that she rejoined the wolves as hardly another howl was heard that night. Only the mark of bare feet within the myriad of tracks left by the wolves provided evidence that she was ever there at all. For some time after, sightings of wolves in the region were rare.

Nothing more was heard about the Wolf Girl of the Devil's River, save for rumor and legend, for nearly six years. In the meantime, gold had been discovered in California and westward travel began to increase. Around 1852, an exploring party of frontiersmen, who were searching a route to El Paso with better water than the trails that already existed, rode down to the Rio Grande at a sharp bend far above the mouth of the Devil's River.

They were almost upon the river when they saw a strange creature, sitting along the edge of a sandbar. As they looked closer, they realized that the figure was that of a naked young woman with two young wolf whelps tugging at her full breasts. When the woman heard the approaching horses, she sprang to her feet and snatched up the pups under each arm and ran off. She ran into the nearby breaks at full speed and vanished from sight.

After that, the Wolf Girl was rarely seen. The Apache, however, claimed that she lived with the wolves for many years afterward. Soon, those tales also came to an end. Was the girl a feral child, raised by wolves? Or was she something else altogether? The passage of time has ensured that those questions will remain unanswered.

The June 2, 1888 edition of the *Dallas Morning News* included a strange story with the eye-opening headline of "A Huge Wolf Killed, Big as a Yearling." The newspaper stated, "Frank Boshire, a farmer living near the city, killed and brought to town yesterday one of the largest gray wolves that was ever killed in this country. It is nearly as tall as a yearling calf. These animals have been a great disadvantage to the community, one man saying that he had been damaged at least $1,000 by them on sheep."

While this creature was certainly not to be mistaken for a werewolf, it was of a size that had never been seen by men who had lived in the area all of their lives and were quite familiar with wolves and other predators. Could, perhaps, some of the sightings of werewolves and unknown creatures really be encounters with wolves of monstrous size? There have been theories raised of creatures now believed to be extinct, known collectively as *Amphicyonidae*, that can best be described as a cross between a bear and a muscular dog. Could some of these creatures have survived extinction to become sightings of beasts believed to be monsters and werewolves?

A similar animal showed up in the same newspaper, the *Dallas Morning News*, on January 29, 1908. This time, the headline read "Hunt for Phantom-Like Animal." The story started that some sort of large animal, described both as a giant dog and a wolf, had been wreaking havoc throughout Waco since the start of the year. Pigs, dogs, ducks, geese and hens had been slaughtered and eaten.

There were also claims that the beast was almost spectral in nature. Those who had seen the wolf described it as "passing like a phantom, jumping fences from one lot to another, elusive and shadowy, except where the use is made of teeth and claws." The story added that, "The McLennan County Fox Hunter's Association with their best hunters declare that while they have been able to capture big wolves, red and gray foxes, bobcats and catamounts, they are baffled by this particular beast."

Whatever the creature was, it soon vanished and was never heard from again.

One of the classic stories of Texas werewolves is a report that came from the East Texas town of Greggton (near Longview) in 1958. On a July night, Mrs. Delburt Gregg was getting ready for bed when she heard scratching sounds on the window screen. When a sudden flash of lightning illuminated the night, she saw a horrific sight outside. It was a "huge, shaggy, wolf-like creature" that was clawing at the screen and glaring at her with "baleful, glowing, slitted eyes." When she jumped out of bed and ran to grab a flashlight, the beast ran off into the darkness and did not return.

But there are few - if any - states with as many werewolf reports as Wisconsin. This can be explained by either the sheer number of encounters or the excellent documentation of Linda Godfrey, a Wisconsin author with a keen interest in mysterious wolves in the state. She was one of the first to bring attention to the "Bray Road Beast," the state's most famous case, as well as many other bizarre reports.

One of the first documented Wisconsin werewolf sightings occurred in 1936. A man named Mark Schackelman reported encountering a talking "wolfman" just east of Jefferson, Wisconsin, on Highway 18. As he was driving along the road one evening, he spotted a figure digging in an old Indian mound. He looked closer and saw that the figure was a strange, hair-covered creature that stood erect and was more than six feet tall. The face of the creature had a muzzle and features of both an ape and a dog. Its hands were oddly formed with a twisted thumb and three fully formed fingers. The beast gave off a putrid smell that was like "decaying meat," he later recalled.

Schackelman returned to the site the following evening, hoping for another look, and this time, he actually heard the creature speak in what he described as being "neo-human." The beast uttered a "three-syllable growling noise that sounded like *gadara* with the emphasis on the second syllable." Schackelman was a religious man and after spotting this obviously "evil" creature, he began to back away from it and to pray. Eventually, the creature was lost to sight.

But did it turn up again? In 1964, another man, Dennis Fewless, had a similar sighting less than two miles away. Fewless was driving home around midnight from his job at the Admiral Television Corp. in Harvard, Illinois. After turning onto Highway 89 from Highway 14, his headlights caught an animal running across the road in front of him. It was dark brown in color and he estimated that it weighed between 400 and 500 pounds. He also described it as being seven or eight feet tall. It ran across the highway, jumped a barbed wire fence and vanished. Fewless returned to the spot in the daylight hours to look for footprints or other evidence but the hard, sun-dried ground offered nothing. He did find where the corn had been pushed aside as the beast entered the field. In an interview, he said, "I was awful scared that night. That was no man. It was all hairy from head to feet."

In 1972, another werewolf was sighted in Wisconsin. One night, a woman in rural Jefferson County called the police to report an attempted break-in at her home. According to an investigation conducted by the Wisconsin Department of Natural Resources, she said that the intruder was a "large, unknown animal" that had come to the house and had tried to get in the door. The creature departed but returned again a few weeks later and injured one of her farm animals. The account stated that the creature had long, dark hair, stood about eight feet tall and walked upright like a man. Its arms were long and it had claws on each hand. After trying to enter the house, the beast went out to the barn and attacked a horse that was stabled there. It left a deep gash on the animal that stretched from one shoulder to the other. A footprint left behind was more than a foot long.

The Wisconsin reports go on and on, but there is no case as celebrated and strange as that of what was dubbed the "Beast of Bray Road."

The first sighting of the monster to go public occurred (perhaps fittingly) on October 31, 1999. Doristine Gipson was driving along Bray Road near Delavan, and as she neared the intersection of Hospital Road, she leaned over to change the station on her radio when she felt her right front tire jump off the ground as if she had hit something. Concerned, she stopped the car and got out to see what it was. Finding nothing on the roadway behind her car, she began to look around. As she peered into the darkness, she suddenly saw a dark, hairy form racing toward her. She did not see what the figure looked like in detail from the distance at which she was standing (about fifty feet) but she did see it was quite bulky, and she would later compare its form to someone who works out continually with weights. Startled by the oncoming figure, and by the sounds of its "heavy feet," she quickly retreated to her car. She jumped in and was attempting to drive away when the beast jumped onto her trunk. Luckily, it was too wet for it to hang on and it fell off onto the pavement. Doristine returned to the site later on that evening with a young girl that she was taking out trick-or-treating and saw a large form on the side of the road. When she saw the creature moving, she ordered the child to lock her door and drove quickly away from the scene.

She had no idea what she had seen but wondered if perhaps it might be a bear, angered because she had struck it with her car. Regardless, she told a neighbor about the encounter the next day and showed her the scratched car. As word spread, more local people began to step forward with their own encounters with the beast, dating back to 1989.

One night in the fall of that year, twenty-four-year-old bar manager Lorianne Endrizzi was rounding a curve on Bray Road (just a half-mile from the site of the later incident) and saw what she thought was a person kneeling hunched over on the side of the road. When she slowed down, she took a closer look at the figure on the passenger side of the car. She was no more than six feet away from it at the time. The sighting lasted for about forty-five seconds and she stated that she clearly saw a beast with grayish, brown hair, fangs and pointed ears. "His face was ... long and snouty, like a wolf," she said.

She also noted that, even though the car's headlights were pointed ahead down the roadway, the creature's eyes glowed with a yellowish glint, just like an animal's will do when reflected in car lights. Like Doris Gipson, she also saw how wide and powerful the creature's chest and build were. She went on to add that the arms of the beast were rather strange. They were jointed as a man's would be and it seemed to be holding food with its palms upward, completely unlike any animal that she had ever heard of. The arms were muscular ("like a man who had worked out a little bit") and the creature seemed to have human-like fingers with claws on the ends. She did not notice any sort of tail but did say that its back legs were behind it, like a person's would be if kneeling.

Endrizzi was completely unnerved by the sighting. She later stated in an interview that the creature "appeared to be so human-like that it was scary." He own answer to what she had seen was that it had been a "freak of nature." She had no idea what it could have been until she saw a book at a library that had an illustration of a werewolf in it. It so closely resembled what she had seen on Bray Road that her "eyes popped out of her head."

After hearing Doris Gipson's account by way of rumor, Endrizzi contacted the Lakeland Animal Shelter and her mother contacted a local newspaper writer named Linda Godfrey, hoping that publicity might encourage other people who had encountered the creature to come forward. The story that followed was published on December 29, 1991, and while it contained basic information about the Gipson and Endrizzi sightings (using pseudonyms for the two women), it also included some information on other sightings. It also mentioned that chickens had been stolen and that another family who lived near Bray Road had experienced their own close encounter with the beast. Karen Bowey, who actually lived along Bowers Road, stated that her eleven-year-old daughter Heather had seen the creature back in 1989. They had been playing outside and thought they had spotted a large dog -- until it stood up. She mentioned the odd shape of its back legs and the speed at which it could move. The county humane officer, John Frederickson, told the reporter that he believed the creature was a "coyote" but he did concede that there were a lot of people who believed that they had seen something out of the ordinary. He admitted that he was not sure what to make of it.

Predictably, large media outlets picked up the story and the witnesses began to suffer from practical jokes and mockery. Monster signs were planted in front yards and "werewolf parties" became common, even at the bar where Endrizzi worked. Werewolf t-shirts were sold and tourists cruised up and down Bray Road, hoping for a glimpse of the creature. As time went by, the excitement decreased and the temper of the community began to wear thin. Despite all of the jokes and humor, there was still an undercurrent of fear in Delavan and Elkhorn. Something was going on out in the vicinity of Bray Road, and soon people began to whisper about other things as well.

Just the summer before the wolf creature had been reported, a dozen or so dead animals had been dumped in a ditch along nearby Willow Road. John Frederickson, the humane officer from Delavan, stated that he believed several of the animals had been used in cult rituals. While Linn Police Chief James Jensen dismissed this idea in June 1991, Frederickson insisted that officials were missing the point. According to the officer, some of the animals had ropes tied around their back legs and their throats were slit, some were decapitated and others were dismembered in various ways. The most recently killed animal was a dog that had its chest cavity split open and its heart removed. Several of the animals matched descriptions of recently missing pets and they certainly had not been killed by passing cars. The mutilated carcasses were almost immediately covered up -- literally. The site was quickly bulldozed, ending Frederickson's investigation. But it did not end the whispers and rumors - or reports of other strange things.

As the bizarre encounters with the Beast continued, along with the animal mutilations, matters were further complicated by all sorts of other sightings in the region, including Bigfoot-like creatures, UFO reports and "men in black." In addition to the chaos of the werewolf stories, all kinds of high strangeness was filtering into the area.

Rumors also swirled about imposters posing as humane officers hunting stray dogs. One incident involved an unidentified man in a black uniform, driving a large, black car, who attempted to intimidate a child who was home alone into giving up his black Labrador Retriever. Around this same time, there were also reports of "occult" graffiti being found in an abandoned house and at the local cemetery, where grave markers were found to be covered with candle wax. The abandoned house was located just a quarter-mile off Bray Road. This led many to ponder whether the Satanic activity and the Bray Road Beast were in some way connected. The strange stories and animal carcasses had been whispered about and discovered just a few months before the first sightings of the monster had been publicized, but the Beast was apparently in the vicinity long before that.

An earlier sighting of "something" was made by a dairy farmer from Elkhorn named Scott Bray, who reported seeing a "strange-looking dog" in his pasture near Bray Road in September or October of 1989. He said that the beast was larger and taller than a German Shepherd and had pointed ears, a hairy tail and long, gray and black hair. He added that it was built very heavy in the front, as if it had a wide chest. He followed the "dog" to a large pile of rocks but the creature had vanished. He did find that it had left behind huge footprints, which disappeared when the creature walked out into the grass of the pasture.

Russell Gest of Elkhorn also reported seeing the creature about the same time as the Scott Bray sighting. He was about a block or so away from an overgrown area and when he heard weeds being rustled, he looked up to see a creature emerge from a thicket. It was standing on its hind feet and took two "wobbly" steps forward before Gest began to run away. He looked back to see that the creature was now on all fours, but it never gave chase. After a short distance, it wandered off in the direction of Bray Road. Gest said that the creature was much larger than a dog and was covered with black and grayish hair. While standing upright, it appeared to be about five feet tall. It had an oversized dog or wolf-like head with a big neck and wide shoulders. The animal's form was mostly dog-like, leading Gest to surmise that it was some sort of dog-wolf hybrid.

Around Christmas 1990, Heather Bowey had her previously mentioned encounter. She had no idea that she had seen the same thing as Doris Gipson until she heard the young woman talking about it on the school bus. The driver, Pat Lester, (who oddly happened to be Lorianne Endrizzi's mother), listened to the girl's story and passed it on to Linda Godfrey. The reporter then contacted

Karen Bowey, also a school bus driver, and then mentioned the sighting in the newspaper. Heather elaborated on the encounter to writer Scarlett Sankey.

The sighting occurred around 4:30 p.m. as Heather and several friends were returning home from sledding near Loveland Road (about a mile and a half southeast of the intersection of Bray and Hospital Roads). They happened to look up and see what appeared to be a large dog walking along a creek in a snow-covered cornfield. Heather estimated that it was about a block away from them. Thinking that it was a dog, they children began calling to it. The creature looked at them and then it stood up on its hind legs. She described it as being covered with long brownish hair. The beast took four awkward steps in their direction and then dropped down on all fours and began to run at the children in what Heather later described as being "a bigger leap than dogs run." It followed the group about halfway to the Bowey home (about 250 yards away) before it turned and ran off in another direction.

In March 1990, an Elkhorn dairy farmer named Mike Etten spotted something unusual along Bray Road one morning around 2:00 a.m. In the moonlight, Etten (who admitted that he had been drinking at the time) saw a dark-haired creature that was bigger than a dog, just a short distance from the Hospital Road intersection. Whatever the creature was, it was sitting "like a raccoon sits," using its front paws to hold onto something that it was eating. As he passed by the creature, it lifted its head and looked at him. He described the head as being thick and wide, with a snout that was not as long as a dog's. The body was covered with dark, thick hair and its legs were big and thick. Not being able to identify the animal, Etten assumed that it was a bear. However, when the other sightings of the Bray Road Beast were made public in 1991, he had to reconsider this assumption.

One of the last reported encounters with the creature occurred in early February 1992. It happened around 10:30 p.m. on Highway H, about six miles southwest of the Bray and Hospital Roads intersection. A young woman named Tammy Bray, who worked for a retirement home, was driving her car when a large, dog-like animal crossed the road in front of her. She quickly punched the brakes and slid to a stop, just about the same time that the creature turned and looked at her. She described the creature as having a broad chest, pointed ears and being covered with matted brown and black fur. The narrow nose, thick neck and shining yellow eyes of the beast quickly convinced her that she was not looking at any sort of dog. Finally, it continued on, unafraid, across the road. She noted that it walked "strong in front, more slouchy, sloppy-like in the rear." Tammy drove home and hurried into the house to tell her husband, Scott Bray, that she had seen the same animal that he had earlier seen in their pasture.

The sightings eventually died out, but the strangeness that seemed to envelope the region took a little longer to fade. In January 1992, just as the furor over the Bray Road Beast sightings was starting to quiet down, a local man described as a "reputable businessman" told reporter Linda Godfrey that he had seen two bright lights emitting sparks and moving erratically across the sky above Delavan. Later that spring, four or five horses that were pastured near Elkhorn were found with their throats slashed. John Frederickson, who investigated, was quoted as saying, "They were almost surgical-type wounds." And after that, things became eerily quiet.

What was the Bray Road Beast? Neither a coyote nor the native red wolf can really match the descriptions that were given of the creature, despite humane officer John Frederickson's comments that a coyote might rear up on its hind legs before running. A gray wolf would be much larger than a red wolf but they are not generally found in the area. In addition, gray wolves are much narrower in the chest than the Bray Road creature was reported to be, and wolves are shy of humans and would not attack a car as the creature from the Doris Gipson encounter did. The creature simply resembled no known animal, but alternately was compared to dogs, bears and wolves. According to Jerome Clark, Dan Groebner of the International Wolf Research Center in Ely, Minnesota, stated that the creature could not be a wild wolf.

Witnesses also insisted that it was not a dog, although some suggested that it could have been a wolf-dog hybrid of some sort. But how does this explain the creature's habit of kneeling, walking on two legs and holding onto food with the flat of its paws turned upward? Also, Lori Endrizzi claimed that the animal had human-like fingers. The idea that the monster may have been a bear is also called into question. While bears do occasionally walk for short distances on their hind legs, they do not hold food with their palms up, do not jump onto moving cars and very rarely do they pursue or try to attack humans.

So, what could it have been? Some cryptozoological researchers suggested that the creature may have been the "shunka warak'in," a wolf-like creature that once existed in the wilds of the Upper Midwest and was known to the Native American population and to the early settlers in the region. It was named by the Ioway Indians and meant "carrying-off dogs." Little is known for about the creature but apparently it was quite fierce, and for a while, a mounted specimen of one was exhibited at various times in the west Yellowstone area and in a small museum near Henry Lake in Idaho. Interestingly, the dog and hyena-type creature fits many of the descriptions of witnesses in southeastern Wisconsin, including its strange look (which would have made many compare it to a wolf or a dog mix), its dark shaggy fur and a sloping weakness to its back legs, which was noted in almost every report.

But even if we accept the possibility that this creature could have been one of the rare - and extinct -- "shunka warak'in," how do we explain the fact that it picked up its food with its paws and walked about on two legs. If the Bray Road Beast was real it had to have been some sort of creature that had never been classified before.

Or more incredible to believe, was it a genuine werewolf? Many came to believe there was an occult connection with the Bray Road Beast. The discovery of the mutilated animal carcasses and the occult activity at the cemetery and the abandoned house coincided with the sightings of the monster in the region. Those who believe in this possibility have demanded that we not dismiss the idea that the Beast was a shape-shifter of some sort, combining the characteristics of man and wolf.

There is also one more theory that we have to consider: that the entire thing could have been an elaborate hoax. Notwithstanding the fact that Doris Gipson's encounter took place on Halloween, there were other problems with the story. The most obvious issue to cause suspicion was the relationships between all of those involved in the case. Endrizzi's mother, Pat Lester, is a central figure in the case. In addition to being one witness' mother, she was also Gipson's neighbor and drove the school bus that Gipson, Heather Bowey and Russell Gest rode. Heather's mother was also a school bus driver. Tammy Bray was a friend of Pat Lester's daughter and the wife of Scott Bray. It was also Lester who took the initiative to contact the newspaper about the sightings. However, it should be pointed out that Lester never tried to influence the reports of the witnesses. It seems more likely that she was simply in a position to hear about the encounters and her interest and compassion towards those involved helped to encourage them to go public.

So, could they have been making the whole thing up? They could have been, but it doesn't seem likely, especially based on the fact that no one had anything to gain by making the sightings public, other than ridicule and embarrassment, which is hardly an incentive to make the story known.

As time has passed, the investigation into the case has grown cold, and with no further sightings of the Beast of Bray Road to continue the news stories, the papers fell silent. One has to wonder if we will ever know the truth of what happened in southeastern Wisconsin between 1989 and 1992. At this point, the mystery remains unsolved.

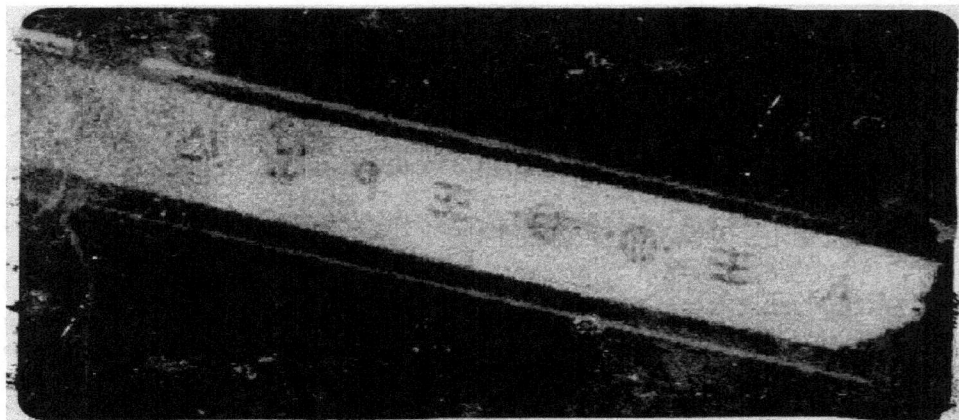

MYSTERIOUS WRECKAGE WITH STRANGE "HEIROGLYPHICS"
AIRSHIPS OVER AMERICA 1896-1897

They have been up there since the beginning of recorded time: those strange objects that seem to have no explanation for being in the skies over our heads. Every civilization in history has told of things in the sky that shouldn't have been there. These bizarre objects have included burning wheels, fiery objects with wings and, during the last years of the nineteenth century, cylindrical shapes that were constructed of weird metals and shiny steel. Reports of these airships circulated around the country in those days, despite the fact that their construction, and very existence, was seemingly an impossibility at the time. No known aircraft, save for hot air balloons, flew under their own power before the Wright Brothers left the ground at Kitty Hawk. So, what were these strange ships? Who had constructed them and perhaps strangest of all, who was flying them?

Reports of the alleged crewmen and pilots usually described them as human-looking, although sometimes the crew claimed to be from Mars, or possibly stranger yet, were worried about the rights of the Cuban people. Most of them carried extraordinary messages to the people on the ground, while others seemed to have superior intelligence, odd skin tones and weird speech patterns. It was popularly believed that the mystery airships were the product of some inventor who was not yet ready to make knowledge of his creation public. Thomas Edison was so widely speculated to be the source behind the alleged airships that in 1897 he "was forced to issue a strongly worded statement" denying his responsibility.

Reports of the aircraft, which had vast metal wingspans and arrays of bright lights, first appeared in California in 1896. Hundreds of people saw the airships as they began what seemed to be a leisurely eastward tour across America.

The first sighting occurred on November 18, 1896 and was reported in the *Sacramento Bee* and the *San Francisco Call* newspapers and had a distinctly Steampunk ring to it. Witnesses claimed that they saw a light moving slowly over Sacramento on the evening of November 17. Some witnesses said they could see a dark shape behind the light. A man named R. L. Lowery reported that he heard a voice from the craft issuing commands to increase elevation in order to avoid hitting a church steeple. There were no churches in the area, but there was a tower on a local brewery. Lowery further described the craft as being powered by two men exerting themselves on bicycle pedals. Above the pedaling men seemed to be a passenger compartment, which lay under the main body of a dirigible. A light was mounted on the front end of the airship. Some witnesses reported the sound of singing as the craft passed overhead.

The next day, a witness claimed to see the airship - or one just like it - on the ground. According to the November 19 edition of the *Stockton Daily Mail*, Colonel H.G. Shaw stated that while driving his buggy through the countryside near Stockton he came across what appeared to be a landed aircraft. Shaw described it as having a metallic surface, which was completely featureless apart from a rudder, and pointed ends. He estimated it had a diameter of twenty-five feet and a total length of around one hundred and fifty feet. Three slender men, each standing close to seven feet tall, were outside the airship "emitting a strange warbling noise." The men reportedly examined Shaw's buggy and then tried to seize him, apparently attempting to force him to accompany them back to the airship. When the doughty Colonel Shaw resisted, they fled back to the ship, which lifted off the ground and sped out of sight. Shaw believed they were "Martians" sent to kidnap an earthling for unknowable but potentially nefarious purposes.

On November 21, the airship with the mystery light appeared again over Sacramento. It was also seen over Folsom, San Francisco and Oakland later that same evening and was reportedly viewed by hundreds of witnesses.

Soon after, the mysterious ship began traveling eastward across the country, wreaking havoc, creating mayhem and leaving very puzzled witnesses in its wake. Some of the stories of the airship were very strange. For instance, one witness from Arkansas - allegedly a former state senator named Harris - was supposedly told by an airship pilot (during the tensions leading up to the Spanish-American War) that the craft was bound for Cuba, to use its "Hotchkiss gun" to "kill Spaniards." In one account from Texas, three men reported an encounter with an airship and with "five peculiarly dressed men" who reported that they were descendants from the lost tribes of Israel. They had learned English, they said, from the 1553 North Pole expedition led by Sir Hugh Willoughby, an early English Arctic voyager. An article in the Albion, Nebraska, *Weekly News* reported that two witnesses saw an airship crash just inches from where they were standing. The airship suddenly disappeared, leaving a man standing where the vessel had been. The airship pilot showed the astonished men a small device that supposedly enabled him to shrink the airship small enough to store the vessel in his pocket.

In April 1897, the *St. Louis Post-Dispatch* published a story reporting that one W. H. Hopkins encountered a grounded airship about twenty feet in length and eight feet in diameter near the outskirts of Springfield, Missouri. The vehicle was apparently powered by three large propellers and was crewed by a beautiful nude woman and a bearded man, also nude. Hopkins attempted with some difficulty to communicate with the crew in order to ascertain their origins. Eventually they understood what Hopkins was asking of them and they both pointed to the sky and "uttered something that sounded like the word 'Mars.'"

The mysterious aircraft arrived in Illinois a short time later. The first sightings were in Evanston and in several other communities near Chicago. The local newspapers quickly spread the news that the airship was filled with "English spies," although why the English would have wanted to dispatch spies to the American Midwest was left unstated. More than five hundred people witnessed a ship that was said to be in full view for over forty-five minutes. One description stated that the airship was "composed of two cigar-shaped bodies attached by girders" and others claimed that it had wings and sails. Still others scoffed at the news. Professor G.W. Hough of the Dearborn Observatory admitted that he didn't even bother to look at the airship when it was over his headquarters in Evanston. He was sure that it was merely the star Alpha Orionis.

The airship reportedly stayed in the Chicago area for three days and was there long enough to be photographed by a newspaper dealer named Walter McCann. He was picking up his daily newspapers at the Northwestern Railway depot when he saw the ship coming toward him from the south. A short time before, his son had won a camera in a contest for signing up newspaper subscribers and McCann ran into his store and snatched it up. He ran back outside and snapped a photo of it. He then ran down the railroad tracks and took another photo a few minutes later. After the plates were developed, McCann gave copies of the photos to all of the newspapers who requested them but he refused to sell the negatives. The staff artists and etcher for the *Chicago Times-Herald* subjected the photos to acid tests and proclaimed them to be authentic. Sadly, the photos have since been lost.

After departing from Chicago, the airship began a tour across Illinois. It was spotted in dozens of cities and there seemed to be no rhyme or reason to its route. It appeared in both northern and southern Illinois, being in one region on one day and the other on the next. For instance, on April 5, it made an appearance in the southwestern Illinois town of Nashville and on April 8 was seen up north in Dixon, Rock Island and Sterling. The craft buzzed over Elgin, Jerseyville, Kankakee, Taylorville, East St. Louis, Edwardsville, Jacksonville, Ottawa, Quincy, Decatur, Lincoln, Hillsboro, Peoria and many other locations. Even if we discount many of the reports as being merely excitement or practical jokes that were generated by newspaper stories, there are still scores of credible and very similar accounts.

Several of the Illinois accounts from April 1897 stand out as even stranger than sightings of the airship itself. One of the encounters took place about two miles outside of Springfield, when two farmhands reported that the airship landed in a field where they were working. The occupants of the ship, two men and one woman, disembarked and told the field workers that they would make a report to the government about their journey "when Cuba is declared free." After their bizarre announcement, the occupants of the airship cheerfully waved to them and climbed back into the craft. It lifted off again into the skies.

The aircraft was seen again near Mt. Vernon a few days after this. The city's mayor was looking at the sky with his telescope when the ship came into range. In addition to the airship, he also claimed to see one of the occupants of the craft hovering in the sky around it. He said that the man had some sort of device strapped to his back that allowed him to fly about and apparently make repairs to his ship.

The airship landed several more times over the next few days in Nilwood, Downs Township and Green Ridge, but the occupants always quickly climbed back aboard and lifted off when they were approached. In two of the cases, the passengers were seen checking over some of the machinery on the airship before they departed. The last Illinois airship sighting took place in Rossville on April 25, and then the ship continued on its strange journey.

In the midst of the airship reports, one of the strangest incidents linked to the craft (or apparently one of many such crafts) allegedly took place in the town of Aurora, Texas. The story appeared in the *Dallas Morning News* on April 19, 1897. According to the reporter:

About 6 o'clock this morning the early risers of Aurora were astonished at the sudden appearance of the airship which has been sailing around the country. It was traveling due north and much nearer the earth than before.

Evidently some of the machinery was out-of-order, for it was making a speed of only ten or twelve miles an hour, and gradually settling toward the earth. It sailed over the public square and when it reached the north part of town it collided with the tower of Judge Proctor's windmill and went into pieces with a terrific explosion, scattering debris over several acres of ground, wrecking the windmill and water tank and destroying the judge's flower garden.

The pilot of the ship is supposed to have been the only one aboard and, while his remains were badly disfigured, enough of the original has been picked up to show that he was not an inhabitant of this world.

As mentioned, the occupant of the craft was dead and mangled, and while UFO researchers believe that the pilot was an alien, the newspaper only states that he was "not an inhabitant of this world." This could have referred to his looks, his dress, or the fact that he was flying an airship that should not have existed - not that he was an alien. However, there was a note that strange "hieroglyphic" figures were seen on the wreckage, which resembled "a mixture of aluminum and silver ... it must have weighed several tons." In 1973, interest was revived in this story and metallic material recovered from the presumed crash site was shown to contain an unusual percentage of aluminum and iron. The story ended by noting that the pilot was given a "Christian burial" in the town cemetery. During the investigation of the possible crash site, researchers discovered the alleged stone marker used in this burial. Their metal detectors indicated a quantity of foreign material might remain buried there. However, they were not permitted to exhume whatever may have lain below, and when they returned several years later, the headstone was gone. Incidentally, there is now a Texas Historical Commission marker in the cemetery mentioning the incident.

According to local legend, wreckage from the crash site was dumped into a nearby well. Adding to the mystery was the story of Brawley Oates, who purchased Judge Proctor's property around 1945. Oates cleaned out the debris from the well in order to use it as a water source, but later developed an extremely severe case of arthritis, which he claimed to be the result of drinking contaminated water from the wreckage that was dumped into the well. As a result, Oates sealed up the well with a concrete slab and placed an outbuilding atop the slab in 1957.

It's not surprising that many have come to believe this story is a hoax. One of the most outspoken believers in the hoax was Barbara Brammer, a former mayor of Aurora. Her research revealed that in the months prior to the alleged crash, Aurora was plagued by a series of tragic incidents. The local cotton crop was destroyed by a boll weevil infestation, a fire on the west side of town destroyed several buildings and killed a number of people, a spotted fever epidemic caused the town to be quarantined and finally, a planned railroad reached a point twenty-seven miles from Aurora, but never made it to town. Essentially, Aurora, which had nearly three thousand residents at the time, was in danger of dying out. Brammer believed the story was designed as a last-ditch effort to keep Aurora alive. Her theory was further supported by the fact that there was never any follow-up to the story. She also pointed to the fact that Judge Proctor never had a windmill on his property.

Unfortunately, Brammer's theories of the hoax also work toward making the story seem legitimate. For starters, Judge Proctor *did* have a windmill on his property. The remains of it have since been found, along with the well that Brawley Oates thought was contaminated. They also found melted metal at the site, which turned out to be aluminum, which was very rare in the late nineteenth century. There was an actual grave marker at the site in the cemetery (later stolen) that supposedly marked where the pilot was buried and ground-penetrating radar has revealed the presence of a casket-shaped object under the ground.

And as far as the idea that the story was a hoax cooked up to save the town? Well, the tragic incidents might also explain why there was no follow-up story to the airship's crash. With all of the terrible things that had just occurred, it's not really that surprising that the pilot was simply buried and the people moved on with their lives. There were more important things going on in Aurora at the time than the crash. It wasn't until the 1970s that anyone really took an interest in the story again.

What really happened in Texas in 1897? Who knows? While I don't think there is any conclusive proof that an airship crashed to earth on that day in April, I do think something unusual happened, but what it was, we'll probably never know.

In time, the airship reports faded away, leaving a mystery behind - and a lot of people to argue about what really happened. As one can imagine, theories abound. Attempts to uncover the truth about the airship reports reveal some unhappy realities: newspaper coverage was unreliable; no independent investigators spoke directly with alleged witnesses or attempted to verify or debunk their testimony; and, with a only one exception, no eyewitness was ever interviewed, even in the 1950s, when some were presumably still living. That single witness was a former *San Francisco Chronicle* employee named Edward Ruppelt. In 1952, Ruppelt stated that he had been a copyboy in 1897 "and remembered the incident, but time had cancelled out the details." He did say that he, along with the newspaper's editor and the news staff had seen the airship but they never told anyone what they had seen because they didn't want people to think they were "crazy."

There will always be many who dismiss the 1896-1897 airship wave as some massive hoax. Even at the time, there were many attempts to explain the airship sightings as hoaxes, pranks, publicity stunts and hallucinations. One man suggested the airships were swarms of lightning bugs that were misidentified by observers. It's also very likely that many of the newspaper reports were, in fact, hoaxes, riding the wave of a national craze for goofy, off-beat tales. Stories created out of whole cloth by enterprising reporters do tend to stand out, though, since most of them have a tongue-in-cheek tone and are heavily sensational. Furthermore, the supposed authors of many such newspaper hoaxes make their hoax obvious by stating - in the last line - that he was writing from an insane asylum, or something to that effect.

Over time, the 1896-1897 airship wave has become probably the best investigated of all historical anomalies. The files of almost 1,500 newspapers from across the United States have been combed for reports, an astonishing feat of research. The general conclusion of investigators was that a considerable number of the simpler sightings were misidentification of planets and stars, and a large number of the more complex sightings were the result of hoaxes and practical jokes. A sizable number, though, remain perplexing.

What were the ships and better yet, who was flying them? In 2009, author J. Allan Danelek made a case for the idea that the mystery airship was the work of an unknown individual, possibly funded by a wealthy investor from San Francisco, who built an airship prototype as a test vehicle for a later series of larger, passenger-carrying airships. Danelek not only laid out a plausible scenario, but demonstrated how the craft might have been built using materials and technologies available in 1896 (including speculative line drawings and technical details). The ship, Danelek proposed, was built in secret as a safeguard from patent infringement, as well as to protect investors in case of failure. Noting that the flights were initially seen over California and only later over the Midwest, he speculated that the inventor was making a series of short test flights, moving from west to east, and following the main railroad lines for logistical support, and that it was these experimental flights that formed the basis for many - though not all - of the newspaper accounts from the era. Danelek also noted that the reports ended abruptly in late April 1897, suggesting that the craft may have met with disaster, effectively ending the venture and permitting the sightings to fall into the realm of legend.

These ideas were not far off from some of the theories posed at the end of the nineteenth century - a time of great popularity for science-fiction writers like Jules Verne and H.G. Wells. In fact, the idea that a secretive inventor might have developed a viable craft with advanced capabilities was the focus of Jules Verne's 1886 novel *Robur the Conqueror*. Steerable airships had been publicly flown in the United States since 1863, and numerous inventors were working on airship and aircraft designs. In fact, two French army officers and engineers, Arthur Krebs and Charles Renard, had successfully flown in an electric-powered airship called the *La France* as early as 1885, making no fewer than seven successful flights over an eleven-month period. Also during the 1896-1897 period, David Schwarz built an aluminum-skinned airship in Germany that successfully flew over Tempelhof Field before being irreparably damaged during a hard landing. Both events clearly demonstrated that the technology to build a practical airship existed during the period in question, though if reports of the capabilities of the California and Midwest airship sighted in 1896-97 are true, it would have been considerably more advanced than any airship built up to that time.

Several individuals, including Lyman Gilmore, Charles Dellschau and Thomas Edison (who issued a strong denial) were later identified as possible candidates for being involved in the design and construction of the airships, although little evidence was found in support of these ideas.

How can we explain the mysterious airship (or airships) that crossed America in 1896-1897? Was it a hoax, a case of mass hysteria? Perhaps, but this seems unlikely based on the unrelated and completely unconnected witnesses who spotted and reported it. In Chicago, there was a sighting that allegedly included several hundred people, all describing it in almost exactly the same way.

If the ship was real, then who were the passengers? They had strange messages to pass along and seemed to be almost constantly at work on their vessel. During one encounter that took place in Texas, an airship passenger actually asked for help in repairing his craft. He handed the witness current American money and asked him to fetch supplies from the local hardware store. But how could ordinary materials function in the baffling airship?

The mystery remains unsolved. It seems unlikely that the airship was built by the mechanical means of the time period and yet it apparently existed. The passengers on the ship appeared to be normal humans, taking what seemed to them to be a normal trip, aboard a machine that could not exist - and yet did.

PATCH OF DEAD GRASS

ORION WILLIAMSON AND THE MAN WHO DISAPPEARED

On the cold evening of November 8, 1878, a sixteen-year-old boy named Charles Ashmore walked out of the back door of his family's farmhouse near Quincy, Illinois. He carried with him a bucket with which to fetch fresh water from a spring a short distance away. When he didn't return, his family became uneasy and his father, Christian Ashmore, accompanied by his oldest daughter, Martha, took a lantern and went in search of the boy. A new snow had just fallen and Charles' footprints were plainly visible as they went out the back door and started across the yard. His father and sister followed his trail for a short distance but after going about seventy-five yards, they saw that the trail abruptly ended. Beyond the last footprint was nothing other than smooth, unbroken snow - the boy's tracks simply came to an end.

Ashmore and his daughter made a wide circle around the tracks, careful not to disturb them, then went on to the spring. They found the water covered with a layer of unbroken ice and it became apparent that Charles had gotten no closer to the spring than his tracks had indicated. The boy had vanished without explanation.

But the story does not end there. Four days later, the grief-stricken mother went to the spring for water and insisted that she heard the voice of her vanished son calling to her when she passed the spot where his footprints had ended. She wandered the area, thinking that the voice was coming from one direction and then another. Later, when questioned about the voice, she said that it was very distinct, and the voice was definitely that of her son, and yet she could make out no message from them.

For months afterward, the voice was heard every few days by one family member or another, or sometimes several of them. It seemed to come from a great distance and yet was entirely distinct, although none of them could determine its message or repeat its words. Soon, the intervals of silence grew longer and the voice became much fainter. By mid-summer of 1879, it was heard no more.

Those with an interest in the strange and the unusual have likely heard of this story before. Or perhaps the reader may have run across a slightly different variation of it, with the name of Charles Ashmore being changed to that of David Lang and the location being moved from Illinois to Gallatin, Tennessee. Or the reader may have heard yet another version - enhanced by the young man piteously crying for help before vanishing. That version has the boy's name as Oliver Larch and the location was South Bend, Indiana. All of these accounts have appeared in various books of supposedly true stories about unsolved mysteries and the unexplained over the years.

The problem with every one of these stories is that not a single one is true! The story of Charles Ashmore first appeared in the writings of journalist Ambrose Bierce, a prolific writer who penned not only newspaper articles, but several books, scores of stories about ghosts and the Civil War and a number of acerbic and cutting essays over the course of his career. Bierce's style and journalistic background gave his stories of war and strange disappearances such an uneasy realism that many mistook them for being true. Such was the case of the story of Charles Ashmore and many others that he wrote. As time has passed, the stories have often been presented as being accounts of real disappearances that took place many years ago.

Critics often scoff at writers who mistake these literary creations for true stories, often because it seems obvious that one cannot simply walk out the door one day and vanish into thin air. Such a thing cannot possible happen. Or can it?

Ambrose Bierce believed that it was possible for people to simply "disappear" and in fact, his fictional stories of Charles Ashmore and others were based on a real-life experience that intrigued Bierce at the start of his journalistic career. Ironically, the author of stories like that of Charles Ashmore, and the chilling tale called "The Spook House," in which two travelers enter a house in Kentucky but only one emerges, himself vanished without a trace in 1913. No clue has ever been found to explain what may have become of the one of the most famous American writers of the early twentieth century. But it cannot be denied that Bierce was a strange and eccentric man whose life was riddled with many mysteries.

In the San Francisco of 1900, Ambrose Bierce reigned as the city's unchallenged literary king and was considered to be the best-known writer west of the Rocky Mountains. In my opinion, he still stands today with Jack London as one of the best writers of the period, but a long road led from the beginnings of his career to his mysterious disappearance. And there were many who believed that if anyone deserved to disappear, it would have been the man known by many as "Bitter" Bierce.

Ambrose Gwinnett Bierce was born in Meigs County, Ohio, in 1842. In his family were nine brothers and sisters, all christened with names that started with the letter "A" - Abigail, Addison, Aurelius, Amelia, Ann, Augustus, Andrew, Almeda, Albert and Ambrose. It might be expected that parents who named their children so whimsically would be warm and devoted but, according to Bierce, they were not. In fact, Bierce grew into a child who saw nothing good in either parent. In time, he wrote five short stories, which he collected under the title of *Parenticide* - the killing of one's own parents. One story, "An Imperfect Conflagration," began, "Early one June morning in 1872, I murdered my father - an act which made a deep impression on me at the time."

Whatever faults his upbringing may have had, lack of literary appreciation was not among them. Bierce's father was an avid reader and had accumulated a large personal library, which Bierce explored as a boy. Through his voracious reading of books and newspapers, he became an ardent abolitionist as a young man and went to work for an anti-slavery newspaper in northern Indiana. As he began writing, he realized his life's work and spent the next years as a journalist. He briefly attended the Kentucky Military Institute but left in 1859 without a degree. This lack of formal education would dog him through his critics for the rest of his life, as they complained of his poor grammatical skills. Bierce never let this stop him, and as a born storyteller, he was able to achieve success with those who mattered: his readers.

Bierce was described as being cynical and aloof. He reveled in the unknown and his life was pockmarked with adventure. Both his writings of war and adventure and his writings of ghosts and horror were influenced by events in Bierce's own life. It's possible that his interest in weird happenings and strange disappearances stemmed from an event about which he wrote, which took place in 1854.

One hot day in July of that year, a planter named Orion Williamson from Selma, Alabama, was sitting on the veranda of his home with his wife and child. As he squinted out into the bright sunshine, his gaze fell on the ten-acre pasture where his horses were grazing. Williamson stood up and announced to his wife, "I forgot to tell Andrew about those horses." Andrew was his overseer. Mrs. Williamson later remembered her husband stepping down from the porch and walking out into the field. He picked up a small stick and he absent-mindedly swished it back and forth as he walked through the ankle-high grass.

At that same time, a neighboring farmer, Armour Wren, and his son, James, were returning from Selma in a buggy, passing by the field on a road on the far side. They stopped when they saw Williamson approaching and Wren stood up and waved to him. At that split second, with four sets of eyes upon him, Williamson abruptly disappeared. A moment earlier, he had been walking away from his family and waving at friends and the next moment, he had vanished into thin air.

Stunned, Wren and his son jumped from their buggy and ran into the field, where they soon met Mrs. Williamson and her child. They breathlessly searched the area where Williamson had vanished but saw nothing but bare ground and sparse grass. It seemed impossible, but the man was gone.

For two hours, the Wrens and the Williamsons searched the field. They found nothing and as the realization of what had happened occurred to her, Mrs. Williamson collapsed in shock. She was taken to Selma and hospitalized. When news spread of what happened, three hundred men from town gathered at the field. They formed three hand-to-hand ranks and moved across the field inches at a time, stopping every few feet to kneel down and examine the ground for openings or holes. They searched the field dozens of times and when night fell, they used torches and lanterns to light up the area. Bloodhounds were brought in, but no trace of the farmer could be found.

The following morning, hundreds more volunteers arrived from nearby communities, along with a team of geologists. They began digging at the point where Williamson disappeared but, a few feet below the surface, they hit solid bedrock. There were no caves, crevices or holes to explain where he had gone. He had simply vanished.

The word of Williamson's sensational disappearance attracted the attention of journalists from around the South and Midwest. Later, one of those was Ambrose Bierce, whose fascination with the unknown brought him to look into the case and to write a short story about it entitled "The Difficulty of Crossing a Field." The unexplained aspects of this particular story inspired him to pen many other variations on the theme.

And while what happened to Orion Williamson was certainly strange, it did not prepare anyone for what happened next. The following spring revealed an odd circle that appeared in the field at the exact spot where Williamson was last seen. The grass within the circle died and this curious event was pointed out to Mrs. Williamson by investigators who were still interested in the mystery. By this time, Mrs. Williamson was still so traumatized by her husband's abrupt disappearance that she was reluctant to mention his name or to speculate on what might have become of him. Her strange behavior brought many questions from volunteers and the authorities alike. Why was the woman still in such a state of shock? True, the disappearance of her husband was undoubtedly bizarre, but why did she refuse to talk about him?

In a quavering and fearful voice, Mrs. Williamson finally explained. She told the searchers that in the days following her husband's disappearance, she and her child distinctly heard Williamson's voice calling for help from the spot where he had vanished. They had run to the spot each time they heard him, but there was no one and nothing there. The calling continued for almost two weeks with Williamson's voice becoming weaker and weaker as the days passed. On the last night he was heard, the family slept at the edge of the spot where he vanished. They heard Williamson's whispers and then he was heard no more.

Ambrose Bierce would interview not only the searchers in the Williamson affair, but also "experts" who claimed to have theories as to where the farmer had gone. One of them, Dr. Maximilian Hern, was a scientist who had written a book called *Disappearance and Theory Thereof*. He stated that Williamson had walked into "void spot of universal ether." These spots, he explained, only lasted for a few seconds but were capable of destroying any and all material elements that happened to blunder into them. Other scientists stepped forward with theories, as well. One of them said that he believed Williamson walked into a periodic "magnetic field" that disintegrated his atomic structure and sent him into another dimension.

None of these theories helped to discover the missing Orion Williamson, though, and while he was immortalized in Bierce's writings, he now seemed to be gone for good. His story refused to die, however. Not only did he appear in a story by Ambrose Bierce, but he would also provide the inspiration for more stories by the writer. In addition, his story would be plagiarized numerous times over the years, starting in 1889.

In that year, a traveling salesman from Cincinnati named McHatten was trapped by a snowstorm in Gallatin, Tennessee. With nothing to do but sleep, eat and drink, McHatten decided to rewrite the Orion Williamson story and sell it to a newspaper as an original report. He changed Williamson's name to David Lang and the site of his disappearance to Gallatin. He also altered the date of the occurrence from 1854 to 1880. McHatten's story, except for the basic facts, was a complete fabrication that has since been accepted and rewritten to appear in many reputable journals and books. Research has revealed that no one named David Lang ever lived in Gallatin.

Orion Williamson, however, was a real person and was not the figment of anyone's imagination. According to census records, he was a resident of Selma, Alabama, in 1854 - although his residence in that city tragically and abruptly came to an end one hot July afternoon.

The accounts of Orion Williamson that Bierce discovered almost surely provided the inspiration for the writer's works on the unknown, but it would be his service during the Civil War that would inspire his gritty tales of death and adventure. Bierce always considered the war to be his finest hour. He originally enlisted at age eighteen with the Ninth Indiana Infantry and through the bloody battles of Shiloh, Murfreesboro, Kenesaw Mountain, Franklin and Nashville, he rose through the ranks to first lieutenant. At the time of his final discharge in 1865, he was a major.

He enlisted three times and the war took a physical toll on him. He was wounded twice, once quite seriously in the head, but he always returned to the battlefield after he had recovered. He seemed to love the war, but his brother, Albert, always believed that it changed him in negative ways. He stated that Bierce was never the same after he was wounded in the head. "Some of the iron of the shell seemed to stick to his brain," he said, "and he became bitter and suspicious."

Following the war, Bierce joined a military expedition that fought its way through Indians to reach the Pacific. He settled in wild San Francisco, among the miners, gamblers and prostitutes. Times were changing in the West and good newspapermen were needed. Bierce was determined to fit the bill and he soon became a popular writer. He earned a reputation for his wit but was considered as unpredictable and as odd as many of the people he wrote about. He was strikingly handsome, and stood six feet tall, carrying himself with an erect military bearing. His eyes, under reddish-blond brows, were blue and piercing. His flowing hair and luxuriant mustache were blond, with red streaks running through the gold. And if his eye-catching looks were not enough, Bierce had a commanding vitality. Women swooned at the sight of him and according to one account, "Young ladies claimed that they could feel him when he stood ten feet away."

Despite his good looks, Bierce was a failure with women. He simply worshipped them too much, placing them on a pedestal from which they were guaranteed to fall. When he discovered their flesh and blood failings, his love turned to dislike and hatred. His tirades against women were infamous and they became even worse after he destroyed his marriage to a lovely society belle named Ellen Day. He was married to her long enough to father two sons and a daughter, but never stopped hating his wife for having failed to live up to his impossible standards. He never had much contact with his sons, both of whom died young, and yet he maintained a loving relationship and voluminous correspondence with his daughter, Helen.

Bierce's bitterness was not only directed at his wife. He made many enemies in San Francisco. His writings contained a level of viciousness and brutality that were unrivaled in journalism of the day and he received scores of death threats. Bets were placed on how long he might live and he took to carrying a pistol with him on the streets. He was not subtle in his criticisms, but he was impartial about how he handed out abuse. In other words, Bierce hated just about everyone.

With his marriage on the rocks, Bierce took a long trip to London, where his reputation as a bitter curmudgeon took hold. His writings became even more acidic, perhaps because of his dislike for England, and yet people seemed to love what he published. He was writing seriously for the first time and ironically, he sold his first efforts to a magazine called *Fun!* They were gloomy, cynical pieces that were amazingly well received. In 1871, they were collected into a book called *Cobwebs from an Empty Skull*.

Bierce's work attracted so much attention that he was hired to write and edit a magazine called *The Lantern*. It was financed by none other than the dazzling Empress Eugenie of France, who was anxious to have the British take a friendly view toward her frivolous activities. Bierce was not above enhancing the truth when needed and he turned out to be a superb creator of propaganda. British opinion swung strongly to the Empress, who decided to show her appreciation to Bierce by commanding him to appear in her presence. It was a costly error. Ambrose Bierce had not allowed himself to be commanded by anyone since he left the Army - and certainly not by a woman. He never showed up to the scheduled meeting and he sent no regrets. The outraged Empress fired him.

In 1874, Bierce returned to San Francisco and found that he was now a celebrity, largely because he had lived in England and published a book there.

He returned to writing, working with two different local newspapers. There was no reconciliation with his wife. Instead, Bierce began to test his mettle as a drinker. He boasted proudly that no matter how much he drank, he always remained on his feet to order, and pay for, the last round of drinks. However, alcohol managed to alter the course of Bierce's life. One night after a long drinking bout, he took a long walk and then stumbled into a graveyard to sleep off the effects of the liquor. While he slumbered on a flat gravestone, he was enveloped by a damp San Francisco fog. The chill that resulted gave him acute attacks of asthma, which plagued him for the rest of his life.

Because of this, he moved to the hills around San Francisco and rarely appeared in the city. He sent his writings to the newspapers by messenger and managed to become the most popular writer west of the Rockies.

Soon, Bierce became one of the star writers in the spreading editorial empire of William Randolph Hearst. Their partnership became an arrangement that would last for more than twenty years, despite frequent arguments and resignations. Bierce and Hearst eventually came to cordially loathe one another. "Working for Hearst has all of the satisfactions of masturbation," Bierce once wrote, to the delight of his audience.

But Hearst, who had no love for his famous writer, cared more about sensationalism and a rising circulation than he did about being insulted. Bierce's writings appeared in the *New York Journal*, *New York American* and *San Francisco Chronicle*, as well as in Heart's tremendously popular magazine, *Cosmopolitan*. His name became a household word and between his sharp attacks on everyone from clergymen to politicians, he wrote short stories of the Civil War and of the bizarre and the curious. Collections such as *Fantastic Fables* and *Can Such Things Be?* began to appear. Many of the stories were based on real-life happenings, or claimed to be, and Bierce's mixing of fact with fiction continues to thrill readers today. In many of his stories, he wrote about unsolved disappearances, seeming to be obsessed by them. On several occasions, he conducted interviews at the sites where people had vanished and while many of the people he talked to expressed skepticism as to the supernatural nature of the vanishing, Bierce's stories did draw attention to the events.

Oddly, Bierce began to joke about the possibility of his own disappearance, which would no longer be a jest in 1913.

In the rustic surroundings of the California hills, Bierce lived alone. Occasionally, a woman joined him, but it never lasted for long. Bierce never had a satisfactory relationship with a woman and he never stopped hating his wife. He seemed to despise the women who were attracted to him, and considered them damaged because they were willing to give themselves to a married man.

Bierce found all the companionship that he needed with animals. He loved cats, and other assorted creatures, except for dogs, which he never liked. He kept a lizard as a pet for many years and the animal contentedly perched on his shoulder each day as he wrote. When the lizard died, he found a humble garden toad to serve as his new writing companion. He grew so fond of the toad that he let it hop around on the table when he ate his meals.

With the publication of the stories "The Damned Thing" and "The Monk and the Hangman's Daughter," Bierce truly became famous. He was never a best-selling author like Mark Twain, but a devout cult of followers sprang up. Bierce was pleased by this, although the misfortunes and tragedies of his life kept him from enjoying any true happiness. His greatest tragedy stemmed from his two sons. Although they had never been close to their father, both men died young. One of them died of acute alcoholism and the other was stabbed to death in a saloon fight.

In 1909, Hearst sent Bierce to Washington, D.C., to cover a story involving the California millionaire Collis P. Huntington. The Washington climate - humid and swelteringly hot in the summer and bitingly cold in the winter - was disliked by most of the residents of the nation's capital, but Bierce loved it. He claimed that his asthma actually improved in Washington and he decided to settle there, write for the Hearst papers in New York and San Francisco, and retire to edit his collected works. He labored over the twelve volumes with the help of his devoted secretary, Carrie Christiansen, the only woman other than his daughter that he could stand. His other published works were selling steadily and Bierce was assured of a good income. With Carrie's help, he was able to take his time and rework every story and poem that he had ever written. This kept him occupied until 1912 and then, apparently, Bierce decided to examine the prospects for the last years of his life.

At the age of seventy, Bierce made two important decisions. One of them was that he would retrace the paths that he had taken on the battlefields of the Civil War, and the second was that he would travel to Mexico, where revolutionary forces were fighting to overthrow the federal troops of the dictator, Victoriano Huerta.

In 1913, no one could foresee that the Great War would break out in Europe just one year later. But in Mexico, there was fighting. Just below the border, the forces of Pancho Villa had risen up to challenge the dictatorship of President Huerta. The United States, much concerned, had adopted a policy of watchful waiting. American troops were stationed at Laredo, Texas, but anyone who stepped over the border would find themselves in the midst of Villa's ragged, yet spirited, troops. Bierce became determined to see what was taking place in Mexico. The Civil War had been one of the greatest experiences of his life and he wanted to see combat one last time before he died.

Bierce first wanted to make a sojourn to the battlefields of his youth and in October 1913, he retraced his steps through Shiloh, Chickmauga, Murfreesboro, Kenesaw Mountain, Franklin and Nashville. After that, he stayed in New Orleans for a short time. While he was there, a reporter managed to land an interview with him and Bierce made the claim that he had never amounted to much after the Civil War. Then he told the reporter, "I'm on my way to Mexico because I like the game. I like fighting. I want to see it."

During his travels, Bierce had written long, almost daily letters to Carrie Christiansen in Washington and, less frequently, to his daughter, Helen, in Detroit. The letters continued until mid-December, when Bierce reached Laredo. His last letter to Carrie, dated December 16, 1913, was full of information, detailing the local color and his excitement about seeing the Mexican Revolution. It also contained a cryptic message: "I am going into Mexico with a pretty definite purpose which is not at present disclosable."

From there, Bierce crossed the border into Juarez, which had recently been liberated by Pancho Villa. The bandit, now turned general, issued Bierce credentials that would allow him to accompany Villa's army. By this time, Bierce was seventy and had not ridden a horse in almost thirty years. The fact that he managed to take up with the soldiers was a remarkable accomplishment for him.

He sent a last letter to his daughter dated December 26. He said that he had ridden four miles to mail it and that he had been given a sombrero as a reward for "picking off" one of the enemy with a rifle at long range. He also told her that he was leaving with the army for Ojinaga, a city under siege, the following day.

After that, the facts behind the disappearance of Ambrose Bierce end and the speculation begins.

Lack of word from Bierce bothered Carrie greatly. Helen, who did not hear from her father as often, was not as concerned. Both of them assumed that Bierce was too busy to write and was doing exactly what he wanted to be doing. Daily, they expected him to return to Texas, or to at least to get another colorful message from him in the mail. But the letters never came.

Finally, ten months after he crossed the border into Mexico, in September 1914, Helen appealed to the state department for help in finding her famous father. The commander of American troops in Texas was ordered to conduct as much of a search as possible under the circumstances. He, in turn, appealed to American consular officials in Mexico. The only information they could find was that Bierce was with Pancho Villa, acting as a military advisor.

But, if this were true, why had he not written to his daughter or to Carrie Christiansen? There were a number of American military correspondents traveling with Villa's army. Bierce could have asked any one of them to send back word that he was safe. Or Bierce himself could have found ways of slipping messages back across the border, just as he had done with the letter to his daughter in late December 1913.

The mystery of Ambrose Bierce began to capture the public's attention. In April 1915, an astounding rumor claimed that Bierce was alive and well and not in Mexico at all. By that time, Europe was also at war and several American newspapers printed a story that Bierce was attached to the staff of England's Lord Kitchener as a major specializing in recruitment. Helen immediately requested Washington to verify this and word came back from London that the story was completely false. There was no doubt that the cantankerous Bierce would have been pleased to learn that he was considered important enough to be the subject of an international hoax.

By 1919, with both European and Mexican wars ended, reporters, writers and friends began to investigate Bierce's disappearance.

George F. Weeks, a friend of Bierce's from California, set out on a personal search for the author in February 1919. No word had come from his old friend since the last days of 1913 and while most assumed that he had long since died, answers were still being sought about his final destination. In Mexico City, Weeks managed to track down an officer who told him that Bierce had been killed during a campaign in January 1914. He had collapsed during the attack on Ojinaga and had died from hardship and exposure. There was no proof of this and no one else could verify it, however, Pancho Villa, fearing world opinion, did have a policy of keeping names of foreigners off the casualty lists.

Other rumors, clues and leads suggested that Bierce was killed by a firing squad, conducted by federal soldiers. He was also said to have been killed by the volatile Pancho Villa himself after the two of them had quarreled. Or that he was killed by guides or by Villa's men after one too many insults from his sharp tongue. Some have suggested that Bierce did not go to Mexico at all and instead committed suicide over his failing health. It was also theorized that he might have been murdered and buried in secret.

Others theorized that Bierce had actually crossed back into the United States to live and die in obscurity and have a last laugh at those who puzzled over his mysterious disappearance. While this sounds like something Bierce might have done, most agreed that the lure of war would have been too strong for him to be able to resist going to Mexico. Odo B. Slade, a former member of Pancho Villa's staff, recalled an elderly American with gray hair who served as a military advisor to Villa. The American called himself "Jack Robinson" and he criticized the Mexican's battle strategies with the eye of a military expert. Slade later stated that "Robinson" quarreled violently with Villa and was shot to death when he announced his intention to leave and ally himself with the enemy.

What really happened to Bierce remains a mystery and will, without a doubt, remain that way forever. He vanished, as he wrote in his own words, into a space "through which animate and inanimate objects may fall into the invisible world and be seen and heard no more."

And that's just the way that Ambrose Bierce would have liked it.

HORNED HUMAN SKULL
AMERICAN ARTIFACTS THAT SIMPLY
SHOULDN'T EXIST

The American continent is often dismissed by researchers of the unexplained as a place that falls far short when it comes to ancient mysteries. We can't claim the length of human habitation here that residents of the Middle East or Europe countries can. Even some of our mysterious sites, like puzzling stone slabs, mysterious chambers and unusual forts seem to point to ancient visitors who came here from somewhere else.

But there are plenty of weird things that have been found in the most enigmatic corners of America. For many years, scientists and ordinary people have happened upon everything from the skeletal remains of visitors that should not exist to ancient coins that logically cannot have ended up where they were found. Other puzzles include bizarre writings and carvings, and mystery stones inscribed in ancient languages. Extensive theories have been formulated to explain such things, along with scores of books, articles and entire religious faiths.

But that's the stuff of mythology and folklore, right? It's not science, or so the skeptics say. Any substantial departure from the normal standard or the usual view of how things should work is considered to be an anomaly and, as such, is dismissed as largely suspect by the scientific community. This, however, does not keep evidence of inexplicable events from cropping up in a variety of ways and in a wide range of places.

America is literally a museum of anomalous history, filled with the weird, the curious and the incredible. However, the scientists and scholars of our country are predisposed to look askance at the following collection of improbable relics. And who can blame them? As rational beings, we tend to feel uneasy about things that we cannot explain. But read this section closely for it's possible that some of your most fondly held beliefs may be shattered beyond repair.

A burial ground of what its 1837 discoverers called "pygmies" was found near Coshocton, Ohio. The skeletons were from three to four and a half feet tall and were buried in wooden caskets. No artifacts were found with the burials, but the number of graves led the observers to suppose there may have been a great number of the little people at one time.

In 1888, seven skeletons were found buried in an upside-down sitting position facing a lake near Clearwater, Minnesota. Each of them had double rows of teeth in the upper and lower jaws. The skulls were described as having unusually low and sloping foreheads and prominent brows.

Another strange discovery took place in 1911 near Lovelock, Nevada. Two miners began working the rich bat guano deposits in Lovelock Cave and had removed several carloads of the substance before coming upon a collection of Indian relics. Soon afterward, they discovered a mummy -- a six-and-a-half-foot-tall person with "distinctly red hair." According to the legends of the local Paiute Indians, a tribe of fierce, red-haired giants (called the Si-te-cahs) had once lived in the area. The giants had been the mortal enemies of the other tribes, who finally took matters in hand by banding together and driving the red-haired ones away. A mining engineer from Lovelock named John T. Reid became convinced that the discovery of the mummy substantiated the Paiute legend. Reed spent years collecting evidence that the mysterious red-haired tribe had existed.

A year later, the discovery of the mummy, along with the other relics, caught the interest of the University of California at Berkeley and the Nevada State Historical Society. They sent archaeologist L.L. Loud to investigate the cave. He managed to salvage a number of other artifacts from the mining operation. His excavations were followed in 1924 by M.R. Harrington, from the Museum of the American Indian in New York. He too collected artifacts, but found no other bones. He also asked that the original mummy be reburied to mollify the Indian workers on the site, who had been complaining that the remains weren't being treated respectfully.

His requests were ignored and over the next few years, more red-haired remains were found in the Lovelock area. After measuring the intact bones and bone fragments, Reid and others were able to determine that the skeletons belonged to people who ranged in height six to ten feet tall.

Today, a few of the remains, including a skull, some bones and a few artifacts, are part of the collection of the Humboldt Museum in Winnemucca, Nevada. There are also artifacts from Lovelock at the Nevada State Historical Society in Reno, but no bones. There is no mention there of giant people, but the fact that the red-haired Indians did exist is no longer disputed.

But there were other giants to be found in America, leading some to speculate that perhaps a race of abnormally tall beings once roamed the continent. For instance, in 1879, a skeleton that measured nine feet, eight inches tall was found in a stone burial mound in Brewersville, Indiana. A mica necklace was found around its neck and a human image formed of burnt clay was nestled at its feet. The mound was excavated by Indiana archaeologists, scientists from New York and Ohio, a local physician named Dr. Charles Green and the owner of the farm where it was found, a man named Robison. The bones were then stored in the Robison grain mill until 1937, when the mill was washed away by a flood.

A History of Livingston County, New York, 1824: According to an account from a man named Jesse Stanley, who had come to Mount Morris in 1811, there had been a large burial mound that covered the site where a General Mills had built his home. The mound was removed around 1820 and inside of it, workmen found arrowheads, a brass kettle, knives and a number of skeletons. Among them was a human skeleton of enormous size, the jawbone of which was so large that a man named Adam Holsander was able to place it, mask-like, over his chin and jaw. He was the largest man in the settlement, but the skull was much larger than his own face.

History of Winona County, Minnesota, 1883: While there had been Indian bones and relics uncovered around the county for years, a startling find was made "not long since" when some men digging near Mineral Bluff, found a skeleton of unusual size about 150 feet above the river. On measuring, the skeleton was found to be ten feet in length, with all of its parts in proper proportion to its size. Embedded in the skull, they found a copper hatchet and an arrowhead that was nine inches long.
Another skeleton, nine feet long, was found in the village of Dresbach while some men were digging a road. The article went on to say of the bones, "Their size, form and structure would lead those well-versed in paleontology to believe they belonged to a race prior to the Indian... Where they came from, when they lived and from whence they have gone, is only conjecture and speculation."

Athens, Georgia, Banner, May 6, 1884: An unusual discovery was made in Carterville, Georgia in May 1884 after committee of scientists opened a nearby burial mound. After removing several feet of dirt, they uncovered a layer of large flagstones that had been carefully fitted together. Beneath the stones was a kind of vault that contained the skeleton of a man. It measured just over seven feet in length. The remaining hair on the skull was coarse, jet black and hung to its waist. It had a cooper crown on its head. Nearby were the bodies of several small children of various sizes, all of which were decorated with beads and bone carvings. When the children's skeletons were removed, they were found to be encased in a basket of reeds, which had been lined with animal skins. All of the bodies had been carefully preserved, suggesting that they had been of some importance in their culture.

New York Times, May 5, 1885: An article in this edition mentioned an archaeological discovery in Licking County, Ohio, an area that holds numerous ancient burial mounds and had been attracting researchers since the early 1800s. In early May, a mound near Homer was opened by several young boys and a further search of the burial site revealed a large vault several feet under the earth. The vault, with a stone floor and bark covering, contained four huge skeletons, three being over seven feet tall and the other, a full eight feet.

The skeletons had been laid out with their feet to the east on a bed of charcoal, in which there were numerous burned bones. Around the neck of the largest skeleton was a necklace made from stone beads. The grave contained about thirty stone vessels and implements, including a curiously carved pipe.

Baltimore American, November 15, 1897: The Maryland Academy of Sciences released the information that the skeleton of an Indian more than seven feet tall was discovered near Antietam. This was the third skeleton of such size that the Academy had discovered in Maryland. The newspaper stated that the "bones of the leg are nearly as thick as those of a horse and the length of the long bones is exceptional." The skeletons were all found in Frederick County, near Antietam Creek, which was once the battleground of two tribes: the Catawba and the Delaware. Legend had it that before the arrival of the white man, there had been a village located there that was occupied by Indians of great stature.

Ohio Morning Sun News Herald, April 14, 1904: Reports stated that the giant skeleton of a man was found on the Wolverton farm, a short distance from Tippecanoe City, Ohio. The skeleton measured eight feet from the top of its head to its ankles, but its feet were missing. The skull was reportedly large enough to fit as a helmet over an average man's head. The giant set of bones was one of seven, buried in a circle, the feet of all being pointed towards the center.

And in addition to giants, other, even weirder things have also been found...

Cincinnati Enquirer, July 14, 1880: A mound that was opened in Muskingum County, Ohio, yielded an unexpected discovery for researchers. A number of skeletons were found buried down about eight feet from the top of the mound. In one grave was a female skeleton, encased in a clay coffin. She was holding the skeleton of a child in her arms and next to her head was a stone tablet, which we'll explore further in a moment. In another grave, there were two skeletons - male and female. The female was facing downward and the man was on top of her, with the face looking upward. The male skeleton measured nine feet in length and the female was eight feet long. There were seven other skeletons, all found in single graves, lying on their sides. The smallest of them was seven feet, nine inches in length and the largest was ten feet long. Oddly, none of the skulls had any teeth, except for the female in the clay coffin.

But giants and teeth were not the strangest things about this discovery. That oddity was a single item: the stone tablet found with the woman in the clay coffin. The stone was an irregularly-shaped piece of red sandstone that weighed about eighteen pounds. Carved into the stone were two lines of Egyptian hieroglyphics.

But that's not the weirdest thing found. According to the archives at Ohio State University, a man named David Wyrick made a bizarre discovery in a burial mound about ten miles south of Newark, Ohio, in 1860. Amidst the bones of the dead, he found an inscribed stone that bore a condensed version of the biblical "Ten Commandments," in a peculiar form of post-exile, square Hebrew letters. The bearded and robed figure on the front was identified as Moses in the letters above the figure's head.

The inscription was carved into a fine-grained black stone that was identified by geologists Ken Bork and David Hawkins of Denison University as limestone - but a type of limestone that was not generally found in the surrounding area. The stone was found inside a sandstone box, smooth on the outside and hollowed out so that it perfectly fit the "holy stone," as it came to be called. The inscription began with a non-alphabetic symbol at the top of the front, ran down the left side of the front, around every available space on the back and sides, and then back up the right side of the front to end where it begins, as though it was meant to be read repetitively.

It was noted that the stone fit well in a person's hand and that the lettering was worn precisely where the stone would be in contact with the last three fingers and palm if held in the left hand. There was also a puzzling handle at the bottom that could be used to secure the stone to the left arm with a strap. Historians concluded that it was a Jewish arm phylactery for prayer, used during the period of the Second Temple. However, they could provide no answers as to how it ended up in an ancient burial ground in the middle of Ohio.

On August 10, 1892, the *Chicago Tribune* reported that a discovery had been made in a field near LaHarpe in Hancock County, Illinois. Two men, Wyman Huston and Daniel Lovitt, were hunting ground squirrels on Huston's farm when one of their dogs chased a squirrel into a hole beneath a fallen, long-dead tree. As they pulled the tree out of the way, the stump was pulled up out of the ground and under its roots they found two sandstone tablets, about ten inches tall and about one-half inch thick. The tablets lay on top of each other and the sides that faced together contained strange inscriptions in Roman-like capital letters that had been cut into the stone with some sharp instrument.

The men brought the tablets to LaHarpe, where they were inspected by several "antiquarians" but none of them could decipher the inscriptions. Huston allowed the stones to be sent to the Smithsonian Institution in Washington, D.C. for investigation but there was never any information released about their findings.

And then there are the skulls - with horns. Oddly, though, this story has become rather garbled over the years, apparently crediting the discovery to several scientists who had nothing to do with it. In September 1916, a newspaper article in the *Charleston Daily Mail* (West Virginia), printed a story about a discovery that had been made a few months earlier, on July 13, by Pennsylvania historian Dr. George P. Donehoo and two professors, A.B. Skinner from the American Indian Museum in Philadelphia and Warren King Morehead, curator of the Robert S. Peabody Museum of Archaeology at Phillips Academy in Andover, Massachusetts. While working at a burial mound at Tioga Point, near Sayre, Pennsylvania, they uncovered the bones of sixty-eight men, which they estimated had been buried at least 700 to 800 years previously. The average height of the skeletons was seven feet, but many were taller.

That's strange enough, but the story got even stranger - although it had nothing to do with these eminent scholars, who were considered to be experts in the field. Morehead has often been referred as the dean of American archaeology. George Donehoo wrote a five-volume history of Pennsylvania and served as secretary of the state historical commission. Professor A.B. Skinner was likely Alanson Buck Skinner (1886-1925). Skinner was educated at Columbia and Harvard universities. He trained as an ethnologist specializing in the study of American Indians and was affiliated with several prestigious museums, including the American Museum of Natural History. They apparently made a strange discovery - but not the really weird one.

A few days after the original article, the *Charleston Daily Mail* revisited the story of the burial mound and added that while the exact date was not clear, another burial mound had been discovered earlier in Sayre, Pennsylvania, likely in the 1880s. During the excavation, several human skulls with horns were reportedly found. Reports say that except for the horns, which protruded from the skulls about two inches above the eyebrows, the skeletons were perfectly normal human males, expect for the fact that they were about seven feet tall. They were estimated to have been buried around A.D. 1200. The bones were allegedly sent to a museum, where they later disappeared.

Over the years, the two stories became intertwined and Donehoo, Skinner and Morehead were also credited with this find, but - if it actually happened - it occurred almost three decades earlier. The confusion was caused by one writer passing along another writer's research multiple times over the years.

Did someone really find horned human skulls? The odds are we'll never know for sure, but the confusion over who found them has added another element of mystery to what already was a very weird tale.

PEDRO

The Mystery of the Wyoming Mummy

Perhaps one of the oddest exhibits in our cabinet of curiosities is the mummy of what appears to be a tiny little man. Dubbed "Pedro" after it was discovered in the mountains of Wyoming, many believed it to be proof of a Native American legend about a race of little people who once inhabited the region. Others immediately dismissed it as a hoax - but was it?

One thing is sure: there has been a lot of confusion about this story over the years, including in my own writings. Hopefully, this account will set some of the story straight - or as straight as it can be with a tale this strange.

In October 1934 (not 1932, as is often reported), two prospectors were seeking gold in a ravine at the base of the San Pedro Mountains, southwest of Casper, Wyoming. Cecil Main and Frank Carr were working along the edge of the rocks and thought they spotted indications of gold in the stone walls of the ravine. They inserted sticks of dynamite into some cracks in the gulch and started blasting away the rock. As the resulting dust cloud began to disperse, they discovered a small cavern behind the wall. They went inside and found what appeared to be a natural cave, the entrance to which had apparently been covered over years before. They looked around, never imagining what they were about to find.

Sitting on a small ledge inside the cave was a mummified man with his legs crossed. His hands were folded in his lap and his skin was brown and wrinkled. The face was oddly proportioned with a flat nose, a low forehead, and a wide mouth with thin lips. In spite of his strange features, he appeared to be an ordinary person -- except for the fact that he was only fourteen inches tall.

As the incredulous prospectors peered closer, they couldn't believe their eyes. The tiny mummy did not appear to be that of a child, but rather a smirking old man. Bewildered, they carefully removed the figure from the ledge and took it back with them to Casper, where it attracted a great deal of interest.

Photographs and a signed affidavit leave little doubt that the discovery of the little figure was real. The affidavit, dated November 13, 1936 and signed by Cecil Main, one of the prospectors, states that the mummy was "found in a sealed cave, on a rock ledge about two and one half feet from the ground...there was nothing else in the cave." The affidavit further states that the mummy was "now owned by Homer F. Sherrill, and located in the Field Museum in Chicago, Illinois." The affidavit was sworn in Scotts Bluff County, Nebraska, and subsequently recorded in Hot Springs County, Wyoming on August 16, 1943.

From the time of its discovery until it was lost in 1950, the mummy traveled a path that will probably never be possible to document fully. A 1979 newspaper article reported that the two prospectors "took the mummy back to Casper with them as a curiosity. Although they were ridiculed for perpetrating a hoax, the body made the rounds of local sideshows in a glass bottle. . . ."

In 1950, reporter Lou Musser wrote that the mummy for years "has been the center of much controversy locally." Musser noted that before it was purchased by Ivan Goodman, a Casper automobile dealer, it was displayed by a prior owner in the Jones Drugstore in Meeteetse, Wyoming. The prior owner was believed to be a man named Floyd Jones, and while the price that Goodman paid for the mummy has never been recorded, a selling price of "several thousand dollars" has been mentioned.

There is also some confusion about where the mummy came from. Floyd Jones said that it was found by a "sheepherder" in the mountains. Even the sworn claim that the mummy was at the Field Museum is open to question. Archivist Armand Esai notes that the Field Museum has no record of the mummy's presence during that time. The item could have been there on loan or for identification, but because it was not part of the museum's official collection, the mummy was not listed in the records.

Thus, facts discovered after the recording of the affidavit are sketchy, but Ivan Goodman's ownership by 1950 is certain. This was confirmed by his son, Dixon Goodman, of Casper. The elder Goodman took the mummy to Dr. Harry Shapiro, curator of biological anthropology at the American Museum of Natural History in New York City. Shapiro examined it, took X-rays and sent the films around that time to George Gill, then professor of biological anthropology at the University of Wyoming.

Most suspected that the mummy was a hoax but Shapiro agreed to examine it. He was intrigued enough by his initial examination to have the mummified remains X-rayed. He was still nearly positive that he would find the mummy was either a clever fabrication, or the body of a deformed child.

Instead, he found that "Pedro" (as the mummy was dubbed on the carnival circuit) possessed an undeniably man-like skeleton, in spite of his size. The figure had a complete set of ribs, fully formed arms and legs, a backbone that had once suffered an injury and even a fractured left collarbone. This broken bone could have been part of the injuries that Shapiro deduced had killed the little man. It seemed that the flat appearance of the mummy's head came about when Pedro was hit with a violent blow to the skull while still alive. A dark substance on the head was found to be exposed brain tissue and congealed blood.

Shapiro, who died in 1990 at age eighty-seven, was considered the dean of forensic anthropologists. He began trying to discover Pedro's age at the time of death. He noted that his skull had been closed (before the injury), which means that he could not have been an infant as a baby's skull does not close for some time. He also found that Pedro had a full set of teeth, along with large and pointed canines. Shapiro estimated that Pedro had been about sixty-five years old when he died and that his death had not been in recent times, but far back in history. He had apparently been given a ceremonial burial.

These findings sparked more interest and debate and many spoke of the legends of the Shoshone and Crow Indians of Wyoming, who told tales of the "little people" that had once lived among them. Could Pedro have been one of these little people? Some believed so (and many still do) but other scientists would later refute Shapiro's findings.

In 1950, after the death of Ivan Goodman, the mummy became the property of Leonard Wadler. What became of it next remains a mystery for it was never seen again. And while it may have vanished from the public eye, interest in it refused to die.

In 1979, Pedro's photos and X-rays were given to Wyoming University anthropologist George Gill, who completely disagreed with Shapiro's theories about the mummy. He announced that the remains were not those of a small adult, but rather those of an infant suffering from anencephaly, a condition in which most of the brain and cranium do not develop. While this could account for the state of Pedro's head, it does not explain his adult features and full set of teeth. But a French zoologist named Dr. Francois de Sarre came up with an explanation for Pedro's features in 1993. He stated that the mummy was that of a deformed infant to which the skin of an adult male had been molded, as headhunters do when creating shrunken heads.

Could he have been right? Who knows? Gill refused to discount the possibility that Pedro might have been a member of an unknown prehistoric race of small people. The race might provide the basis for the Native American legends of the "little people," descriptions of which are very close to the way Pedro may have looked when he was alive. According to these traditions, the small people sometimes killed their own when they became terminally ill by smashing their skulls in with a rock.

Interest in the mummy continues today. In 2005, a Wyoming man put up a $10,000 reward for anyone who was able to reveal Pedro's current whereabouts. So far, the reward has not been claimed.

DOWN OZARK WAY: CAMP AT NIGHT AND SEE,
FREAK SPOOK MYSTERY LIGHT, AT LOGCABIN
ON 43 HI. BETWEEN JOPLIN AND SENECA MISSOURI.

PICTURE POSTCARD

The Hornet Spooklight

Located about twenty miles southwest of Joplin, Missouri, is a roughly paved road where my favorite American spook light puts in a regular appearance. This old and otherwise forgotten track runs across the Oklahoma border but is only about four miles long. Nearby is the border village of Hornet and close to that is the site of what once was a spook light museum. The place is remote and far from civilization, so why do so many people come here?

They are searching for an unexplained enigma, a puzzle that many of them find. It has been seen along this road since 1866 and has created such a mystery that even the Army Corps of Engineers officially concluded that it was a "mysterious light of unknown origin." It has been called by many names since it started appearing near what is called the Devil's Promenade, but it's most commonly known as the Hornet Spook Light.

Over the years, the enigmatic light has attracted scores of visitors, who used to drive or hike in to the area and have "spook light parties" along the road. They came in droves, hoping to photograph, track down or just get a glimpse of the light. They wore spook light t-shirts, bought postcards and watched the light through a telescope at the museum for twenty-five cents. But like so many roadside attractions of yesterday, fascination with the spook light has waned - just as the light itself has faded over the last couple of decades. It's not seen nearly as often as it used to be, and like old Route 66, which once passed by just a short distance away, the spook light seems as though it's becoming just a memory of days gone by.

But it wasn't always this way. The spook light danced along the old road, looking like a ball of fire, for nearly a century and a half, varying in size from that of a softball to a basketball. It spins down the center of the road at great speed, rises up high, and bobs and weaves to the right and left. It appears to be a large lantern, but there is never anyone carrying it. The light has appeared inside vehicles, seems to retreat when it is pursued and never allows anyone to get too close to it. Does it have some sort of intelligence? This remains just one of the many mysteries connected to this light.

No one has ever been injured by the light but many claim to have been frightened by it while walking or driving down this road at night. Sometimes it seems to come out of nowhere and a few witnesses claim they have felt the heat from it as it passed close to them. Occasionally, some observer will even take a shot or two at the light, like Franklin Rossman, who lived near the Devil's Promenade for years. He twice attempted to shoot the light with a hunting rifle but the shots had no effect on it whatsoever. He told a spook light investigator that he was unable to judge the distance to the light because it had such an odd look to it. When asked what he meant by this, Rossman was unable to explain. It just looked "sort of blurry," he said.

There have been many theories that have attempted to explain why this mysterious light appears on this lonely stretch of roadway. In the nineteenth century, a number of legends sprung up around the place. One of them claimed the light was connected to the spirit of two young Quapaw Indians who died in the area many years ago. Another claimed the light was the spirit of an Osage Indian chief who had been beheaded on the Devil's Promenade and the light was said to be his torch as he searched for his missing head. Another legend tells of a farmer whose children were kidnapped by Indians and he set off looking for them with only a lantern to light his way. The light is said to be that very lantern as the farmer's ghost continues to search for the children.

Locals claim that the stories of the Hornet light originated back in the 1800s but most printed accounts are of a much more recent vintage. As far as is known, the first account of it appeared in the *Kansas City Star* in 1936 and then in the 1947 book "Ozark Superstitions" by Vance Randolph, the famed Missouri folklorist. Randolph was the first to put into print the oral legends of the light's origins, from beheaded Indians to lost children.

In 1958, a writer for *Ford Times* investigated the light and described it as a diffused, orange glow that floated and weaved along the roadway. He also noted that it seemed to change size as he watched it, varying between the size of apple to that of a bushel basket. He also saw the light split off into three different lights and then merge into a single light, as it settled down upon the branch of a tree and changed colors from orange to blue.

Over the years, the light has been studied, researched, chased, photographed and shot at -- but what is it? While legends give one reason for the light, its genuine origins seem to present a formidable problem. Many suggestions have been offered as to what could cause the light to appear, and for many years the most popular theory was that it was merely a will-o'-the-wisp, the name given to a biological phenomenon that is caused by the decay of wood and organic materials. The emission of light that comes from the decay often glows brightly and can be seen on occasion in wooded areas and damp regions. As fascinating as this is, it really doesn't explain the Hornet light. Instances of will-o'-the-wisp simply do not give off the intensity of light that has been reported along the Devil's Promenade.

Another suggestion has been the ever-popular "marsh gas." Unfortunately, while an abundance of marsh gas in a marsh or swamp would certainly be flammable, it cannot spontaneously light itself. Even if it did, wind and rain would soon extinguish any flame that appeared. Strong winds that have been reported during sightings of the Hornet light do not seem to disturb it and they don't keep it from moving in whatever direction it pleases.

There have also been suggestions that the light might be a glow coming from minerals in the area. This seems doubtful too, as the light does not always appear in the same place. One plausible suggestion theorizes that the light might be formed by electrical fields in areas where earthquakes and ground shifts take place. This is a possibility since there are fault lines in the region. Four large earthquakes took place in the area in the early nineteenth century that had a devastating effect on this part of the state. It is possible that the lights starting appearing around the time of the earthquakes but were not reported until the population in the area started to grow around the time of the Civil War.

Other "experts" claim they have the mystery solved and that the light is caused by the headlights of automobiles driving on the highway about five miles east of what's known as "Spook Light Road." They say the highway is on a direct line with it but at a slightly lower elevation. When it is pointed out that a high ridge separates the area from the highway, the experts explain how refraction causes light to bend and creates the eerie effect that so many people have reported as the spook light.

Believe it or not, several investigations that have been conducted at the site have shown that some of the sightings may be attributed to this. Dr. George W. Ward, formerly of the Bureau of Standards in Washington, D.C., and later with the Midwest Research Institute, investigated the light in 1945. He said that shortly after arriving at the site, he saw a diffused glow appear over some low hills. A few moments later, a sphere of light appeared that looked to be four to six feet in diameter. Ward humorously added that the publicity director of the Midwest Institute remarked to the others assembled that he had seen all that he cared to, and as the light approached the group, he quickly locked himself inside their car.

But Ward was critical about the source of the light. During his study, he decided that the light must originate to the west of the viewing site and over the range of hills in the distance. He surmised that the refraction of auto headlights from a road that was in line with the country lane could create an illusion of a traveling light. Dr. Ward checked his maps and found that such a road did exist, a section of highway that ran east and west between Commerce and Quapaw, Oklahoma. He suggested that an airplane might be used to spot cars on the highway and relay the information to observers at the spook light site. If the lights could be shown to correspond with the Hornet light, the mystery would be solved.

Captain Bob E. Loftin followed these speculations with his own experiments a few years later. He discovered that colored test lights that were placed on the suspected areas of Route 66 could be seen from Spook Light Road. He further reasoned that the presence of moving cars along the highway would appear as spheres of light, closely grouped together. He also added that changing humidity and temperature would cause the lights that were created to behave strangely. This, they reasoned, would explain the number of unusual stories told about the way the light acted.

And while this would admittedly explain some of the sightings of the Hornet light, it is impossible that it could explain them all. The most important point to remember is that the light was being seen before the invention of automobiles.

These were far from the only investigations conducted at the site. Author Raymond Bayless embarked on an extensive study of the spook light in October 1963. Around dusk on the evening of October 17, he and several assistants spotted the light for the first time, as it appeared as a bright light some distance along the roadway. He reported that the light fluctuated in intensity and at times became two separate lights, hovering one above the other. The light returned again about an hour later and according to Bayless, was so bright that it caused a reflection on the dirt surface of the road. A few minutes after the light appeared, the investigators began moving westward along the road in pursuit of it. The light receded backward (or appeared to) as they got closer to it. The group began navigating the hills and ravines of the road and the light vanished. It did not reappear until they reached a point near the spook light museum, which was still in operation at that time.

The "Spooksville Museum," then operated by Leslie W. Robertson, offered not only photographs and a collection of accounts about the light but also a viewing platform for people to observe the light with the naked eye or through telescopes and cameras. A member of Bayless' group set up a small refracting telescope on the platform and they were able to learn that what appeared to be a single light was actually composed of a number of smaller lights. Bayless stated that they moved very close together, weaving slightly, expanding and contracting back and forth. It was amber and gold in color and sometimes gained a reddish tint for a few moments at a time. Through the telescope, the edges of the light were observed to be like a "flame" in that they were not uniform and constantly changed.

Bayless was fascinated with the many explanations given for the light and was able to rule out almost all of the ones that had been proposed, including the theory that all of the sightings could be explained away as the refraction of auto headlights. In fact, Mr. Arthur Holbrook, a resident of the area and a man who had investigated the light many times, told Bayless that he had first seen the light in 1905. At that time, Holbrook explained, there were only about a dozen automobiles in Joplin, the closest large town. He also added that there had been no highways at that period and because of this, headlights could not have explained his sightings of the light. The few cars that were in existence in the area at that time did not travel about on remote, dirt lanes that were best suited for horses and any autos that would have traveled around the region were only fitted with oil and carbide lamps, which would not have been capable of creating the long, intense beams of modern headlights. To add even more credibility to his account, Holbrook was in the automotive profession and would have been very aware of the number of autos in the region in those days and the state of the roads and highways.

But did the light actually exist before automobiles came to southwest Missouri or was this merely a part of the local legend? Many skeptics claimed that the enigma's longevity was merely a part of the light's folklore, but Bayless did not agree. After conducting a number of interviews in the area, he began to believe that it had been seen in the 1800s. He did not feel that his own sighting of the light was comparable to auto headlights but as it had been shown that some lights would appear on the road as refraction from the highway, he needed to gather as much evidence as possible to show the light pre-dated automobiles. Holbrook had experienced his first sighting of the light in 1905 and had heard of the light for several years before that. After that first sighting, he rode out in a buggy to see the light many times and told Bayless that the light was the same in the 1960s as it had been in 1905.

Bayless also interviewed Leslie Robertson, the curator of the Spooksville Museum, who first saw the light in 1916. He was only fourteen years old at the time and during his lifetime he had seen the light literally "thousands of times."

John Muening of Joplin first saw the light around 1928 and had heard stories about it for a number of years before that. He told Bayless, "We have watched it all night... Highway 66 has nothing to do with the light. It couldn't have, as it didn't exist when the light was first seen, of that I am sure."

Bayless also collected testimony from Rene Waller of Joplin, who also said that she had seen the Hornet light before Route 66 was put in through Quapaw, Oklahoma. She stated that the original highway was a dirt road that was traveled infrequently. She had first seen the light in the late 1920s, when auto headlights would have been too seldom on the road to have created the effect of the spook light.

Mr. and Mrs. L.C. Ferguson of Joplin also stated that they had been familiar with the Hornet light since 1910 and at the time they first saw it, they were told that the light had been seen along the road for many years already.

These claims of the light's longevity were substantiated in the early 1960s by J. Leonard, a member of the Miami Indian tribe. He told Bayless that his parents had spoken of the light many times when he was a boy. He could personally remember seeing it for as long as he had been alive (he had been born in 1896) and according to stories at that time, the light had been in existence for several generations or at least one hundred years. Another Native American from the area, Guy Jennison, recalled hearing about the light when he was a boy attending the Quapaw Mission School in 1892. By that time, it was a local topic of conversation, implying that reports of the light had been around for at least a few years. Jennison, like Leonard, believed that the light might have appeared several generations before, based on the Indian legends that had been suggested to explain its origin. Unfortunately, during the time of the Bayless investigation, there were few Native Americans left who had knowledge of when the stories originated.

Even without the earlier dates, Bayless was able to show that the Hornet light existed prior to the use of automobiles in the area. He did not dispute the idea that some sightings could be caused by headlights, but he debunked the idea that headlights could be the *only* cause. Others have suggested that perhaps lights from Quapaw or from mining camps in the area could have caused a refraction of light, thus creating the Spook Light, but there is little evidence to suggest this or to suggest that these stationary lights could manage to create a light that moves about and comes and goes as the Hornet light does.

With that in mind, Raymond Bayless' investigations of the light should be considered groundbreaking. Although he certainly did not solve the mystery of the Hornet light, he did manage to present some compelling evidence for its early existence. The only problem to come out of his investigations was that he managed, by showing how long the light had been around and by showing that not all of the sightings could be dismissed as having a simple explanation, to make the mystery even more perplexing.

Bayless was not the first, nor would he be the last, to investigate the Hornet Spook Light. Literally thousands of curiosity-seekers have visited the Devil's Promenade over the years and many of those are serious researchers of the unknown. The old "Spook Light Museum" is gone now but long after Leslie Robertson came Garland "Spooky" Middleton, who also operated the place for a time. Along with displaying photographs and newspaper articles about the light, Middleton sold soda to tourists and entertained them with anecdotes about his own encounters with the mysterious light, like the time he saw it in a field near the museum. He said that the light appeared one night on the road, just after sunset, and began to roll like a ball, giving off sparks as it traveled along the gravel road. It entered a field where several cattle grazed and managed to move among the animals, not disturbing them at all.

What is the Hornet Spook Light? No one knows but I think that it's still described best in the words of the Army Corps of Engineers as a "mysterious light of unknown origin." Regardless of what it may be, one thing is certain: it's something that has to be seen, if possible. There are those who believe that the Hornet light is slowly burning itself out, that sightings of the light are going to become more and more infrequent in the years to come. I hope that this is not the case, and not only for my own selfish desire to see the light again, but also for all of those who have not had the chance to experience this wonder first-hand.

The Hornet Spook Light is one of America's greatest unsolved mysteries and since no one has managed to puzzle out the answers to this enigma just yet, we need the spook light to be around for future generations to ponder for themselves.

ROCKS, ICE AND LITTLE FISH
STRANGE THINGS THAT FALL FROM THE SKY

Throughout the strange history of America, there have been many bizarre instances recorded when things have fallen from the skies that simply shouldn't have been up there in the first place. There have been showers of frogs and toads, along with fish, snakes and worms. Blood has been said to fall from the heavens, as well as chunks of meat. Reports of these things and others have been around for centuries. The stories of such things range in believability from the logically possible to the downright incredible.

And for those who believe such things only date back to recent times, it should be noted that the earliest reports of strange falls from the sky appear in the Bible: the Book of Joshua in the Old Testament to be exact. According to one story, the Israelites, led by Joshua, routed the Amorite army and were in hot pursuit of the survivors when a shower of stones fell from the sky and killed more of the enemy than died by the Israelite sword. The Bible goes on to mention other strange happenings in regards to falls from the sky, with the frogs that plagued Egypt and the mysterious "manna" that fell from the heavens to feed the Israelites after they crossed the Red Sea not being the least of them.

The earliest reports that I could find of such happenings in America date back to 1828. It was said that after ten to twelve days of rain, a partially dug ditch that belonged to a Joseph Muse of Cambridge, Maryland, was found to contain hundreds of fish. The creatures ranged in size from four to seven inches long and were apparently jack perch and sun perch. There had been no water in the ditch before the rainfall and the nearest river was over a mile away. There was no explanation as to how they could have gotten there.

In 1833, something more unusual than fish fell from the sky over the town of Rahway, New Jersey. On November 13, locals saw what they described as "fiery rain" falling to the ground. When the glowing masses struck the ground, they turned into "lumps of jelly." The lumps were said to be transparent and became round, flattened masses when they landed. Within hours, the jelly disintegrated and became a pile of small white particles that crumbled into dust when touched. The strange masses were reported at the same time that a meteor shower was taking place over the eastern United States and may have been connected to it in some way.

Troops stationed at an army post near San Francisco had their own encounter with strange objects from the sky on July 24, 1851. On that afternoon, soldiers who were on the drill field reported being pelted with spatters of blood and pieces of meat, which were apparently beef. The blood and meat fell from a cloudless sky and ranged in size from a pigeon's egg to that of an orange. Several pieces of meat were given to the post surgeon and he described some of them as being slightly spoiled, as if they had been left out in the sun too long.

A similar event was said to have taken place in Simpson County, North Carolina, on February 15 of that same year. Witnesses reported that pieces of flesh, liver, brains and blood rained down from the sky over an area that was roughly thirty feet wide and about 250 yards long.

On June 15, 1857 a farmer who lived in Ottawa, Illinois, reported that he heard a hissing sound in the sky and he looked up to see a shower of cinders falling to the earth. They landed on the ground in a V-shaped pattern about fifty feet from where he was standing and caused the ground to steam and the grass to catch fire. The larger cinders buried themselves in the earth and even the smallest pieces were inserted into the ground at least partially. The farmer, whose name was Bradley, noticed a small, dense, dark cloud "hanging over the garden" at the time of the fall. The weather that day had been damp and a little rainy but no thunder or lightning had been reported.

The children of Lake County, California, must have been happy on the nights of September 2 and 11, 1857. According to the History of Napa and Lake Counties by Lyman L. Palmer, a shower of candy apparently fell on some portions of the county on those evenings. The report states: "It is said that on both of these nights there fell a shower of candy or sugar. The crystals were from one-eighth to one-fourth of an inch in length and the size of a goose quill. Syrup was made of it by some of the lady residents of the section."

Another shower of flesh and blood was reported in California on August 1, 1869. The shower lasted for three minutes and covered about two acres of J. Hudson's farm near Los Nietos. The day was clear and windless and the bloody flesh fell in strips that were from one to six inches long. Many of them were reportedly covered with fine hairs, as if stripped from the body of an animal.

In August 1870, a deluge of "water lizards" hit Sacramento, California. The small reptiles were from two to eight inches long and they were alive when they hit the ground. The initial shower rained the lizards down so that they nearly covered the roof of the opera house. The little reptiles slid down the roof and into the rain spouts, from which they emerged onto the pavement around the opera house, covering it. The *Sacramento Reporter* stated that hundreds of them survived for several days in rainwater that flooded a partially dug cellar that was located nearby.

One of the strangest stories of this sort took place on March 3, 1876 when flakes of meat fell over an area 100 yards long and fifty yards wide near the Bath, Kentucky, home of Mr. and Mrs. Allen Crouch. The sky was clear at the time and the flakes of meat were described as being one to three or four inches square and appeared to be fresh beef. At any rate, according to two men who (for some reason) decided to taste the meat, it was neither mutton nor venison.

Or perhaps it wasn't meat at all, wrote Mr. Leopold Brandeis, whose article on the strange fall appeared in a July issue of the *Sanitarian*. He explained that the so-called "meat" was really nothing more than a substance that he called "nostic" -- "a low form of vegetable substance." He did not, however, explain how this substance managed to fall from the sky. His opinion on the matter did not last for long for he was soon contacted by Dr. A. Mead Edwards, president of the Newark Scientific Association, who asked for a sample of the material that had been collected from Bath County. Brandeis was kind enough to give him the entire specimen, along with the information that he had obtained it from a doctor in Brooklyn, who had in turn been given it by a Professor Chandler.

Shortly after this, a letter from Dr. Allan McLane Hamilton was posted to the *Medical Record*, saying that he and Dr. J.W.S. Arnold had examined the material from the Kentucky meat shower under a microscope. The material, which had been given to them by Professor Chandler, was identified as being lung tissue from either a human infant or a horse! According to the letter, "the structure of the organ in these two cases" was apparently "very similar."

After reading the letter, Dr. Edwards called on Dr. Hamilton and was given a sample of the material that he had been studying. He was told that the samples had been sent from Kentucky to the editor of the *Agriculturist*, who had given them to Professor Chandler. And while the trail of where the samples had come from seemed to be growing longer and longer, Edwards noted that they seemed to be similar in character and age, although the sample given to him by Brandeis was less well-preserved. Soon after, Edwards was shown a microscopic slide of a third sample of the Kentucky meat, which had been given to Professor J. Phin of the *American Journal of Microscopy* by a Mr. Walmsley of Philadelphia, who had in turn received it from Kentucky. The slide contained something that was "undoubtedly striated muscular fibre."

Phin also showed Edwards a fourth sample that had been collected by A.T. Parker of Lexington, Kentucky. This sample also turned out to be muscle tissue but Edwards wanted to see more. He wrote to Parker and was sent three more samples, two of which turned out to be cartilage and the third, more muscle tissue. Edwards also passed along an explanation for the bizarre event that was currently making the rounds in Kentucky.

Locals believed that the meat had been vomited up by buzzards, "who, as is their custom, seeing one of their companions disgorge himself, immediately followed suit." Parker did not explain just how many buzzards would be required to vomit that much meat, how much they would have had to have eaten, or just how high they had been flying as to render themselves invisible to those on the ground, never mind the question of whether they had been dining on horses or human infants!

Perhaps almost as strange was the rain of living snakes that fell over the southern part of Memphis, Tennessee, in 1877. These creatures reportedly ranged in length from about a foot to 18 inches, and were presumed by the people of Memphis to have been swept into the air by a hurricane. Although even *Scientific American* asked where so many snakes would exist "in such abundance" (they fell by the thousands) concluding that their source "is yet a mystery."

Scientific American also reported another strange occurrence in late October 1881 when Milwaukee, Green Bay and other towns in that part of Wisconsin saw falls of strong, very white spider webs. They ranged in size from a few inches to strands more than sixty feet long. The webs all seemed to float inland from above Lake Michigan in thick sheets, fading upward into the sky for as high as the eye could see. There was no mention of any spiders being seen in the webs. Where the substance could have come from was a mystery.

On September 4, 1886, a shower of warm stones purportedly fell on the offices of the *News and Courier* in Charleston, South Carolina. The first shower occurred around 2:30 in the morning and was repeated at 7:30 a.m. and then again at 1:30 in the afternoon. As far as any observers could see, the stones fell only over a small area directly above the newspaper offices. They came down with great force and even broke apart on the pavement. The rocks were described as polished pebbles of flint with the smallest being about the size of a grape and the largest as big as a hen's egg. Many of the stones were gathered up and saved but I was unable to learn what may have become of them.

Scientific American from February 1891 had another tale of strangeness from the skies concerning the Valley Bend District of Randolph County, West Virginia. It seems that over the course of that winter, there were several occasions when the ground was thickly covered with worms. Since the snow had been two feet deep at the times when the worms were discovered, and there was a hard crust on the top of it, they seemingly fell from the sky along with the fresh snow. They were said to be a species of ordinary "cut worms" and were abundant enough that a "square foot of snow can scarcely be found on some days without a dozen of these worms on it."

During the early morning hours of a day in November 1896, a deluge of dead birds fell from a clear sky above Baton Rouge, Louisiana. They fell in such numbers that contemporary accounts say that they "cluttered the streets of the city." The avian shower included wild ducks, catbirds, woodpeckers and many birds of strange plumage, some of them resembling canaries. The birds fell in heaps throughout the city. The only plausible theory advanced as to their source was that they had been driven inland by a recent storm along the Florida coast and had been killed by a sudden change in temperature around Baton Rouge. The editors of the *Monthly Weather Review* stated that storms and temperature changes were common, but bird falls were most assuredly not.

From birds to fish again... In June 1901, hundreds of small catfish, trout and perch fell during a heavy rain at Tiller's Ferry, South Carolina. After the rain showers ended, the fish were found swimming around in pools of water that had accumulated between the rows of cotton of a farm owned by Charles Raley. There is no record of what the Raley family had for dinner that night, although one can guess that it may have had fins.

In November 1921, rocks began to fall from the sky over the town of Chico, California. J.W. Charge, the owner of a grain warehouse along the Southern Pacific Railroad tracks, complained to City Marshal J.A. Peck that someone was throwing rocks at his building every day. Peck, believing it was nothing more than local youngsters playing pranks, paid little attention to the report. His conclusions, after a very brief investigation, were that he had seen the stones fall but could not explain where they came from. He suspected that "someone with a machine was to blame." The stones remained a nuisance to Charge but were largely ignored by everyone else until a few months later, on March 8, 1922. On that day, stones ranging in size from peas to baseballs came raining down on the warehouse, seemingly from nowhere. They continued to fall for days and a search of the area by police officers failed to find anyone throwing them.

In the days that followed, Charge's warehouse sustained quite a bit of damage, from broken windows to split boards and collapsed roof shingles. Stones also began to rain down on a cluster of houses that were located near the railroad tracks. Individuals who stood in the open, perhaps trying to determine the source of the mysterious projectiles, were often struck. The investigators and officials present often became targets. Fire Chief C.E. Tovee and Traffic Officer J.J. Corbett were narrowly missed by a large boulder that seemingly came from nowhere and slammed into a wall behind the spot where they had been standing just moments before. The force of the stone's impact left a large dent in the wood.

The fall of stones continued throughout most of the rest of the month, attracting a large amount of publicity and a number of curiosity-seekers. The origin of the stones was never solved. Professor C.K. Studley said that some of the rocks were so large that they "could not be thrown by ordinary means." He also noted that they did not seem to be of meteoric nature. Charles Fort the famous chronicler of anomalies, asked a friend, mystery writer Miriam Allen de Ford, to go to Chico to investigate personally. Throughout March, a series of articles appeared in the San Francisco Chronicle in which the rocks were described as being warm to the touch and "oval-shaped." Miriam Allen de Ford wrote: "I looked up in the cloudless sky and suddenly saw a rock falling straight down, as if becoming visible when it came near enough. This rock struck the earth with a thud and bounced off on the track beside the warehouse, and I could not find it." She also stated that at one point a rock fell from the sky to "land gently at my feet."

Fish fell again on October 23, 1947, this time over the town of Marksville, Louisiana. The weather at the time was calm and it was not raining, although it was somewhat foggy. The fish came raining down without warning and included largemouth bass, sunfish, shad and minnows. Some of them were frozen and others merely cold to the touch, but all were said to be "fit for human consumption." The fish came down into an area that was about 1,000 feet long and seventy-five or eighty feet wide. A number of them struck people who happened to be on the street at the time. The weather bureau in New Orleans reported that there were no tornadoes in the area at the time of the incident.

On the night of September 26, 1950, two Philadelphia police officers, John Collins and Joe Keenan, encountered something that was far beyond the range of their experience as veteran cops. As they were patrolling the streets in their squad car, they made their way down a quiet side street near Vare Avenue and 26th Street. Coming around a corner, their headlights picked up a large, shimmering object that seemed to be drifting down into an open field about a half-block away from them.

When they stopped to investigate, their flashlights illuminated a domed mass of quivering purple jelly. It was about six feet in diameter and about a foot thick in the center. It gently sloped down toward the edges, where it was an inch or two thick. The pulsating movements of the mass made the astonished officers wonder if it might be alive. They quickly radioed for help and were soon joined by Sergeant Joe Cook and Patrolman James Cooper. Cook suggested that the four of them try and pick the thing up but when Officer Collins attempted to reach underneath it, the mass fell apart in his hands. Fragments of it clung to his skin but they, too, began to slide off, leaving only a sticky, odorless scum behind.

Within a half-hour after Cook and Cooper arrived on the scene, the entire mass had evaporated, leaving no trace behind.

On September 7, 1953, a downpour of frogs and toads "of all descriptions" began falling from the sky over Leicester, Massachusetts. The streets seemed to be alive with them and children gleefully gathered them into buckets, making a game of the astounding event. Officials attempted to explain the sudden appearance of thousands of the creatures by saying that they had escaped from a nearby overflowing pond. However, this explanation did not provide a logical reason as to why so many of them were found on the roofs of houses and in the rain gutters.

Carpenters who were working on the roof of a house in Shreveport, Louisiana, had to take cover on July 12, 1961 when a brief deluge of green peaches began falling from the sky. They were all about the size of golf balls and were believed to have fallen from a dark cloud that was spotted overhead. According to the local weather bureau, the conditions around the city that day were not sufficient to cause whirlwinds, tornadoes or water spouts. Even a strong updraft would not have been enough to carry peaches into the sky, leaving those who witnessed the event scratching their heads in confusion.

In January 1969, hundreds of badly injured ducks came crashing to the earth in St. Mary's City, Maryland. Wildlife officials surmised that the ducks had received their injuries, which included broken bones and mysterious hemorrhages, while they were flying. What may have caused the damage, or why so many ducks were flying in one large mass, was unknown.

Those are just a sampling of the bizarre falls from the sky that have plagued America. Many hundreds more incidents like this have occurred in other places around the world. How do we explain such a thing?

There are naturally many theories but the standard explanation for the seemingly inexplicable falls from the sky is that the objects that come down were carried up into a whirlwind or a waterspout. This is the most logical explanation and admittedly, storms do often manage to pick objects up from one place and deposit them in another. A great variety of natural debris (like plants, dust, feathers, etc.) requires little force to lift it up into the air and larger storms could certainly move rocks or perhaps even pull fish or frogs from a body of water. Much larger items have often been found moved by tornadoes, including automobiles, people and even entire structures. Few of us have any doubts (especially those living in the Great Plains or the Midwest) as to what a major storm can do. I will never forget one of my first visits to the Illinois State Museum as a child during which I saw on display a single piece of straw that had been driven through a solid wooden fence post.

Less is known about waterspouts, but records show that they have also accomplished extraordinary things. There are records of fish being emptied from bays, ponds being sucked dry and on at least one occasion, all aquatic life being pulled from a lake in England and then being deposited on dry land.

That seems to show that the energy generated by tornadoes and other storms is sufficient to lift into the sky those things that have been seen to fall from it, but does this theory really provide a solution for all of the strange incidents that have been recorded? How, for example, have these storms managed to be so selective about depositing items? Things that fall from the sky are usually neatly segregated in that only stones, or only frogs, or only fish fall in one location. If a storm has swept up everything in its path, then how does it manage to only let fall a certain type of item?

Another interesting question would be how the fish, frogs and other assorted creatures usually manage to land on the ground alive? The whirlwind/tornado theory asks us to believe that the animals must survive being pulled from the water and then exist on nothing more than the moisture inside of the storm cloud for an extended period of time. This must be a relatively long time, we have to note, because in many cases, there are no records of storms or tornadoes present in the area where the falls occur at the time they take place. Also for this theory to work, we have to believe that forces powerful enough to lift the creatures from their normal habitat and into the sky are insufficient to do them any physical damage (in most reported cases) and that the sudden changes in pressure and temperature that would undoubtedly take place are just as harmless.

Needless to say, this theory does make sense but really lacks the evidence for it to be seen as the only explanation for the phenomenon. Unfortunately, though, many of the other explanations that have been suggested to explain how such falls happen are nearly as hard to believe. These explanations fall into categories of extraterrestrials, the supernatural and shifts in time and space.

Those who proffer theories of aliens from outer space suggest that perhaps the otherworldly visitors have gathered up large supplies of earthly items, only to jettison them from their spacecrafts before returning to wherever they came from. The falls from the upper atmospheres might seem as if the objects were falling from nowhere. In addition, the rains of blood and meat could be waste matter from the crafts that was dumped to lighten the load for the journey.

In the supernatural theory, gods, spirits or other unnamed entities are responsible for falls from the sky, or at least some of them. Others suggest that perhaps poltergeist-like instances of psychokinetic energy may be responsible for falls of rocks and stones. When it comes to the falls of fish, frogs and other creatures, there have been suggestions that perhaps they are examples of some kind of supernatural benevolence. Proponents of this theory point to instances when dry ponds or new ditches have been found to contain full-grown fish after a rainstorm. This was one of the first theories to explain falls from the sky that I ever heard. As a child, a minister once told me that the oceans and lakes were stocked every time that it rained as God made the fish fall from the heavens. This fascinated me until I reached the age of perhaps ten. After that, I looked elsewhere for the answers to a number of questions that the minister's explanation created for me.

One of the most popular theories to deal with falls from the sky is that our world consists of many different times and dimensions. These parallel worlds intersect occasionally with our own and perhaps things sometimes vanish from our world and in turn, items mysteriously appear in our own. Many researchers of strange phenomena are inclined to this theory of teleportation -- the paranormal transportation of an object from one place to another -- as a sort of blanket explanation for everything from falls from the sky to mystery animals that appear in places where they don't belong. In this case, even if we accept the idea that teleportation is possible (which is not certain, of course) it still asks the same questions as the more logical explanations for these weird events: how is it that the falls manage to be so selective with the items that rain down and the locations where they happen?

As the discerning reader must have already noticed, the virtue of these types of paranormal explanations is that they account for all possibilities, no matter how bizarre. Their only flaw is that they provide explanations using untested ideas and circumstances that go beyond the fantastic. This is not to say that there may not be some truth to the theories, but there is simply no way to know at this time. For now, our explanations for why these things occur are nearly as strange as the unsolved mysteries themselves.

EMPTY BOTTLES

"Popper the Poltergeist"

Ghosts can be very pesky creatures at times. They have been accused of tearing up houses, breaking things and making objects fly about rooms. In days gone by, paranormal researchers always believed that spirits were to blame for any violent or destructive activity reported in what were thought to be haunted houses. But today, most investigators don't think so. While rambunctious spirits may be the culprits in some cases, many hauntings have a force behind them that, while not supernatural, remains mysterious just the same.

In a poltergeist case, there can be a variety of phenomena taking place. There are reports of knocking and tapping noises, sounds with no visible cause, disturbance of stationary objects like household items and furniture, doors slamming, lights turning on and off, fires breaking out and much, much more. Is this the work of ghosts? Maybe, but probably not, according to recent research into the paranormal.

The most commonly accepted theory behind this "poltergeist-like" activity is that it is caused by a person in the household, dubbed the "human agent." The agent is usually an adolescent girl frequently one who is troubled emotionally. It is believed that she unconsciously manipulates physical objects in the house by psychokinesis (PK), the power to move things by energy generated in the brain. This kinetic type of energy remains unexplained, but even some mainstream scientists are starting to explore the idea that it does exist.

It is unknown why this energy seems to appear in females around the age of puberty, but documentation of its existence is starting to appear as more and more case studies have become public. It seems that when the activity begins to manifest, the girl is usually in the midst of some emotional or sexual turmoil. The presence of the energy is almost always an unconscious one and it is rare when any of the agents actually realize that they are the source of the destruction around them. They do not realize that they are the reason that objects in the home have become displaced and are usually of the impression that a ghost (or some sort of other supernatural entity) is present instead. The bursts of PK come and go and most poltergeist-like cases will peak early and then slowly fade away.

It should be noted that while most cases such as this manifest around young women, it is possible for puberty-age boys (and even older adults) to show this same unknowing ability. As with the young women, the vast majority will have no idea that they are causing the activity and will be surprised to find there is even a possibility that strange things are happening because of them.

But not all such cases involve disturbed individuals. The paranormal is never easily classified and in many cases, a weird energy seems to be at work all on its own, rather than a disturbance caused by an individual. Where does this energy come from? And how does it cause a house to become seemingly "haunted?" That's a mystery that, as yet, remains unsolved.

In 1958, a series of ghostly events that were occurring on Long Island transfixed television viewers and readers all over the country. A house belonging to a family named Herrmann was being beset by strange and inexplicable incidents that were attributed to a ghost who was dubbed "Popper" (for reasons that will soon become obvious). But what was really happening in the house? Was it an unseen force from beyond -- or was it something else?

The "Popper" case remains unique in the annals of the supernatural for a variety of reasons, not the least of which is the fact that this became the first haunting that was actually shown on television. Wide-eyed audiences all across the country stared at their television screens in amazement as Popper performed for the cameras. These films became the ghost's claim to fame, but they were not the first incidents to take place in the Herrmann house.

"Popper" first made itself known at around 3:30 in the afternoon of February 3, 1958. The James Herrmann family lived in Seaford, New York, a middle-class suburb on Long Island, about thirty miles from New York City. Their white and green ranch-style home at 1648 Redwood Path had been built in 1953 and contained three bedrooms, a bathroom, a kitchen, a small dining room, a living room and a basement that was divided between a utility room and a playroom. In other words, it was a typical 1950s-era home in a quiet, conservative neighborhood with public parks and tree-lined streets. It was the last place that you would expect anything out of the ordinary to occur.

That February 3 was a day like most any other. It was clear and cold outside and Lucille Herrmann, a registered nurse, was there to welcome her children home from school and to prepare dinner. The children were Lucille, 13, and James, 12, two ordinary kids with ordinary interests. Their ordinary world, however, was about to change.

Soon after the children entered the kitchen, chaos erupted in the house. In a matter of moments, various bottles containing liquid in different rooms of the house suddenly began to pop their caps and dance around. No one saw the bottles move or explode, but all of them heard the caps as they popped loose and the bottles' contents went spewing into the air.

They would later discover an opened bottle of bleach in the basement utility room, a bottle of liquid starch in the kitchen, bottles of shampoo and medicine in the bathroom and a bottle of holy water that had opened in the master bedroom and was lying on its side with the contents spilled. Each of the bottles had been sealed with twist-off metal or plastic caps. There were no corks or crimped caps that might have somehow come loose.

Puzzled, Mrs. Herrmann called her husband, who worked for Air France in New York City, and reported the strange "popping" sounds they had heard. Herrmann was just as confused by the incident as his wife was, but since no one had been hurt, he decided there was no need for him to go home early.

Following his usual schedule, Herrmann took the train to Long Island and arrived home just before 7:00 p.m. During his commute, he pondered his wife's call and was sure that he had a solution for the mystery. He believed that some sort of chemical reaction in the products had caused the bottle lids to blow and the fact that they did so at the same time was merely a coincidence. Perhaps it had been caused by some sort of excessive humidity in the house? He examined the bottles when he arrived home and confessed to being baffled when he found that they were screw-top lids. How could they have simply popped off?

The excitement over the event having passed, and since nothing more had happened, the family decided to write the experience off as "just one of those funny things." Two uneventful days passed and the popping bottles were almost forgotten.

Then, on Thursday, once again at about the same time that the Herrmann children came home from school, another half dozen bottles popped their lids. A bottle of nail polish burst open, as did a bottle of rubbing alcohol, a bottle of bleach, detergent, starch and the bottle that contained holy water on Mrs. Herrmann's dresser. It was an almost exact repeat performance of February 3.

On Friday night, it happened again. Only this time, when the bottles began to pop open, James Herrmann began to suspect that he knew the culprit responsible for the multiple containers' strange behavior. He surmised that his science-loving son had somehow rigged the bottles to pop in order to scare his family. He thought that perhaps his son had planted some carbonated capsules inside the bottles and timed it so that he could get home from school in time to see the startled expression on his mother's face.

As he developed this theory, Herrmann spent the entire weekend secretly observing Jimmy. He was determined to catch him in the act of tampering with a bottle. It's no wonder that he was surprised on Sunday morning, February 9, when several caps popped off bottles of starch, turpentine and holy water, leaving the containers rocking back and forth on the shelves. Herrmann had kept a close eye on Jimmy, so how could the boy have managed to put something inside the bottles without his father seeing him do it? Feeling baffled and a bit angry, Herrmann burst into the bathroom, where Jimmy was brushing his teeth, and accused him of rigging the bottles to pop. The boy vigorously protested his innocence and as if to prove the point, Herrmann was startled to see a bottle of medicine suddenly move across the top of the sink and fall into the basin. A moment later, a bottle of shampoo also slid across the sink and fell with a thud to the floor.

Still skeptical, Herrmann immediately examined the bathroom, searching for hidden wires or strings. He found nothing and finally realized that there were things going on in the house that he could not explain. Unsure of what else to do, he called the Nassau County Police Department and spent the next several minutes on the phone trying to get Lieutenant E. Richardson, the desk officer who answered the call, to take him seriously. When he heard the story, Richardson accused Herrmann of either playing a practical joke or drinking too much, but he was soon swayed by the earnest tone of the man's voice. It helped that Herrmann had a good reputation in the community. Richardson promised to send someone to investigate.

Officer James Hughes went to the house feeling skeptical and perhaps wondering how he always managed to wind up with the nutcase calls. Within a few minutes, though, he had changed his mind about the nature of the case when several bottles in the bathroom popped their lids and fired them in his direction. He quickly concluded that the Herrmanns did indeed need help.

Detective Joseph Tozzi was assigned to look into the case. He read Hughes' report of the incident in the bathroom with interest. While not willing to pass judgment without actually visiting the scene, he was relatively sure the Herrmanns were experiencing some natural phenomenon or were simply imagining things. Or, he noted with the cynicism of a veteran police officer, the popping bottles could be getting some help a human source.

On February 11, Detective Tozzi began his vigil at the Herrmann house. That same evening, a perfume atomizer overturned and spilled perfume in the daughter's bedroom. There was no one in the room at the time, according to reports. Over the next few days, the disturbances seemed to center around the bottle of holy water in the parents' bedroom. On several occasions, the lid of the bottle popped off and once, after hearing the distinctive sound, Mr. Herrmann dashed into the room and found the bottle on the floor. He picked it up and found it strangely warm to the touch.

Later that same day, on February 15, the activity took another turn. As the Herrmann children were watching television in the living room with Marie Murtha, their middle-aged second cousin, a porcelain figurine on an end table next to the couch began to wiggle and then shot two feet through the air, making a loud crashing sound as it landed on the floor. To the amazement of Miss Murtha and the children, the figurine was unbroken.

After this last demonstration, the Herrmanns decided to turn to another source for comfort and to aid the stumped Detective Tozzi in his investigations. They contacted Father William McLeod of the Church of St. William the Abbott for help. As devout Catholics, the Herrmanns believed that the Church could help them where ordinary methods had failed. Father McLeod came to the house and sprinkled holy water in each of the rooms. Unfortunately, "Popper," as the poltergeist came to be called, had decided that he didn't want to leave.

During the two weeks since Popper had made his first appearance in the Herrmann house, news of the strange happenings had leaked to newspapers, radio and television reports. The story received a great deal of publicity, even meriting articles in *Time* and *Life* magazines. Tozzi was interviewed on the *Armstrong Circle Theater,* a live television docudrama. If the beleaguered family thought that mopping up spilled liquids and having their possessions broken by an unseen force was bad, then the onslaught of public attention was worse. During the day, the Herrmann home was surrounded by reporters, photographers, curiosity-seekers and an astounding array of television equipment. While the Herrmanns managed to get used to these intrusions into their lives, they weren't quite prepared for some of the strangeness that came with it.

Letters and telephone calls came every day. Many of them proposed logical solutions, while others assured the Herrmanns that Martians had landed nearby or that the problem in the house was caused by the spirit of a long-dead Indian chief or that the Russians were tunneling under Long Island to invade New York. The Herrmanns managed to stay patient with everyone. They never turned anyone away and they listened attentively to all the calls and suggestions that came in, even those who shouted "Repent!" into the telephone at midnight or proclaimed that "the Sputniks are here!"

Many of the letters and visitors were less easy to tolerate, however. Letters arrived in barely intelligible scrawl, condemning the Herrmanns for their sins and suggesting that they had invited these "tricks of Satan." Ministers from all sorts of dubious faiths conducted rituals on the front lawn of the house. One man in a blue serge suit, who claimed to be a "holy man from Center Moriches," (a nearby town on Long Island) knelt in the yard and prayed for ten minutes. Then he stood and announced: "Everything is all right. You have been forgiven." With that, he left -- but "Popper" remained.

But not all of the suggestions and attempts to help were so bizarre. One man who came to the house, Robert Zider, was a physicist from Long Island's Brookhaven National Laboratory. He brought a set of dowsing rods with him and went over the property with them. When he was finished, he stated that he believed there were underground streams below the house. He thought that the water might be creating a "freak magnetic field." Detective Tozzi examined this idea at length, but a geological survey suggested that the information was inaccurate.

Tozzi's case file grew thicker and thicker with added notes, observations, research and facts that he collected. At one point, he had been walking down the basement stairs with Jimmy Herrmann when a bronze statue of a horse weighing nearly 100 pounds flew across the basement and hit the detective in the legs. Jimmy had been nowhere near the statue and no one else was down there. How had it happened? Tozzi had absolutely no idea.

He had checked with the Air Force and after studying their flight plans, they had told him that sonic booms from passing jets could not have caused the disturbances. He also ruled out radio waves by contacting the Radio Corporation of America (RCA). The Long Island Lighting Company had set up a delicate oscilloscope in the basement, but it detected no underground vibrations. Building inspectors from the town of Hempstead pronounced the house structurally sound. The Seaford Fire Department even inspected a well on the property to see if changes in the water level could be causing the disturbances. However, they found that the water level had been stable for at least five years. Although puzzled, Tozzi remained determined and he tried valiantly to discover a source for the happenings.

He finally found hope in a letter from a woman named Helen Connolly of Revere, Massachusetts. She wrote that she had experienced odd events in her living room, where chairs and furniture moved about. She didn't have a ghost in her house, but rather a heavy downdraft through her fireplace. When capped with a rotary metal turbine, the flying tables and chairs ceased to fly. Mr. Herrmann immediately had one installed on his own chimney, convinced that the strangeness was finally coming to an end.

But that wasn't meant to be.... No sooner had the workmen completed the installation than a porcelain figurine launched itself from a table and smashed against a desk. The figurine had managed to travel a distance of more than twelve feet. It left a dent on the wood that was broadcast to rapt television audiences all over the New York metropolitan area.

On February 20, events became even more violent. Another figurine was smashed against the desk, a bottle of ink popped its screw cap, then sailed into the air and splashed its contents on the wall and a sugar bowl flew off the table under the startled gaze of Detective Tozzi. It had been close to Jimmy but not within his reach. Needing a break, the Herrmann family spent the night with a relative. Tozzi stayed in the house, but the rest of the night passed without incident. When the family returned the next evening, though, the sugar bowl again flew from the table and this time, it shattered into pieces.

On February 24, Tozzi was startled to his feet by the sound of a loud noise from Jimmy's room. No one had been in the room or near it, yet a large bookcase had managed to fall facedown onto the floor. The next night, while Jimmy was in the room doing his homework, his record player lifted and moved fifteen feet across the room. A small statue of the Virgin Mary flew more than twelve feet and struck a mirror frame in the master bedroom. A bookcase filled with encyclopedias was upended. A heavy glass centerpiece from the dining room table flew up and stuck a cupboard, chipping away a piece of molding before falling to the floor. A world globe shot down the hallway from Jimmy's room and just missed Detective Tozzi. A newspaper photographer named John Gold from the *London Evening News* witnessed his flashbulbs lift off a table and fly through the air to strike a wall. In addition, Popper had begun knocking on the walls to get attention, although no attempts to "communicate" with the ghost (if indeed it was a ghost) were ever made.

Tozzi had become concerned about the new violence in the disruptions. Until that point, the activity had been limited to popping bottle tops. He had explored every possible explanation that he could come up with, and while he was not prepared to say the house was haunted, he was out of fresh ideas. About this same time, the staff of scientists at the Parapsychology Laboratory at Duke University, North Carolina, became interested in the events reported in the Herrmann home. This group of researchers, under the leadership of Dr. J.B. Rhine, had already compiled a mass of evidence that supported the idea that certain people, under the right circumstances, could influence the behavior of objects without touching them. They called it psychokinesis, or PK.

As the disturbances at the home continued (and in fact, increased) Dr. Rhine's assistant, Dr. Joseph Gaither Pratt, traveled to New York and arrived at the Herrmann house on February 26. Pratt believed that someone in the house was unknowingly causing the strange incidents to occur. Meanwhile, other researchers came to believe that the incidents in the house were being caused by an actual ghost, a poltergeist, or "noisy spirit." These prankster ghosts traditionally targeted religious items, like the holy water and the Virgin Mary statue in the Herrmann house.

On the other hand, strong evidence remained for the idea that there was a human component behind the haunting. It had been noted by the Duke researchers that an adolescent child, usually a girl, was almost always among the members of the household being plagued by poltergeist phenomena. They believed it was possible that this young person might be capable of psychokinesis during the height of puberty. In every case, the young person was apparently unaware that she or he was unconsciously causing the events to happen, making them as bewildered as the adults around them. In the case of the Herrmann house, Jimmy (according to Detective Tozzi's notes) was at or near the scene of the poltergeist disturbances more than seventy-five percent of the time. He was the sole witness to many of the incidents. However, the detective had cleared the boy of deliberately causing any of the disturbances.

Like the others who came before him, Dr. Pratt was welcomed into the Herrmann residence and greeted warmly. He explained that he had come as an observer and he spent most of the time there chatting with Jimmy, playing cards with him, helping him with his homework and generally just being around the young man. There was no sign of strangeness during the visit. Popper was absolutely quiet.

Pratt then summoned another colleague from North Carolina, William G. Roll. Together, they interviewed the family members and were convinced that none of them were perpetrating a hoax. "The family was much too shaken for it to be a colossal hoax," Pratt told a *United Press* reporter.

Things were quiet for the next several days, as though the poltergeist did not want to perform for the scientists. Then, on March 2, one month after Popper first arrived, he decided to make himself known again. All of the Herrmanns were in the house to witness what took place. First, a dish vaulted from a kitchen cabinet and shattered on the floor. Then, a night table flipped over in Jimmy's room. Popper was back and yet there was still no explanation as to who, or what, he was. Two days later, a bowl of flowers slid down the dining room table and jumped into the air. A bookcase turned end over end in the cellar.

But this would not be Popper's farewell performance. That event would occur on March 10 while Mrs. Herrmann, Jimmy, and Lucille were getting ready for bed (James Herrmann was away on business). Pratt and Roll suddenly heard a loud popping sound in the cellar and they hurried downstairs to see what it was. They found that a bleach bottle, sitting in a cardboard box, had somehow lost its plastic lid.

For reasons unknown, this became the last act of the Herrmann family poltergeist. There had been a record of sixty-seven recorded disturbances between February 3 and March 10. The Herrmanns had been visited by detectives, building inspectors, electricians, plumbers, firemen, parapsychologists and half of the "nutcases" on the East Coast, and yet none of them had been able to present a satisfactory explanation for what had occurred in their home.

Weeks after the household returned to normal, "experts" still came to investigate and to theorize about what had taken place. As late as August 1958, the scientists at Duke still had no clue as to what had happened and why. By this time, the Herrmanns had had enough of investigations and just wanted their lives to get back to normal. James Herrmann no longer cared why the disturbances had taken place; he was just happy they were over. Mrs. Herrmann told an *Associated Press* reporter: "I don't think there is a definite solution. It was just one of those things with no rhyme or reason to it. But there was a definite physical force behind it."

Tozzi later moved to Texas, where he became chief of the Colleyville Police Department. He died in 2003 at age 78, certain that "Popper" had not been a hoax, and still baffled by what he had seen and heard in a seemingly ordinary Long Island home in 1958.

What did happen at the Herrmann house? No one really knows. "Popper" the Poltergeist, and the strange incidents that followed in his wake, is just as puzzling today as "he" was in 1958.

BURNED FURNITURE
THE MACOMB FIRESTARTER

In most reports of poltergeist cases, the displaced energy in the house wreaks havoc by moving physical objects from household items to furniture, books, kitchen utensils and, in the "Popper" case, by opening bottles. But not all poltergeist cases involve the mere movement of objects. In some cases, the bizarre energy that is expended comes in other forms: like the creation of fire.

Over the years, I have become acquainted with a number of both professional and volunteer firemen and they can tell you that they always make an attempt to be certain that a fire is totally extinguished before they leave the scene. The image of a department can be badly tarnished if its personnel have to return to a scene because they missed some smoldering spot that causes the building to burst back into flames. For just this reason, there are a few cases when firefighters have been forced to return to a scene a second time but rarely do they have to come back a third or fourth time. In these latter cases, the fires have almost always been in warehouses and factories where combustible materials were present, and almost never in a private home.

But some fires are different. They obey a different set of physical laws that we are only beginning to comprehend. The origin of such fires is not only bizarre but terrifying as well.

In February 1959, Mr. and Mrs. George Byrnes were awakened in their Miami, Florida, home by the screams of their fourteen-year-old daughter, Evelyn. The girl had been sleeping in the living room and her blankets were on fire. She helped her parents drag the smoldering bedding into the front yard but when the Byrneses returned to the house, they discovered that their living room curtains were also on fire, as were the curtains in the dining room and kitchen. After these blazes were put out, the terrified family found that the curtains in an enclosed patio, closed off from the rest of the house, were also burning. No one was hurt and the cause of the fires was never determined.

In Paris, Kentucky, the Charles Johnson family had thirteen small fires break out in their home over a three-day period in December 1958. The family living in the house consisted of Johnson and his wife, a daughter-in-law, nine children and a grandchild. After the first few fires, one member of the family stayed awake at all times to keep watch but the fires continued to break out. Nearly all of the bedding and the children's clothing were destroyed. Nothing else in the house was damaged and the source of the fires was never discovered.

On Sunday, September 9, 1945, Mrs. Annie Bryan of Midland, Arkansas, discovered a fire burning inside the drawer of a table in her home. By Friday, more than thirty mysterious fires had damaged curtains, clothing, wallpaper and furniture. A barn had burned down on Wednesday and on Thursday afternoon nine objects had burst into flame, apparently without cause. Mrs. Bryan had no insurance, which made the cause of the fires even more confusing. There was no reason for a hoax and no answer as to how the fires had started.

As strange as these cases were, though, one of the most famous fire-starter cases in American history took place in Illinois in 1948, galvanizing the residents of the small town of Macomb. The case became so well known that it appeared in almost every newspaper in the country, often on the front page. The case of the "Macomb Poltergeist" created a mystery that remains unsolved to this day.

In the summer of 1948, a disturbed teenager named Wanet McNeill was forced to live with her father after her parents' bitter divorce. The girl and her father moved to a farm that belonged to an uncle, Charles Willey, located just south of Macomb. The situation with her father and mother had plunged Wanet into a deep depression. She had been uprooted from her home, school and friends and didn't understand what had occurred between her parents in the divorce. She was unhappy about being forced to live on the farm, which was very rural compared to her former home in Bloomington, and her emotions were in turmoil. Soon, those emotions took a dangerous turn, and it is believed that in the weeks that followed her arrival, Wanet somehow managed to start fires all over her uncle's farm. She didn't do this with a box of matches and some oily rags, as some might suspect. Instead, it is believed that the fires occurred due to a force that was projected from Wanet's mind. She had no idea that she was causing the phenomenon to take place. The kinetic energy in her body inexplicably caused an eruption of power that ignited combustible material all over the house and property.

The mysterious fires began on August 7. The farm where the events took place belonged to Charles Willey and was located about twelve miles outside of Macomb. The residents of the farm included Willey, his wife, his brother-in-law and Wanet's father, Arthur McNeil, and McNeil's two children, Arthur Junior, 8, and Wanet, who had recently turned 13. As mentioned, McNeil and his wife had recently divorced and contrary to the standard practice of the day, the father had received custody of the children. His former wife was living in Bloomington, where Wanet wanted to be. There is no information available as to what had caused the marriage to end or what may have occurred that would have given McNeil custody of the children. Whatever the situation had been, it had apparently been a volatile one and it had caused a horrible family situation, which the McNeils brought with them to Macomb.

The first fire began as a small brown spot that appeared on the wallpaper in the living room of the Willey farm house. That first spot was followed by another and then another. The spots would appear, spread out several inches as they smoldered and then, when they became hot enough, they burst into flames. The brown spots occurred day after day, leaving the family frightened and befuddled. They searched for some cause for the fires, thinking that perhaps the electrical wiring was faulty, but they could find no reason for them. Willey called on several of his neighbors to investigate but they were as mystified as he was. Many of these neighbors stayed on the property, crowding into the house and even sleeping on the floor in an attempt to help keep watch over the situation. Pans and buckets were filled with water and placed all over the house, and each time one of the small fires broke out, it was quickly dowsed.

In spite of this, fires materialized right in front of the startled witnesses. As word spread, more people came to see what was going on and to offer assistance. Volunteers stood by with hoses and buckets of water to put out the blazes. They were quick to extinguish them but no one could come up with a reason as to why they were occurring. The fire chief from Macomb, Fred Wilson, was called in to investigate. He was just as perplexed as everyone else, but he did have some ideas that he believed could help the situation. Wilson directed the family to strip all of the wallpaper from every wall in the house. Since the brown spots were burning on the wallpaper, he surmised that perhaps there was something in the paper or the glue that held it in place that might be causing the fires. The paper was quickly torn down but then dozens of witnesses, including Chief Wilson, watched as the anomalous brown spots appeared on the bare plaster and again, burst into flames. And then, a new development occurred as small fires began to appear on the ceiling as well.

"The whole thing is so screwy and fantastic that I'm almost ashamed to talk about it," Wilson said. "Yet we have the word of at least a dozen reputable witnesses that say they saw mysterious brown spots smolder suddenly on the walls and ceilings of the home and then burst into flames."

In the days that followed, fires also appeared outside the house on the front porch. Curtains were ignited in several of the rooms, an ironing board burst into flame and a cloth that was lying on a bed burned so hot that it turned into ash. In a bizarre turn, the bedding beneath the scorched cloth was untouched. According to witnesses, the quilt that covered the bed was not even warm. Later on, though, the bed itself was completely engulfed by flames. Bafflingly, the floor beneath it, as well as a nearby rug, was not burned at all.

Chief Wilson was still convinced that the wallpaper in the house was somehow to blame for the fires. He had never seen anything like what was happening on the Willey farm before and this small town firefighter was searching for some sort of explanation that made sense. He sent a sample of the paper to the National Fire Underwriters Laboratory and they reported that the wallpaper was coated only with flour paste, which was a flame retardant, and that no flammable compound, such as an insect repellant that might contain phosphorus, was present in the material. They had no explanation for what could be causing the fires in the house.

Thanks to the damage that was being done in his house, Charles Willey contacted his insurance company. After receiving the report, the company immediately sent investigators to the farm, looking for any evidence that Willey, or a member of the family, was starting the fires in an attempt to commit fraud. They could find nothing to suggest that the fires were caused by arson and could provide no explanation for the blazes.

The insurance investigators were not alone. Deputy State Fire Marshal John Burgard was contacted by Chief Wilson and he, too, came to the Willey farm. He admitted to being confused by the strange events. "Nobody has ever heard anything like this," he announced to the press, "but I saw it with my own eyes."

In the week that followed, more than two hundred fires broke out at the house, an average of nearly twenty each day. Finally, on Saturday, August 14, one of the blazes raged out of control and before the Macomb fire department could be summoned, the entire Willey farm house was consumed. Charles Willey drove posts into the ground and made a tent shelter for himself and his wife, while McNeil and the children moved into the garage. The next day, while the Willeys were milking cows in the barnyard, the barn burst into flames and the building was destroyed. Willey, already distraught, was now shattered. He had only $1,000 insurance on the house and $400 on the barn. Neither policy would come close to replacing the buildings. To make matters worse, at this point, the insurance company was still unwilling to pay even those small amounts. Their investigators were still perplexed about the cause of the fires but believed that further investigations might reveal the source.

Two days later, on Tuesday, several fires broke out on the walls of the milk house, which the family was using as a kitchen and dining room. On Thursday morning, there were two more fires and a box that was filled with newspapers was found burning in the chicken house. A few minutes later, Mrs. Willey opened a cupboard door in the milk house and discovered more newspapers smoldering on a shelf inside. There had been no one else in the building and the cabinet had not been opened. There was no logical reason for the newspapers to have caught fire.

Later that day, at about 6:00 p.m., the farm's second barn caught fire. The blaze burned so hot that the entire building was destroyed in less than a half hour. Firefighters who arrived on the scene were unable to get close to the inferno. A company that sold fire extinguishers was on hand with equipment, but it did little good. An employee of the company stated that "it was the most intense heat that I've ever felt."

Only six small outbuildings remained on the farm, so the family escaped to a nearby vacant house. Regardless, the fires continued. The United States Air Force even got involved in the mystery. They suggested that the fires could be caused by some sort of directed radiation, presumably from the Russians, but could offer no further assistance. Why the Russians would target a humble Illinois farm was unknown. Lewis Gust, the chief technician at Wright Field, Ohio, sent an expert to the farm to test for "very high frequencies and short waves." He thought the fires might be related to several unsolved airplane fires in which radiation was suspected of playing a part. Again, the Russians were believed to be the culprits. "We can't afford to take any chances," he told reporters. "We must test anything, even if it sounds a bit far-fetched. Suppose you had material that could be ignited by radio and wanted to test it for sabotage value. Wouldn't you pick some out of the way place like the Willey farm to make the test?"

Gust explained that scientists believed that powerful, high-frequency or extremely short radio waves could cause fires to start. For example, radar waves set off photographic flash bulbs inside of airplanes that were in flight. An interview with an unnamed scientist in Chicago confirmed these theories and agreed that radioactivity or radio waves could cause "such disturbances" but also added that it was "highly unlikely because there had been no other reactions in the area." If Russian spies were shooting radio waves at the Willey farm, it would have been impossible, the scientist noted, to direct them in such a way that no other homes or farms near Macomb would be affected.

By the end of the following week, the farm was swarming with curiosity-seekers, official and self-appointed investigators, and reporters. Over 1,000 people came to the farm on August 22 alone! Theorists and curiosity-seekers posed their own ideas and explanations. These ran the gamut from fly spray to radio waves, underground gas pockets, flying saucers and more. The authorities had a more down-to-earth explanation in mind. They suspected arson. They realized that they couldn't solve the riddle as to how fires could appear before the eyes of reliable witnesses, but things were getting out of hand on the Willey farm. An explanation needed to be produced, and quickly.

Two investigators noted that there seemed to be a difference between the fires in the house and the later blazes. Professor John J. Ahern, from the Illinois Institute of Technology, suggested that combustible gases inside the walls might have caused the house fires, while the fires that destroyed the barns seem to spring from "other causes." State Fire Marshal John Craig said that the burning of the house "looked like an accident but that the barn fires might have been "touched off by an arsonist." This was enough for some of the officials involved. They overlooked the mysterious nature of the fires and heard only the fact that some of the fires *might* have been started by arson. There was no conclusive evidence of this but the case had to be closed as soon as possible.

On August 30, the mystery was publicly announced to be solved. The arsonist, according to officials, was Wanet McNeil, the slight, red-haired niece of Charles Willey. They claimed that she was starting the fires with kitchen matches when no one was looking, ignoring the witness reports of fires that sprang up from nowhere, including on the ceiling. Apparently, this little girl possessed some pretty amazing skills, along with a seemingly endless supply of matches.

According to Deputy Fire Marshal Burgard, there had been a minor fire at the farm house where the family had moved after the other buildings had been destroyed. He had placed a box of matches in a certain position and the box had been moved. Wanet was nearby but she was never seen touching the box or holding a match. This didn't matter, however. Burgard and State's Attorney Keith Scott had taken Wanet aside for an hour's worth of "intense questioning." After that, she had allegedly confessed. She stated that she was unhappy, didn't like the farm, wanted to see her mother and most telling, that she didn't have pretty clothes. The mystery was solved! This was in spite of the fact that witnesses to the fires had seen them appear on walls, floors and furniture, all when Wanet was not even in the room.

This explanation pleased the authorities but not all of the reporters who were present seemed convinced. The hundreds of paranormal investigators who have examined the case over the years have not been reassured either. One columnist from a Peoria newspaper, who had covered the case from the beginning, stated quite frankly that he did not believe the so-called "confession." Neither did noted researcher of the unexplained Vincent Gaddis, who wrote about the case. He was convinced that it was a perfect example of poltergeist phenomena.

He noted that many poltergeist cases made it necessary for the authorities to figuratively -- and sometimes literally -- slap little girls into confessing. In many cases, there is no doubt about the paranormal nature of these manifestations and yet there is a general prejudice against real mystery. Perhaps it stems from fear of the unknown. And so, no matter how incredible the phenomena and no matter how impossible it would be for a person to produce the results by trickery, we have "confessions." The agent, not realizing that she is unconsciously causing the phenomena, seems at times to have a sense of guilt or perhaps even some small awareness of her part in the matter. Such people can be pressured into a confession, despite the fact that the events could not have been caused by normal means.

Irritated investigators and worried parents occasionally use force to wring confessions out of children, and the history of poltergeist manifestations is riddled with examples of boys being whipped and girls slapped. In other cases, the agent may be told to either reproduce the phenomena by paranormal means or confess that it was fraudulent. Frantic, some may resort to crude trickery, only to be caught, or may simply make a false confession. And these false confessions occur much more commonly than people outside the field of psychology realize, according to experts. Dr. Ian Stevenson, from the University of Virginia School of Medicine, stated that "a vague impression of guilt about something often suffices to motivate a false confession. Innocent persons have frequently confessed to serious crimes like murder, sometimes implicating innocent persons as accomplices..."

For just this reason, confessions in poltergeist cases are often worthless unless they include an explanation for how the manifestations were accomplished that is reasonable, practical and fits the known facts. In the case of the "Macomb Fire Starter," the confession certainly didn't fit the facts, but by the time it came, people were too worried, tired and traumatized to care.

What really happened on the Willey Farm? We will probably never know because the story just went away after that. Wanet was taken to Chicago for examination at the Illinois Juvenile Hospital and was found to be mentally normal by Dr. Sophie Schroeder, a psychiatrist. "She's a nice little kid caught in the middle of a broken home," Schroeder reported. She was later turned over to her grandmother and spent the rest of her teenage years untroubled by mysterious brown spots that appeared, spread and burst into flames.

The insurance company paid Willey for the damage done to his home and farm and the farm house was later rebuilt. Arthur McNeil and his son moved back in with the Willeys for a time before eventually moving out of state.

Fire officials abandoned the case after Wanet's "confession" cleared up the mystery for them, but privately, many of those involved continued to question what really occurred on the Willey farm for years afterward. Fire Chief Fred Wilson talked about the case for quite some time and later retired from his position convinced that something unexplainable had taken place.

The reporters who descended on the Willey farm all received closure for the stories, whether they believed the conclusion or not, and the general public was given a solution that could not have possibly been the truth, although it may have been comforting to believe that a naughty child playing with matches was to blame, and not the Russians or some mysterious, destructive force that could seemingly burst out anytime, anywhere, without warning. Not surprisingly, the case is still listed as "unexplained" today.

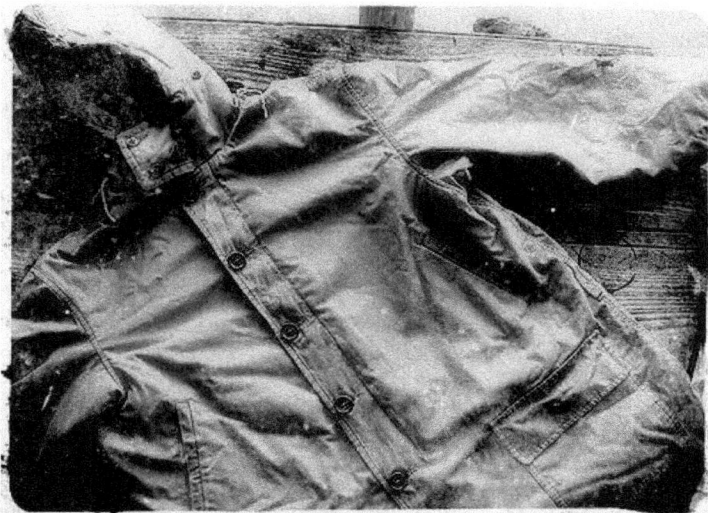

RED WINTER PARKA
THE MYSTERY OF VERMONT'S LONG TRAIL

The historic Green Mountains of Vermont have been described as being part of the most beautiful stretch of wilderness in New England. The warm weather months make this a place of tranquil shade, soaked in a pleasing array of greens and browns. In the autumn, the hills come alive with a symphony of breath-taking color. But at other times, a darker side emerges from these rugged mountains. It occurs when the shadows grow long and the snow starts to fall, covering the landscape in a monotonous blanket of white.

There are places, like the most eerie corners of these mountains, where the fabric of time and space seems to be stretched a little bit thinner. Places where things that are not supposed to do so, slip through into our world. And where things from our world sometimes slip out.

Odd secrets hide in the Green Mountains near Bennington, Vermont. The area has always had a reputation for strangeness. It is a spot that is remote and often inaccessible and since colonial days, it has been plagued with reports of mysterious lights and sounds, Bigfoot sightings, UFOs, ghostly tales and unknown creatures. Master of weird fiction H.P. Lovecraft based his story "The Whisperer in Darkness," near Glastonbury. The local Native Americans shunned the region and according to tradition, used it as a place to bury their dead.

And while stories of spook lights and Indian curses may stretch the limits of credulity, there is no denying that nearby Glastonbury Mountain, and its scenic Long Trail, has been the site of a great American mystery. This unsolved puzzle involves the disappearance of a number of people who have never been found. Thousands of hours were spent searching for them, but not a single clue was ever discovered. They just walked off into the woods one day and never returned, vanishing without a trace.

The string of bizarre disappearances began on November 12, 1945, with the vanishing of Middie Rivers, a seventy-four-year-old hunting and fishing guide. He was reportedly in perfect health and knew the area well, having been a native of the region for most of his life. The day that he disappeared was an unusually mild one for late fall, and Rivers led four hunters up onto the mountain. After spending the day away from camp, they packed up to return with Rivers leading the way. He got a little bit ahead of them, walked around a bend in the trail - and vanished without a trace. One minute he was there and the next he wasn't. The old man simply disappeared.

The hunters searched frantically and then notified the authorities. State police, soldiers, Boy Scouts and local residents combed the woods for hours. They refused to lose hope, knowing that Rivers was an experienced outdoorsman and could survive in the woods, even under icy cold conditions. When no sign of him turned up, efforts were expanded and the search continued for a month. It was eventually called off, and Middie Rivers was never seen again.

On December 1, 1946, a second person vanished from the Long Trail. Her name was Paula Welden, and she came from Stamford, Connecticut. Paula was a sophomore at Bennington College. She was eighteen, the eldest of four daughters of Archibald Welden, an industrial engineer who was employed by Revere Copper & Brass Co. She had come to Bennington College because of the school's excellent reputation for progressive teaching. Paula had blue eyes and usually wore her hair pulled back from her pleasant face. Descriptions of her from 1946 spoke of her being soft-spoken, polite and well-behaved, like the average girl of her time and background. She was a fair student whose favorite subject was botany. Her interest in trees and plants gave her an excuse for solitary walks along the local forest trails.

On the afternoon of Sunday, December 1, Paula told her roommate, Elizabeth Johnson, that she was going out for a short hike. She changed into outdoor clothing - blue jeans, white sneakers and a red parka with a fur-trimmed hood - but failed to take into account the miserable conditions outside. It was a particularly gloomy day, her roommate later recalled, and a cold rain had made the ground slippery and muddy. Despite the fact that it seemed a much better idea to stay indoors and study rather than to go out, Elizabeth, knowing her friend's affinity for being outside made no effort to dissuade her from going.

Paula Welden's actions from the moment that she left her dorm cannot be traced exactly. Against the drab December day, she should have made a conspicuous figure in her bright red coat, but only a handful of people were outdoors to notice her. An attendant at a gas station across Route 67A from the Bennington College gates said he saw her hitchhiking a short distance from the gas station at around 3:15 in the afternoon.

Paula was picked up on the road by Louis Knapp, a contractor who lived about fifteen miles east of the college in the direction of Glastonbury Mountain and the beginning of the Long Trail. That was Paula's goal that day and during the summer, the picturesque trail was one of the area's greatest attractions, with thriving tourist cottages and cabins lining it. In the winter, though, it was barren and neglected. Only four families lived along it in the winter months, which made Paula's choice for her hike that day a strange one. Nevertheless, Knapp agreed to take her up the highway as far as his home in Woodford Hollow, just three miles from the start of the Long Trail. When Knapp stopped the car at his driveway, Paula asked him the distance to the trail and then she got out and started walking. She soon vanished into the mist that had replaced the cold rain of the early afternoon.

About an hour later, she encountered another resident of the area, Ernest Whitman, a night watchman for the *Bennington Banner* newspaper. Whitman was surprised to see a young girl sloshing along the desolate road, especially since it was growing dark. He spoke with Paula for a few minutes and gave her directions. After that, other witnesses spotted her on the trail, remembering her distinctly because she had been wearing a bright red parka. It was very visible, even though the sun was setting by this time. They would be the last ones to see her alive.

Paula did not return to wait on tables at the Commons, the Bennington College dining hall, that evening, nor did she appear by her usual bedtime. Although worried, Elizabeth Johnson decided to wait until morning to report her absence. After a sleepless night, she left her room at dawn and made her way to the Dean's residence. The Dean offered the opinion that Paula might have made a last-minute application to stay away from the college all night, but a quick check of the sign-out records showed that this was not the case. The two of them hurried across campus to the home of Bennington president Lewis Webster Jones. He had no solution to the problem, except to make a careful telephone call to the Welden home in Stamford to see if Paula had unexpectedly turned up there. She had not, and so Jones next called the local Sheriff Clyde W. Peck, who came straight to the college. He was later joined by Vermont State Police detective Almo Fronzoni, a veteran of more than twenty-five years with the department.

Fronzoni took charge of the investigation and started by questioning Elizabeth Johnson. He accompanied her to the dorm room that she shared with Paula and saw that there was no sign that the young woman had taken any clothing with her. Nor, apparently, had she taken any extra money. He found $8.26 on her bureau, along with an un-cashed check for $10. Elizabeth told him that Paula rarely ever had more cash than that on hand.

Fronzoni next drove to the local bus and railroad stations. There, he ran into a taxi driver who told him that he had driven a Bennington girl to the bus station that day but this later turned out to be a mistake. At the railway station, Fronzoni mentioned Stamford, Connecticut, and the ticket seller perked up. On Sunday afternoon, three hunters had purchased tickets to New York and then at the last minute, had changed their destination to Stamford. The ticket seller remembered this because it required quite a bit of adjustment on his part. No matter how Fronzoni tried, though, he was unable to see a connection, other than coincidence, between the three hunters and Paula. All it did was, like the confusion with the taxi driver, slow down the investigation and lessen his chances of finding the missing girl.

The detective returned to the Bennington campus and began questioning other students who knew Paula. Since she had not told anyone where she was going that day, only that she was going for a hike, no one knew where she was headed when she left campus. However, several of her friends mentioned her fondness for a place called Everett's Cave on Mount Anthony. It was three miles south of the college. If Paula had hiked there, it was suggested, she might have fallen and been injured. Fronzoni, Sheriff Peck and several deputies immediately drove to Everett's Cave but Paula, injured or otherwise, was not to be found there.

By this time, word of the disappearance was beginning to spread and when newspaper reporters from the *Bennington Banner* picked up the story, night watchman Ernest Whitman heard about the missing student. He immediately reported to Fronzoni that he had met Paula near the entrance to the Long Trail. After the story hit the newspapers on Tuesday, the authorities also heard from the gas station attendant who had seen Paula hitchhiking and from Louis Knapp, as well. The officials now realized that Paul had been heading for the Long Trail when she vanished and an immediate search was started. It was feared that the young woman had met with an accident while hiking on the trail in the dark, and not being dressed for the bitterly cold nighttime temperatures, she could be dead or badly injured. There was hope that, injured or lost, she could have broken into one of the empty summer cottages on the trail and that she could have found food or at least a fireplace where she could warm herself.

The search commenced on Monday afternoon, headed by Bennington game warden Jesse Wilson. He was assisted by five other game wardens, some sheriff's deputies and several search dogs. It was hurriedly put together and badly organized but they believed that if Paula was injured, time was crucial.

As they searched along the trail, Detective Fronzoni questioned members of the families who lived on Long Trail year round. He found two leads. One person stated that he had seen a half-ton truck driving along the trail late Sunday evening at a time when Paula might have been on it. The other lead was more definite. A woman had been walking along the trail on Sunday and had been forced to step aside to permit a maroon-colored car to pass by. She saw a young couple inside and the girl had been a blonde, the same as Paula. She had not looked very closely at the couple but it did raise the question as to whether or not someone had given Paula a lift. If they had, though, what had happened to her?

On Tuesday, December 3, a more comprehensive search was organized. Classes at Bennington College were suspended and nearly 400 students took part in the effort. Faculty members, students from nearby Williams College in nearby Williamstown, Massachusetts, Boy Scouts, trappers, woodsmen, local residents and search dogs joined deputies and law enforcement officials as they scoured the area. The group was also joined by a number of employees from Revere Copper & Brass and the huge contingent was organized into smaller search teams by expert mountain climbers from the National Guard. The Navy also sent nine Marine search planes from the Squantum Air Base in Quincy, Massachusetts, and a helicopter was brought in to fly low over isolated areas.

As the National Guard climbers worked their way up Glastonbury Mountain, the army of searchers sloshed in long lines up and down the wet foothills. The weather was drab and drizzling, soaking everyone to the skin. It was cold, wearying work that continued for hours. The Bennington student body and friends of the Welden family had started a reward-for-information fund, which was soon up to $5,000. The offer of a reward brought in even more volunteers and the search continued for two full days. On December 5, though, it was called off thanks to overhanging clouds that had grounded the search planes, followed by several inches of snow that blanketed the landscape.

By this time, the Welden family and most of the volunteers were exhausted. The fact that Paula had written no farewell note and that no ransom letters had been received indicated that whatever happened to her must have been spontaneous. It was feared that she was a victim of amnesia, an accident, or homicide. Many feared that Paula was dead but her parents refused to give up hope, insisting that their daughter had been kidnapped. With no evidence of this, the FBI refused to get involved. When the official refusal became public knowledge, well-known novelist Dorothy Canfield Fisher, a Bennington College trustee, wrote letters to J. Edgar Hoover and several political figures in Washington. "Paula is not in these hills," she stated. "She was taken away against her will."

Others felt the same way and made determined pleas that were all turned down. The governor appealed to both New York and Connecticut for skilled investigators to assist them but only Connecticut responded, sending two state detectives who had succeeded with puzzling missing person's cases in the past. Their laborious investigations still failed to produce the missing girl. One of the investigators, Robert Rundle, agreed with Detective Fronzoni when he had declared Paula's case to be the most perplexing of his career. "We have not a single clue," Rundle admitted.

Paula was simply gone. They found no clues: no blood, no clothing, nothing. In the end, helicopters, aircraft, bloodhounds and as many as 1,000 people combed the mountain for the young woman but no trace of her was found.

On December 16, the Weldens returned to Connecticut, taking with them all of Paula's belongings from her dorm room. Even her family had given up hope of seeing their daughter alive again. Classes resumed at Bennington and after the shock of Paula's disappearance passed, students began to think more of going home for the holidays than about the missing girl. The townspeople still talked and speculated but few were still willing to spend time combing the hills for her. Detective Fronzoni moved on to other cases and Paula Welden began to become a part of Bennington's past.

But over five months later, Archibald Welden urged a second organized search, once the winter snows had thawed. On May 23, several hundred volunteers assembled and spent two days in the rain, crisscrossing more than twenty-four square miles between Glastonbury and Bald Mountains. When the search ended, it had accomplished nothing.

When Bennington College reconvened again the following autumn, Paula Welden seemed a forgotten, shadowy figure. People still walked the Long Trail and wondered about her sometimes but few spoke of her again - until the next person vanished into the mountains.

On December 1, 1949, three years to the day of Paula Welden's disappearance, an elderly man named James E. Tetford also vanished near Bennington. Tetford had been visiting relatives in northern Vermont and his family had placed him on a bus in St. Albans for the journey back to Bennington, where he lived at the Vermont Soldiers' Home.

For some reason, he never arrived. Where he actually disappeared is just part of the mystery. Witnesses recalled him getting on the bus and several were sure that he was still on board at the stop before Bennington. At some point, though, he apparently got off along the road. He left no clues behind. No one saw him disappear, including the bus driver, but he was never seen again.

Another disappearance took place near Bennington in October 1950. An eight-year-old boy named Paul Jepson vanished from the town dump, where his parents were caretakers. Paul was waiting in the family's truck while his mother relocated some pigs. She was away for only a moment but when she looked up, the boy was gone. It was between 3:00 and 4:00 in the afternoon and was a sunny day. Paul was wearing a bright red jacket and should have been easily spotted - but he was nowhere to be seen. Mrs. Jepson searched frantically and called for him and after a little while, went for help.

Volunteers assembled to start another search and hundreds of local residents joined police officers in combing through the dump, walking the roads and hunting in the mountains. They even instituted a "double check" system so that after one group checked an area, another would follow them and search it again. But even with the search parties and aircraft brought in by the Coast Guard, there was no sign of the boy.

The only clues came from a group of bloodhounds that were borrowed from the New Hampshire State Police. The dogs managed to follow Paul's scent, only to lose it at the junction of East and Chapel Roads, just west of Glastonbury Mountain. According to locals, this was the same spot where Paula Welden had last been seen. The search was eventually called off and another person was lost to the mountains.

About two weeks later, on October 28, the mountain claimed another victim. Her name was Freida Langer and she was on a hike that day with her cousin, Herbert Elsner. The fifty-three-year-old Langer was described as a rugged outdoorswoman with long experience in the woods and skilled with firearms. She was also very familiar with the region, and like Middie Rivers before her, was an unlikely person to simply get lost or to wander off the trail. Somehow, though, she managed to disappear.

At about 3:45 that afternoon, Freida slipped and fell into the edge of a stream, soaking her boots and pants. Since she and her cousin were only about a half-mile from camp, she said that she would run back and change clothes and then catch up with him. Elsner sat down to wait but after Freida had been gone for a while, he began to grow concerned. After an hour or so, he started back up the trail to their camp. When he got there, he discovered that no one had seen her come back and from the looks of her gear, she had never returned to change her wet clothing. He immediately contacted the authorities.

Alarmed by another disappearance in the same area, local officials quickly launched another massive search. Again, hundreds of volunteers combed the woods, tracing and re-tracing what should have been Freida's route between the stream where she had fallen and the camp.

On November 1, General Merritt Edson, the state director of public safety, started a second search. He vowed that they would find Freida, dead or alive, and he ordered his men to keep searching around the clock. More helicopters, aircraft, officers and volunteers were brought in, but once again, they found no clues. Another search was started on November 5, with the volunteers divided up into groups of thirty. They lined up and marched side by side along trails and through the forest, scanning every inch of ground. There was still no sign of the missing woman.

On November 11, the largest search so far was organized. Over three hundred volunteers joined police officers, firefighters and military units as they scoured the woods. A few days later, Freida's family gave up hope and the search was called off.

Strangely, Freida Langer was the only person to go missing on the Long Trail who was later found. On May 12, 1951, seven months after she had vanished, her body was discovered lying in some tall grass near the flood dam of the Somerset Reservoir. It was nowhere near the spot where she had vanished and impossibly, this site had been thoroughly searched while the hunt for the missing woman was being carried out. The volunteers swore that the body had not been there during the initial search. The site where the corpse was found was an open and clearly visible area and it was simply impossible that the searchers could have missed it. Unfortunately, no clues could be gathered from Freida's body and no cause of death was ever determined by the medical examiner. Her remains were too decomposed and the newspaper stated they were in "gruesome condition."

Could someone have placed the body there after the search was concluded? Rumors swirled about a killer who was hiding on Glastonbury Mountain, claiming victims that were chosen from those who vanished into the woods. In those days, the term "serial killer" had not come to public attention and later examinations of the cases do suggest that a killer might have been at work. The disappearances occurred over a limited length of time and all in one central area, around the mountain and the Long Trail. Perhaps the killer was someone who came to Vermont each fall, committed his crimes, and then left. That might explain why no one ever became a suspect in the vanishings but why were no bodies, save for that of Freida Langer, ever found?

What happened in the mountains near Bennington, Vermont, between 1945 and 1950? Was a madman preying on lone hikers or were darker and more mysterious forces at work? Could these people have simply gotten lost or were they carried off against their will, to a place that none of us can imagine?

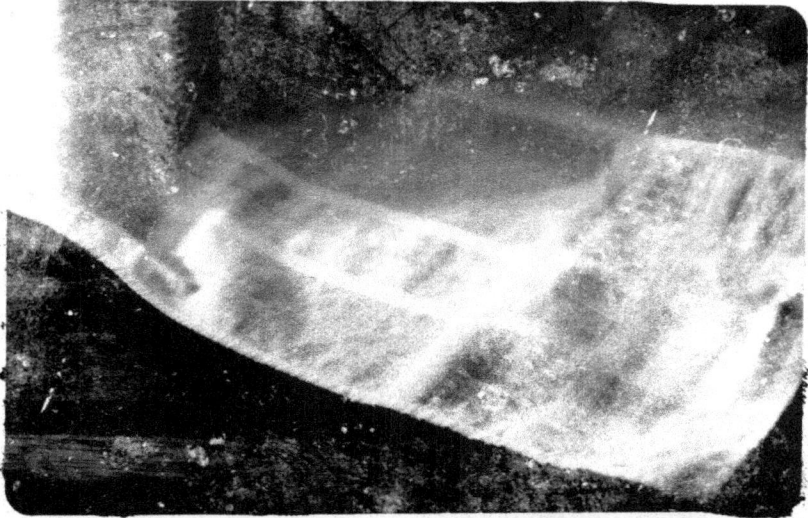

POISON-SCENTED HANDKERCHIEF

The Mad Gasser of Mattoon

The annals of the paranormal in America have been filled with strange histories of phantom attackers and inexplicable events. Many reports, often filled with a mix of legend and truth, have told of mysterious figures that wreaked havoc on an area for a time and then seemingly vanished without a trace, leaving no clue as to their purpose or why they committed the strange acts that they did.

There is no greater "phantom attacker" in the history of the unexplained in America than the legendary "Mad Gasser of Mattoon," a bizarre figure who preyed on a small Illinois town in 1944. This creature turned out to be so elusive that law enforcement officials eventually declared him nonexistent, despite dozens of eyewitness reports and physical evidence that was left behind at the scene of some attacks. Making matters even more interesting was a series of nearly identical attacks that took place in Botetourt County, Virginia, in 1933 and 1934. Social scientists declared that the attacks in Mattoon had been nothing more than mass hysteria, but how could the Illinois residents have known anything about the events in Virginia, which were barely publicized, in order to duplicate them so closely?

Both of these series of attacks involved a mysterious, black-clad figure who came and went without warning, left little in the way of clues behind and for some reason, sprayed a paralyzing gas into the windows of unsuspecting people. The gas was never identified in either case and both cases took place in fairly isolated areas. The homes that were attacked in Virginia were in a rural county and Mattoon, at that time, was a small, central Illinois town with no large cities in the vicinity. Police officials were totally stumped in both cases.

Perhaps what makes this mystery so great is the fact the central figure in the "Mad Gasser" case is such a mystery. Who (or what) attacked the unsuspecting citizens of Virginia and Illinois? Was it a mad scientist carrying out secret experiments? A government agency? A visitor from another planet? No one will ever know for sure, but the annals of the unknown are plagued with cases of inexplicable attackers who appear and vanish without explanation, prey on the unsuspecting without warning and then vanish completely, leaving no trace behind. Could such attackers come from another time and place? Another dimension? I'll let you judge that for yourself. Just remember, though, if these attacks can happen in rural Virginia and small-town Illinois, then they are capable of happening anywhere -- even where you live!

The Botetourt Gasser

In 1933, Botetourt County, Virginia, was a quiet place that had never really experienced much out of the ordinary. That began to change on December 22 in Haymakertown, a community of fewer than thirty people in western Botetourt County. That night, the home of Mrs. and Mrs. Cal Huffman and their six children, was attacked by a mysterious figure that was unlike anything seen, or even heard of, in the region before.

At around 10:00 p.m., Mrs. Huffman grew nauseated after smelling a strange, gassy odor. She decided to go to bed, along with the children, but her husband remained awake and alert. He thought he had glimpsed a shadowy figure outside earlier in the evening and he wanted to see if whoever was lurking around the property might return. A half-hour later, another wave of gas filled the room and Huffman immediately went to the home of his landlord, K.W. Henderson, and telephoned the police. Botetourt County Special Officer O.D. Lemon was dispatched to the scene and he stayed until around midnight, when he was called away. As soon as he left, another gas attack was launched on the property, filling both floors of the Huffmans' 165-year-old stone house. This time, all eight members of the Huffman family, along with Henderson's son, Ashby, were affected by the gas. Ashby and Cal Huffman had been keeping watch for the return of the prowler and they thought that they saw a man running away after the attack.

According to reports, the gas caused the victims to become very nauseated, gave them a headache and caused the mouth and throat muscles to restrict. Alice, the Huffman's 19-year-old daughter, was the most affected by the gas; she passed out and had to be given artificial respiration. She was said to have experienced convulsions for weeks afterward. Her doctor, Dr. S.F. Driver, later reported that while part of her reaction was caused by extreme nervousness over the attack, he had no doubt that the mysterious gas was responsible for the fact that her condition continued.

However, no one could determine what kind of gas was used (Dr. W.N.

Breckinridge, the county coroner, who assisted with the police investigation, ruled out ether, chloroform and tear gas.) The authorities had no idea who could have sprayed it into the house. The only clue that Lemon found at the scene was the print of a woman's shoe beneath the window through which the attacker was thought to have sprayed the gas.

The next attack took place on Christmas Eve in the Botetourt County town of Cloverdale. Clarence Hall, his wife and their two children came home from a church service at around 9:00 p.m. Five minutes after they entered the house, they smelled a strange odor. Hall went into one of the back rooms to investigate and came back moments later, staggering and swaying. His wife, who also felt nauseated and weak, had to drag him outside. The effects of the gas did not linger with Mr. Hall but Mrs. Hall experienced eye irritation for the next two days. Dr. Breckinridge again helped the police and he noted that the gas "tasted sweet" and that he detected a trace of formaldehyde in it. He still had no idea what the gas was, though, and investigators again found only one clue at the scene. Apparently, a nail had been pulled from one of the windows. Was this to make is possible to spray the gas inside?

Another attack occurred on December 27 when A.L. Kelly, a welder from Troutville, and his mother were sprayed in their home. A man and a woman in a new 1933 Chevrolet had been seen driving back and forth in front of Kelly's house around the time of the attack. A neighbor managed to get a partial license plate number but the police were unable to locate the vehicle.

No attacks took place over the next two weeks, but on January 10 the Gasser struck again at the home of Homer Hylton, near Haymakertown. Hylton and his wife were upstairs asleep and their daughter, Mrs. Moore, whose husband was out of town on business, was sleeping downstairs. Around 10:00 p.m., she got up to attend to her baby and later recalled that she heard mumbling voices outside and someone fiddling with the window. Moments later, she said that the room filled with gas and as she grabbed her child, she experienced a "marked feeling of numbness." The window where the noises came from had been slightly broken for some time and this may have allowed the Gasser access to the house. Author Michael T. Shoemaker, in an excellent article on the subject for FATE Magazine in 1985, suggests that we could theorize that Mrs. Moore was simply spooked by the wind blowing through the crack in the glass if not for the voices that she heard. Again, some might say this was only her imagination as well, except for the fact that a neighbor, G.E. Poage, also heard voices around the same time.

Also on January 10, a Troutville man named G.D. Kinzie was also attacked. This case was not reported until later and was different from the others. Apparently, Dr. Driver investigated his case and stated that the gas used in the attack was chlorine. Chlorine was then mentioned in several subsequent accounts until a Roanoke chemistry professor later ruled it out as a possible cause.

After a few quiet nights, the Gasser returned on January 16, this time attacking the home of F.B. Duval near Bonsack. Duval left the house to summon the police, and as he reached a nearby intersection, he saw a man run up to a parked car and speed away. He and Officer Lemon spent several hours driving around searching for the car, but they found nothing. The next day, Lemon again found the prints of a woman's shoes, this time where the car had been parked.

On January 19, the Gasser struck again. This time, gas was sprayed into the window of a Mrs. Campbell, a former judge's wife, near Cloverdale. She was sitting near the window in question and moments after seeing the shade move, she became sick.

A few nights later, the gas attacks reached their peak with five attacks taking place over a period of three nights. The first attack took place on January 21, when Howard Crawford and his wife returned to their home between Cloverdale and Troutville. Mr. Crawford went into the house first to light a lamp but quickly came stumbling back out. He was overwhelmed by the gas, which Dr. Driver again said was chlorine. Police officers were able to find only a single clue at the house: the crank from an old automobile. There were still many cars that had to be cranked by hand on the roads in those days, so the police were unable to trace the item back to its owner.

On January 22, three separate attacks occurred in Carvin's Cove, which is located a few miles northeast of Cloverdale. In just one hour's time, the Gasser covered a distance of about two miles, attacking the homes of Ed Reedy, George C. Riley and Raymond Etter. In each of the houses, the victims all claimed to experience numbness and nausea. Riley called his brother, a Roanoke police officer, and a blockade of the nearby roads was quickly put into place. Although the Gasser managed to elude the authorities, one of Mr. Etter's sons claimed to see a figure disappearing from the direction of the house. He gave chase and even fired a few shots at the man from a distance of 30 yards, but he got away.

On January 23, Mrs. R.H. Hartsell and her family returned to their home in the town of Pleasantdale Church at 4:30 a.m. after having spent the night with neighbors. They discovered that the house had been filled with foul-smelling gas. For some reason, someone had also piled wood and brush up against their front door during the night. The only possible motive that I can see for this would have been to keep the family from easily escaping once the house was filled with gas. This means that the elusive Gasser must have believed the family was home at the time of the attack.

This new series of gassings had the entire community in an uproar. Families who lived in isolated areas began spending the night with friends and neighbors, hoping to find security in numbers. Local men began patrolling the roadways at night, armed with shotguns and rifles. The local newspaper, the Roanoke Times, stated that it was sure the gassers would be caught and pleaded with the farmers not to shoot anyone.

The authorities were now growing more concerned. Prior to this, they had believed the gassings had been nothing more than pranks played by some mischievous boys. Now the county sheriff's office was forced to admit that if this had been the case, the boys would have been caught long before. They had begun to investigate the idea that a mentally deranged person might be the culprit, perhaps even an unhinged gas victim from the trenches of World War I.

The story became a nationwide sensation when the *New York Times* reported on the nocturnal "gas thrower." Realizing that news of the gas attacks had spread far beyond the borders of Botetourt County, the Virginia General Assembly did what lawmakers invariably do when the public becomes sufficiently terrified or annoyed about something: they passed a law making "gassing" a felony punishable by up to 10 years in prison. The law is still on the books.

On January 25, the Gasser may have attempted to strike again, but this time was foiled. Around 9:00 p.m. that evening, a dog at the home of Chester Snyder began barking. Alerted, Snyder jumped out of bed and grabbed his shotgun. Darting outside, he ran across the yard and fired a shot at a man that he saw creeping along a ditch about 20 feet from the house. The shot went wide and Snyder only had one shell in his gun. He ran back inside for more ammunition but by the time he returned, the man was gone.

He called the police and a deputy sheriff named Zimmerman investigated the scene. He managed to find footprints that led from the road to the ditch and signs that the prowler had hidden behind a tree on the property for some time before the dog sounded the alarm. More tracks led from the tree to the house and then stopped, marking the point where the man had retreated. Visitors who had left the Snyder home shortly before the happening recalled seeing a man about one-half mile away on the road. There was no real evidence to say that the prowler was actually the Gasser, but based on the events that had been occurring, any sort of incident like this was immediately suspect.

On January 28, the Gasser managed to pull off another attack, and he would actually return again to this same residence. The home belonged to Ed Stanley of Cloverdale and Stanley, his wife and three other adults were all affected by the still-mysterious gas. Frank Guy, a hired hand on the farm, ran outside immediately after the vapor filled the house and stated that he saw four men running away in the direction of the Blue Ridge Mountains. He ran back inside to get his gun and when he returned to the yard, he could no longer see the fleeing figures, but he could hear them in the woods. He fired several shots in the direction of the voices but felt that it was unlikely that he hit anything.

The Gasser returned to the Stanley house two nights later. This time, Stanley heard a sound outside the window before the attack took place. What happened after that remains a mystery as no further details were reported in the contemporary accounts.

The last of the likely authentic gas attacks took place in Nace, two miles from Troutville, on February 3. The house that was attacked belonged to A.P. Skagges and he and his wife, along with five other adults were all affected by the gas. The group was so badly affected by the gas that Sheriff Williamson would tell the skeptics who later expressed doubt over the gassing cases that "No amount of imagination in the world would make people as ill as the Skagges are."

The attack became as dramatic as the first attack on the Huffman family and author Michael T. Shoemaker noted that perhaps the Gasser wanted to mark his entrance and exit with a splash. Another similarity to the Huffman attack was that it seemed as though the gas was sprayed into the house two times that evening, although Officer Lemon stated that he believed lingering gas near the ceiling could have been responsible for what seemed to be a separate attack. The gas had some pretty strange effects on the people in the house, as one of Skagges' nephews began screaming hysterically that he was "trapped" in the house, and on the family dog as well. Officer Lemon returned to the house to continue his investigation the next day and one of the children came in crying that the dog was dying. Lemon went out and saw that the animal was rolling over and over in the snow, just as dogs do when they are sprayed by a skunk. As no skunk odor was present, this certainly seemed odd. A witness later told Michael Shoemaker that the well-trained dog was sick and would not pay attention to commands for some time after the incident.

It was at this point that the story began to deteriorate. During the following week, there were 20 attacks reported in nearby Roanoke County and a number of other reports in Lexington, about 30 miles away. And while a few of the later "attacks" may have been genuine, they lacked the detail of the original incidents and most were likely hysterical reactions to ordinary odors or the result of hoaxes perpetrated by pranksters. In one of these hoaxes, a teenager threw a bottle of insecticide into a woman's window. A similar incident on February 9 gave the police and the newspapers the opportunity to declare that the Gasser mystery was over.

The last "insecticide" case did have some interesting aspects to it, however. At the time when J.G. Shafer of Lithia believed his house was gassed on February 9, he went outside and scooped up some snow that contained a sweet-smelling substance. It was analyzed and was determined to contain sulfur, arsenic and mineral oil, all of which was commonly used in insecticide sprays. This caused the police to dismiss the attack as a hoax, but was it really? Strangely, investigators found footprints leading from the front porch of the house to the barn, but no trail that led away from this building. It was as if whoever had been on the porch had then walked into the barn and simply vanished. Also, as with some of the other earlier cases, a "woman's tracks" led from the yard to the road.

The later cases that came along led the general public to swallow the unconvincing theory that faulty chimney flues and wild imaginations had caused the entire affair. Those who were attacked and the police officers involved never accepted this explanation. However, the ongoing cases of panic did not convince the non-believers to reconsider. Looking back on the case now, the later cases actually helped to show that the original cases were not hysteria. The later cases didn't follow the pattern of the original attacks. They occurred outside of the already-established area, took place at no particular times and did not cause any lasting physical effects. It should also be noted that the original attacks, while taking place in Botetourt County, were spread out enough throughout the area that neighbors could not infect one another with hysteria.

So if mass hysteria was not the answer in the Mad Gasser of Botetourt County case, then could there be a natural explanation? This also seems unlikely, for explanations like pollution and faulty chimney flues don't hold water when considering all the similar factors in the initial attacks. The gassings all happened under cover of darkness in rural areas and often, a fleeing figure (sometimes more than one) was seen running away. The hoaxer, or even the lone lunatic, theories are not much better, either. Even though a mysterious figure was often seen, there were never any useful clues left behind and the identity of the Gasser was never discovered.

It was almost as if the strange figure left Virginia and vanished without a trace. And while perhaps the Gasser did not return to Botetourt County, could he have possibly surfaced in Illinois eleven years later?

The Mad Gasser of Mattoon

Mattoon, located in the southeastern part of central Illinois, is a fairly typical Midwestern town. The strange events that took place there in 1944, however, were anything but typical. These events would place the small city under the scrutiny of the entire nation and would one day become a textbook case of what psychologists call "mass hysteria." But was it really?

The whirlwind of events would begin in the early morning hours of August 31. A Mattoon man was startled out of a deep sleep and complained to his wife that he felt sick. He questioned her about leaving the gas on in the kitchen because his symptoms seemed very similar to gas exposure. The woman tried to get out of bed to check the pilot light on the stove, but found to her surprise that she could not move. Just minutes later, according to published reports, a woman in a neighboring home also tried to get out of bed and discovered that she, too, was paralyzed.

The next evening, a woman named Mrs. Bert Kearney was awakened by a peculiar smell in her bedroom. The odor was sweet and overpowering and as it grew stronger, she began to feel a peculiar prickling feeling in her legs and lower body. As she tried to get out of bed, she realized that her limbs were paralyzed. She began screaming, which drew the attention of her neighbors, who alerted the police. The following day, she would complain of having burned lips and a parched mouth and throat from exposure to the fumes. A hasty search of the yard by police officers and questioning of her shaken neighbors revealed nothing. But that would not be the last strange event to occur at this particular house...

Around midnight, Bert Kearney returned home from work, completely unaware of what had happened in his home earlier that night. As he turned into his driveway, he spotted a man lurking near the house who would later fit the descriptions of the "Mad Gasser." The stranger, according to Kearney, was tall and dressed in dark clothing and wore a tight-fitting black cap. He was standing near a window and he ran away when Kearney spotted him. Kearney pursued the tall man but was unable to catch up with him.

These events soon became public knowledge and panic gripped the town. The story was badly handled by the authorities and the local newspaper reported the Kearney case, and subsequent others, in a wildly sensational manner. The newspaper is believed by many to be the culprit behind the "Gasser hysteria." Years later, the newspaper would be blamed for everything that happened in the case and for manufacturing the scare. The frightened citizens, according to these skeptics, took leave of their senses and began to imagine that a "mad gasser" was wreaking havoc in the town. Many people still believe that overactive imaginations were to blame for the affair, but it certainly does not eliminate all of the evidence that something very bizarre happened in Mattoon.

By the morning of September 5, the Mattoon police department had received reports of four more "gas attacks." The details in each of these cases were eerily similar, even though none of the witnesses had time to compare notes. The newspapers had published a skewed version of the events but the subsequent reports were not only almost identical but were accurate as to what had actually occurred. In each of the cases, the victims complained of a sickeningly sweet odor that caused them to become sick and slightly paralyzed for up to 30 minutes.

Late on the night of September 5, the first real clues in the Mad Gasser case were discovered. They were found at the home of Carl and Beulah Cordes, but what these clues meant has yet to be determined. The Cordeses returned home late that evening to find a white cloth lying on their porch. Mrs. Cordes picked it up and noticed a strange smell coming from it. She held it up close to her nose and immediately felt nauseated and light-headed. She nearly fainted and her husband had to help her inside the house. Within minutes, her lips and face began to swell and her mouth began to bleed. The symptoms began to subside in about two hours but needless to say, she was terrified. Carl Cordes called the police and officers came out to investigate. They took the cloth into evidence, along with a skeleton key and an empty tube of lipstick that were found on the porch. They decided a prowler had probably tried and failed to break into the house.

The police surmised that the cloth was connected to the other gas attacks. It should be noted however, that the odor on the cloth caused different symptoms in Mrs. Cordes than in the other victims. She did become sick to her stomach but there were no sensations of paralysis. This incident is also different because if this was the Gasser at work, then it is the only time when he actually tried to gain access to the home of his victims. Could his intentions in this incident have been different?

The Gasser attacked again that same night, but he was back to his old tricks and sprayed his gas into an open window. There would only be one other report that even hinted that the attacker tried to break into the house. The woman in this instance claimed that a person in dark clothing tried to force open her front door. Was it really the Mad Gasser or could it have been an ordinary burglar?

The attacks continued and Mattoon residents began reporting fleeting glimpses of the Gasser, always describing him as a tall, thin man in dark clothes and wearing a tight black cap. More attacks were reported and the harried police force tried to respond to the mysterious crimes that left no clues behind. Eventually, the authorities summoned two FBI agents from Springfield to look into the case, but their presence did nothing to stop the strange reports. Panic was widespread and rumors began to circulate that the attacker was an escapee from an insane asylum or a German spy who was testing out some sort of poisonous gas.

Armed citizens took to the streets, organizing watches and patrols to thwart any further attacks, but several took place anyway. The gas attacks were becoming more frequent and the attacker was leaving behind evidence like footprints and sliced window screens. This evidence would become particularly interesting after the revelations of the authorities in the days to come.

A local citizens' "vigilance group" did manage to arrest one suspect but he was released after he passed a polygraph test. Local businessmen announced that they would be holding a protest rally on Saturday, September 10, to put more pressure on the already-pressured Mattoon police force to arrest the culprit. Now, the Gasser was becoming more than a threat to public safety; he was becoming a political liability and a blot on the public image of the city.

The Gasser, apparently not impressed by armed vigilantes and newspaper diatribes, resumed his attacks. The first residence to be attacked was that of Mrs. Violet Driskell and her daughter, Ramona. They awoke late in the evening to hear someone removing the storm sash on their bedroom window. They hurried out of bed and tried to run outside for help, but the fumes overcame Ramona and she threw up. Her mother stated that she saw a man running away from the house.

A short time later that night, the Gasser sprayed fumes into the partially opened window of a room where Mrs. Russell Bailey, Katherine Tuzzo, Mrs. Genevieve Haskell and her young son were sleeping. At another home, Frances Smith, the principal of the Columbian Grade School, and her sister, Maxine, were also overwhelmed with gas and fell ill. They began choking as they were awakened and felt partial paralysis in their legs and arms. They also said that the sweet odor began to fill the room "as a thin, blue vapor." They heard a buzzing noise from outside and believed that it was the Gasser's "spraying apparatus" in operation.

By September 10, Mad Gasser paranoia had peaked. FBI agents were trying to track down the type of gas being used in the attacks and the police were trying to not only find the Gasser, but also to keep the armed citizens off the streets. Neither law enforcement agency was having much luck with any of these tasks. By the following Saturday night, several dozen armed farmers from the surrounding area had joined the citizens' patrols in Mattoon. In spite of this, six attacks took place anyway, including the three just mentioned. Another couple, Mr. and Mrs. Stewart B. Scott, returned to their farm on the edge of Mattoon late in the evening to find the house filled with sweet-smelling gas.

This period seemed to mark a turning point in the case. It was almost as if the idea of the gas attacks moving from the city of Mattoon to the outlying countryside had pushed the scales of official acceptance in the wrong direction. In the words of Thomas V. Wright, city commissioner of public health: "There is no doubt that a gas maniac exists and has made a number of attacks. But many of the reported attacks are nothing more than hysteria. Fear of the gas man is entirely out of proportion to the menace of the relatively harmless gas he is spraying. The whole town is sick with hysteria and last night it spread out into the country."

At this point, newspaper accounts of the affair began to take on a more skeptical tone. Despite claims by victims and material evidence left behind, the police began to dismiss new reports of attacks and suggested that local residents were merely imagining things. The episode had gone so far without being resolved that it was really the only thing left for them to do. The Gasser, if he existed at all, could not be caught, identified, or tracked down. They started to believe that if they ignored the problem, it would go away. After all, if the man were real, how could he have escaped detection for so long?

Psychology experts opined that the women of Mattoon had dreamed up the Gasser as a desperate bid for attention, as many of their husbands were overseas fighting in the war. This insulting theory ignored the fact that many victims and witnesses were men and that this so-called "fantasy" was leaving behind physical evidence of his existence.

On the night of September 11, the police received a number of phone calls from people who reported smelling gas or hearing suspicious noises, but after half-hearted attempts to investigate, they dismissed all of them as false alarms. Just days before, Richard T. Piper, a crime specialist with the State Department of Public Safety, told reporters, "This is one of the strangest cases I have ever encountered in my years of police work," but now new calls were only worthy of perfunctory examination. This is in spite of the fact that a doctor who appeared on the scene shortly after one of the evening's attacks stated that there had been a "peculiar odor" in the room. The officials were simply no longer interested.

The Mattoon police chief issued what he felt was the final statement on the gas attacks on September 12. He said that large quantities of carbon tetrachloride gas were used at the local Atlas Imperial Diesel Engine company and that this gas must be causing the reported cases of illness and paralysis. It could be carried throughout the town on the wind and could have left the stains that were on the rag found at one of the homes. As for the Mad Gasser himself, well, he was simply a figment of people's imaginations. The whole case, he pronounced, "was a mistake from beginning to end."

Not surprisingly, a spokesman for the Atlas plant was quick to deny the allegations that his company was to blame for people getting sick. He maintained that the plant only used that particular type of gas in their fire extinguishers and any similar gases used there caused no ill effects. Besides, why hadn't this gas ever caused problems in the city before? And how exactly could gas vapors cut the window screens on homes before causing nausea and paralysis?

The official explanation also failed to account for how so many identical descriptions of the Gasser had been reported to the police. It also neglected to explain how different witnesses managed to report seeing a man of the Gasser's description fleeing the scene of an attack, even when the witness had no idea that an attack had taken place!

The last Gasser attack took place on September 13, and while it was the last appearance of the attacker in Mattoon, it was also possibly the strangest. It occurred at the home of Mrs. Bertha Bench and her son, Orville. They described the attacker as being a woman dressed in men's clothing who sprayed gas into a bedroom window. The next morning, footprints that appeared to have been made by a woman's high-heeled shoes were found in the dirt below the window. And while this report does not match any of the earlier attacks in Mattoon, readers will undoubtedly recognize the reports of a woman's shoe prints being left behind from several attacks in Botetourt County, Virginia, in 1933.

After this night, the Mad Gasser of Mattoon was never seen or heard from again.

The real story behind what happened in Mattoon and Botetourt County is still unknown and it's unlikely that we will ever know what caused these strange events. It is certain that *something* took place in both locations, and theories abound as to what it may have been. Was the "Mad Gasser" real? And if he was, who was he? If he was real, could he have been responsible for both series of attacks, despite the fact that they occurred eleven years apart? It's hard to ignore the similarities between the two cases, from the method of operation to the unusual form of attacks. In Virginia, though, the Gasser was not always reported as being alone, as he was in Mattoon, but then again, what about the identical reports of prints left by a woman's shoe?

Stories have suggested that Mattoon's Gasser was anything from a mad scientist to an ape-man (although who knows where that came from?) and researchers today have their own theories, some of which are just as wild.

Could he have been some sort of extraterrestrial visitor using some type of paralyzing agent to further a hidden agenda?

Could he have been a mentally unbalanced inventor who was testing a new apparatus? Interestingly, I received a letter in 2002 from a woman who said that her father grew up in Mattoon during the time when the gas attacks were taking place. He told her that there had been two sisters living in town at the time who had a brother who was allegedly insane. A number of people in town believed that he was the Gasser and so his sisters locked him in the basement until they could find a mental institution to put him in. After they locked him away, her father told her, the gas attacks stopped.

Or could the Gasser have been an agent of our own government, who came to an obscure Midwestern town to test some new type of military gas that could be used in the war effort? It might be telling that once national attention came to Mattoon, the authorities began a policy of complete denial and the attacks suddenly ceased. Coincidence?

Whoever, or whatever, he was, the Mad Gasser of Mattoon has vanished into history and, real or imagined, is only a memory in the world of the unknown. Perhaps he was never here at all -- perhaps he was, as Donald M. Johnson wrote in the 1954 issue of the *Journal of Abnormal and Social Psychology*, simply a "shadowy manifestation of some unimaginable unknown."

But was he really? How do we explain the identical sightings of a tall, black-clad figure by independent witnesses who could not have possibly known that others had just spotted the same figure? Was the Gasser, as some have suggested, a visitor from a dimension outside of our own, thus explaining his ability to appear or disappear at will? Was he a creature so outside the realm of our imaginations that we will never be able to comprehend his motives or understand the reason why he came to Mattoon?

Which brings us back to questions posed earlier: could the Mad Gasser have been some sort of mysterious presence that could pass from one dimension to another, coming and going without explanation? Could this solution to the mystery explain the appearance of not only the Mad Gasser but other mystery figures as well? And perhaps more chilling is this question: If this is the case, where might the next phantom attacker appear?

BIBLIOGRAPHY

Barker, Gray - *The Silver Bridge*; 1970
Bell, Horace - *On the Old West Coast*; 1930
Blackman, W. Haden - *Field Guide to North American Monsters*; 1998
Bord, Janet & Colin - *Alien Animals*; 1981
-------------- - *Bigfoot Casebook*; 1982
-------------- - *Evidence for Bigfoot & Other Man-Beasts*; 1984
Churchill, Allen - *They Never Came Back*; 1960
Citro, Joseph A. - *Passing Strange*; 1996
Calvert, Stephen - *Mysterious 1876 Bath County Shower of Flesh Still Unexplained*; 1994
Canning, John - *Great Unsolved Mysteries*; 1984
Childress, David Hatcher - *Lost Cities of North & Central America*; 1992
Clark, Jerome - *Unexplained!*; 1999
---------- - & Loren Coleman, *The Unidentified*; 1975
Coleman, Loren - *Bigfoot*; 2003
------------ - *Curious Encounters*; 1985
------------ - & Patrick Huyghe - *Field Guide to Bigfoot*; 1999
------------ - *Mothman & Other Curious Encounters*; 2002
------------ - *Mysterious America*; 1983 / 2000
Corliss, William R. - *Handbook of Unusual Natural Phenomena*; 1977 / 1983
Dewhurst, Richard J. - *The Ancient Giants who Ruled America*; 2014
FATE Magazine - Various Issues
Fortean Times Magazine - Various Issues
Floyd, E. Randall- *Great American Mysteries*; 1990

Fort, Charles - *Complete Books of Charles Fort*; 1941
Godfrey, Linda - *Beast of Bray Road*; 2002
----------- - *Real Wolfmen*; 2012
Godwin, John - *This Baffling World 2*; 1968
Gregg, Mrs. Delburt - *Werewolf?* (*FATE Magazine* - March 1960)
Green, John - *On the Track of the Sasquatch*; 1973
---------- - *Year of the Sasquatch*; 1973
Guiley, Rosemary Ellen - *Atlas of the Mysterious in North America*; 1995
Hansen, Frank - *I Killed the Ape-Man Creature of Whiteface* (*Saga* Magazine - July 1970)
Hunt, Gerry - *Bizarre America*; 1988
Hunter, Don with Rene Dahinden - *Sasquatch*; 1973
Keel, John - *Complete Guide to Mysterious Beings*; 1970 / 1994
-------------- - *Disneyland of the Gods*; 1988
-------------- - *The Mothman Prophecies*; 1975
-------------- - *Our Haunted Planet*; 1971
McCloy, James F. & Ray Miller Jr. - *The Jersey Devil*; 1976
------------------------ - *Phantom of the Pines*; 1998
Miller, R. DeWitt - *Impossible, Yet it Happened!*; 1947
Monaco, Richard - *Bizarre America 2*; 1992
PURSUIT - Journal of the Society for the Investigation of the Unexplained (Various Issues)
Rife, Phillip L. - *Bigfoot Across America*; 2000
Sanderson, Ivan T. - *Abominable Snowman: Legend Come to Life*; 1961
Sankey, Scarlet - *Bray Road Beast* (*Strange Magazine* - 10); 1992
Shoemaker, Michael T. - *The Mad Gasser of Botetourt* (*FATE Magazine* - June 1985)
------------------ - *Searching for the Historical Bigfoot* (*Strange Magazine* - 5); 1990
Shuker, Karl P.N. - *The Unexplained*; 1996
Stewart, George R. - *Ordeal by Hunger*; 1936
Strange Magazine - Various Issues
Taylor, Troy - *Into the Shadows*; 2002
--------- - *Mysterious Illinois*; 2006
--------- - *Out Past the Campfire Light*; 2003
--------- - *Without a Trace*; 2009
West, Rick - *Pickled Punks & Girlie Shows*; 2011
Wilson, Colin - *Unsolved Mysteries Past & Present*; 1992
Wilson, Colin & Damon Wilson - *Mammoth Encyclopedia of the Unsolved*; 2000

Personal Interviews & Correspondence

Special Thanks to:
Jill Hand - Editor
April Slaughter - Cover Design
Orrin Taylor -- Who came up with the idea to keep this series going
(Yes! There will be more to come)

The Family:
Rene Kruse
Rachael Horath
Elyse & Thomas Reihner
Bethany & Jim McKenzie
Haven & Helayna Taylor

Friends & Assorted Characters:
John Winterbauer
Ginger Collins Justus
Loren Coleman
Jerry Coleman
Mark Chorvinsky
John Keel
John Brill
Linda Godfrey
Raymond Bayless
Mark Scuerman
Mark Moran
Michael Shoemaker
Nick Redfern
Hannah Gray
Lisa Taylor Horton (& Lux)

ABOUT THE AUTHOR: TROY TAYLOR

Troy Taylor is an occultist, crime buff, supernatural historian and the author of more than 100 books on ghosts, hauntings, history, crime and the unexplained in America. He is also the founder of the American Hauntings Tour company. When not traveling to the far-flung reaches of the country in search of the unusual, Troy resides part-time in Decatur, Illinois.

See Troy's other titles at: www.whitechapelpress.com